The

CROWN MAPLE

GUIDE TO

MAPLE SYRUP

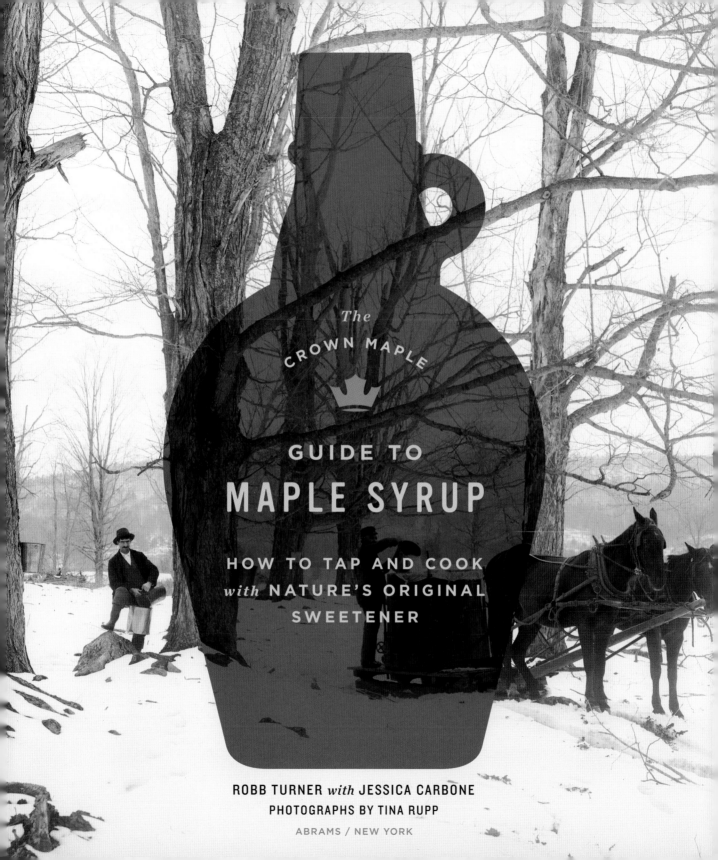

The
CROWN MAPLE

GUIDE TO
MAPLE SYRUP

HOW TO TAP AND COOK
with **NATURE'S ORIGINAL**
SWEETENER

ROBB TURNER with **JESSICA CARBONE**
PHOTOGRAPHS BY TINA RUPP

ABRAMS / NEW YORK

EDITOR: Sarah Massey
PRODUCTION MANAGER: Denise LaCongo

Library of Congress Control Number: 2015955671

ISBN: 978-1-4197-2248-6

TEXT COPYRIGHT © 2016 Madava Holdings, LLC
PHOTOGRAPHS COPYRIGHT © 2016 Tina Rupp
ILLUSTRATIONS by Kate Francis
Woodgrain illustration © Shutterstock.com / adehoidar

Published in 2016 by Abrams, an imprint of ABRAMS.
All rights reserved. No portion of this book may be
reproduced, stored in a retrieval system, or transmitted
in any form or by any means, mechanical, electronic,
photocopying, recording, or otherwise, without written
permission from the publisher.

PRINTED AND BOUND IN THE UNITED STATES
10 9 8 7 6 5 4 3 2 1

Abrams books are available at special discounts
when purchased in quantity for premiums and
promotions as well as fundraising or educational use.
Special editions can also be created to specification.
For details, contact specialsales@abramsbooks.com
or the address below.

ABRAMS The Art of Books
115 West 18th Street, New York, NY 10011
abramsbooks.com

TABLE OF

CONTENTS

INTRODUCTION

T'S AN ODD WAY TO START A COOKBOOK, I KNOW, BUT I HAVE TO SAY IT: I never set out to be a maple syrup producer. It's not something a private equity executive would think to do, especially one who spent the majority of his career investing in power and energy infrastructure. But little did I know that maple syrup—one of the most revered natural food products available today—would challenge me to think like an energy innovator, to be resourceful with science and respectful of a tradition that not only predates me, but predates almost every kind of food technology. To me, maple syrup isn't just a food; it's a natural resource—an edible bounty created in a self-sustaining environment, alone in a world of easily depleted resources, where vast swaths of forest have been bulldozed to make way for industrial spaces. But buildings don't produce food; plants do. In that sense, maple syrup is the most American of products, a food sourced straight from nature that demands we use our modern technology to properly unlock it from the untamed wilderness. It's a seemingly simple yet profoundly sophisticated delicacy, and I fell in love with this hobby and the challenge it presented: to apply my modern sense of business, science, and technology to the oldest and most beautiful of American foods.

I wish I could say I saw the possibilities of maple syrup from the very start, that I purchased huge tracts of land in eastern Dutchess County, New York simply to build my own sugar shack. But that could hardly be further from the truth. In fact, I bought the first patch of land for pure pleasure, a weekend country retreat for my wife, Lydia, and our growing daughters, Madeline and Ava. Though we were living in suburban New Jersey at the time, and have always loved spending time in nearby Manhattan, I am still a farm kid at heart. I grew up in Forreston, a small town of about twelve hundred people outside Rockford, Illinois, where agriculture was the primary business. My dad made his living that way—he was a veterinarian who raised livestock, mostly pigs, and ultimately bought half a dozen farms across the region, where he grew corn and soybeans. This is before the era of commodity crops; this was food grown for eating, and for spreading to livestock, and the revenue was intended to go back into the farm. As a boy, I was expected to work on the farm as well—and when I wasn't roaming the streams and patches of forest for fun, I was at work feeding the pigs, cleaning their pens, and mucking out our stores of hay. I was at home in the countryside, in the wild, and would often go out on vet calls with my dad as he visited animals on other farms.

Maybe I was destined to work with maple syrup—after all, I spent much of my infancy just a little bit sticky.

I left my bucolic background to make a career in finance, so Lydia and I could raise our family, but after almost three decades away from nature, memories of my semiwild childhood drew me back to my roots. I knew I wanted to get my family reacquainted with the natural wonders of a noncity life while I still had the health and resources to enjoy it. We bought the first part of our property in Dover Plains, a mountain-studded area of Dutchess County, in 2007, on a 450-acre plot of stunning, untouched woods on which we intended to renovate a small getaway cabin with plans for a later, larger house. This plot of land had belonged to John Mack, a friend and political confidant of President Franklin D. Roosevelt. We suspect from old newspaper stories that FDR spent leisure time here trout fishing and bird-watching with his friend and former colleague.

When John died, the land was then passed on to family members, who eventually contemplated a housing development. That's where we came in. After buying our initial plot from Mack's descendants, we learned that developers were also courting other neighbors. I didn't know how much land I wanted, but I knew I loved the expansive untouched forest too much to see it torn down in favor of construction trailers and later McMansions. So as each new lot came on the market, I bought it. In just a year and a half, we had accumulated eight hundred acres. What started as a family estate soon gave me a new mission; I was buying land like a baron, but thinking like an environmentalist. This was going to be our sanctuary, a place where my school-aged kids and eventually their kids could run wild in nature the same way I had, and I wanted to keep it as intact as possible. Perhaps it's a selfish motivation, but it's the one I had.

When I first bought the acres of forest that would become Madava Farms, I didn't even know what I'd bought into until we were already well into construction projects. I'd been working with a neighbor to construct some new pathways around the property and a bridge over the trout stream, as the few that remained had been there since the early 1800s. This neighbor had lived near my woods for many years and, after two years of having me in the neighborhood, asked what I intended to do with the maple trees on the property. Well, what *could* I do with them? Could I actually be a maple syrup producer? I dove into finding out—I was thinking of the land as "God's country," and once I discovered the fact that we were sitting on a nearly pristine plot of twenty-five thousand trees, it felt even more so.

After an initial six-month review period, in which we confirmed that we could indeed use our property as a world-class maple operation, we asked ourselves, "How is it we're just sitting on this richness, and what are we doing, hogging it all to ourselves?" I began asking questions of the friendly band of maple syrup producers throughout New York and New England, as well as the brilliant advisors at the maple research center at Cornell University. What would it take for us to tap into—pun very much intended—this natural resource and still keep the land as wild and beautiful as we found it? How could we make sure our syrup was the best possible quality? Would we be able to sell such a large quantity of product?

I learned an enormous amount in those early days, about how the trees would best be tapped and still maintained, and about the essential technology needed to purify and preserve the syrup in its most natural form. I was equally intrigued by the void in the retail marketplace. There is, after all, no one name-brand syrup company in this market—none that truly produces pure maple, anyway. If our biggest shelf space competitors wouldn't even be *real* maple syrup, but instead table syrups with artificial flavoring and only the tiniest amount of maple, if any, mixed in, then we had a real opportunity to break open this entire industry.

When we're putting in our taps, we're riding on faith that the sap will flow—though exactly when, we cannot be sure.

Our greatest realization about the consumer marketplace potential came from Lydia. As she experimented in the kitchen with our extremely pure syrups and sugar, she felt it was the most flavorful sweetener she had ever used in her cooking. The applications were almost endless. We wanted others to discover our syrup and put it to use, and not just enjoy it with their pancakes. If we were going to help maple more broadly break into the food marketplace, we wanted to do it right: to introduce people to maple syrup by giving them something well beyond the artificial syrup they were used to and expand their overall appreciation of what a pure food can taste like when prepared in the very best way possible.

Every year when we're getting ready to tap our sugar maples, we're going into it a bit blind. While we can set up our taps well in advance of the sap flowing, we never know exactly which day will be the first to yield sap. The trees give when they're ready, so we have to respond to their needs—that's our business model, paying attention to and learning from the land, not forcing the land to our will. I never set out to be a businessman in the maple syrup industry—and I still consider it a hobby—but I did love the idea that this could be my family's way to give back: to create a new and sustainable food business, to introduce consumers to an old product, and to put my years of work in the energy business to use in a completely new way. In meetings with Michael Farrell, director of Cornell's Sugar Maple Research and Extension Field Station, I learned that if we directed our resources to maintaining the sugarbush as we tapped, we'd not only keep the forest and all its natural wildlife safe, but also ensure that the forest would be taken care of properly for many centuries to come. We've tried to keep the ecosystem of Madava intact, and in return the trees give us some of the sweetest, purest sap for syrup

imaginable—the very best kind of reward. I was also becoming acutely aware of what this would mean to the surrounding community of the Hudson Valley. Opening a large maple syrup operation would mean jobs, many of them, for people who had made Dutchess County their home. By opening up the land as an agricultural business, it meant that we could no longer use it as our own private hideaway, and for a moment that did give me pause. Was I going to lose my ability to protect the land, which was the whole reason we bought it to begin with?

As you can see from this spectacular drone photograph over our estate, the natural beauty of the sugarbush in mid-autumn simply cannot be beat.

But then I knew that by owning this profoundly local and natural business, our family could play a role in helping bring a whole community back to life, and suddenly my wish for a sanctuary didn't seem so important anymore. Maple syrup wasn't a project for me to retire on; it was a project that would inspire our family, and does inspire us, every day.

And that's what we want you to taste in this book—how extraordinarily inspiring, unique, and complex the story of maple syrup really is, and what part we've played in keeping the sugaring tradition alive. We want anyone who tastes our syrup to be able to appreciate it, to be awakened to the complexity and clarity of the flavor the second it hits their taste buds. But we also know that to truly appreciate the magic of maple syrup, you have to understand the history of the people who've processed it and the changing science and nature of making this product. Part One will take you through the history of maple trees and maple sugaring in America, in the northeastern United States and beyond, from the indigenous uses of maple sap and sugar to what the settlers and early maple industrialists were able to achieve. We'll explore the historical challenges of keeping up with the cane sugar industry, and the industrial tides of American progress in general, and how a new sense of environmental responsibility and economic viability has transformed the future of the maple industry. In Part Two, we'll get into the secrets of the trees themselves, and how we tap and process the sap from our trees here at Crown Maple. This is our deep dive into the botany, biology, and chemistry of maple syrup, and I've discovered that tapping old trees requires as complex a processing system as any in the environmental industry today. Finally, we'll explore the beauty of maple syrup as a sweetener—its innate healthfulness, naturalness, and adaptability—and show you some of our favorite ways to put it to good use.

Crown Maple has been open almost five years now, and even with what our team has learned about this work, we're still learning how to respond to the natural environment we're working in, and to let it guide our business. We only get maybe a month—six weeks if we're lucky—to tap, process, and store all of the hundreds of thousands of gallons of sap our trees produce. This is an industry of profound luck and blessing. If there is a place for us to be arrogant in this business, we haven't found it yet. While we may have found the best technology to work with, and the best team to support us, we're constantly learning from our colleagues in this business, producers both large and small across New England and Canada. And while we can do as much as possible to deliver for our customers, at the end of the day it's still a question of what the trees are able to give us. Because it's just that—a gift. And one of the primary upsides of entering this business when I did is that now I get to be an environmentalist the way I would want to be: with the resources to really make a big impact on the land around me. Every year, we learn new lessons about how to do this better. And in the process, we've come to care deeply about our product, from the tap to the evaporator to the barrel to the bottle, and out to you, the consumer.

It's only made life sweeter for us; let it be sweeter for you.

PART ONE

The
HISTORY OF OUR TASTE
FOR MAPLE SYRUP

— 1 —

The Early American Experience of Maple Syrup

MUCH OF WHAT WE EXPERIENCE of maple syrup today remains untouched by time and history. This is true not only of the maple landscape itself, but also of the processes for producing maple syrup. These have remained largely intact—a true rarity in our modern food landscape. While we've found new ways to produce almost every kind of food product in America, from tomatoes to fish to chickens to wheat, the maple tree remains unique in continuing to need the same basic conditions to produce syrup.

There are several species of maple trees, but the king of all of these is the sugar maple (*Acer saccharum*), and it is the type most frequently used for maple syrup production. Sugarbushes (clusters of maple trees) can be found throughout New England, New York, and Pennsylvania, as well as spread across parts of the Great Lakes region and southern Canada. They reach as far south as Tennessee, and stretch to the west as far as Missouri. Each of these trees needs a good sloppy spring, with warm days that melt winter's base of snow and lightly freezing nights, to release its sap, and the syrup that results is never too far away from the taste of the tree itself. It is one of North America's most recognizable flavors and most symbolic foods, as significant to the Northeast as wild salmon is to the Pacific Northwest, pecans to the Deep South, or corn and maize to the Southwest. When I taste our maple syrup each sugar season, I know that I taste the place it's from, the time it was grown, and the many legacies of the people who have tapped it before me.

THE TREES

However, these trees are not limited to North America. The roots of the maple family tree (genus *Acer*) extend to Asia, originating in China during the Cretaceous period (over 130 million years ago). The plant spread west into Europe, and far south to the Philippines. It may have first appeared in North America by way of eastern Siberia, initially appearing on American soil in Alaska and spreading to the East Coast. Fossils tell us that the biggest boom of maple tree growth was during the Miocene epoch, about 23 to 5.3 million years ago, with hundreds of thousands of species flourishing across the world. Today there are still 124 different species of maple trees present and growing throughout the world. Thirteen of those species are native to North America—the climate that the trees require can be found throughout the Midwest and mid-Atlantic all the way up to Ontario, Quebec, and New Brunswick. There are even a few species of maple on the West Coast and in the Deep South—you can find bigleaf and Douglas maples in Washington State and Oregon,

This fossil shows a leaf from the species of Acer lesquereuxi, *ancient maple or sweet gum, and dates back to the Eocene period, about 45 million years ago.*

There are 124 different species of maple trees in the world, but here are three native to the United States, from left to right: bigleaf maple, canyon maple, and Florida maple.

canyon maples in the Rocky Mountains and scattered throughout Texas and Oklahoma, and Florida or hammock maples running from southern Virginia to central Florida. While all maple trees can be tapped for edible sap, sugar maples are widely considered to produce the most superior flavor and quality of finished syrup.

The botany of sugar maples is fairly similar to that of other hardwood trees; like oak and willow trees, maples are deciduous, meaning that they release their leaves seasonally. (For more on the differences between sugar maples and red maples, and the different ways to spot them, see pages 53–54) Sugar maple flowers are generally wind-pollinated (rather than by bees), and produce samaras, a winged papery fruit that allows the seeds to be carried far from the tree to pollinate elsewhere. (You might recognize them as the flat paperlike propellers that catch on the wind like a helicopter blade, and are

TOP AND BOTTOM RIGHT: *The seeds of sugar maples, otherwise known as samaras or "spinning jennys," are ubiquitous in most New England forests; Sugar maple beginning to flower.*

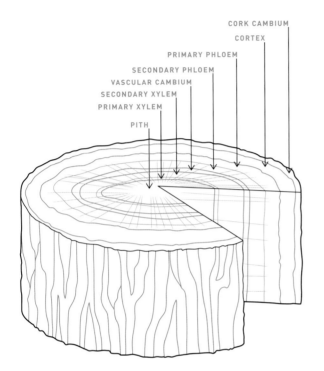

CORK CAMBIUM
CORTEX
PRIMARY PHLOEM
SECONDARY PHLOEM
VASCULAR CAMBIUM
SECONDARY XYLEM
PRIMARY XYLEM
PITH

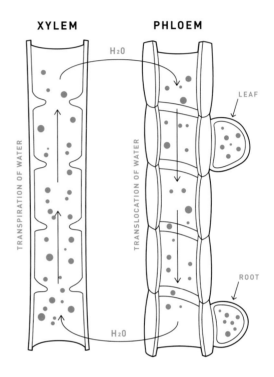

XYLEM **PHLOEM**

H_2O

TRANSPIRATION OF WATER

TRANSLOCATION OF WATER

LEAF

ROOT

H_2O

The vascular system within each maple trunk allows for the steady flow of water and plant sugars within the tree, keeping it strong and healthy over decades of growth.

also known as spinning jennys or whirligigs.)[1] Also like oaks and willows, maples are vascular plants, with the **xylem** in the tree's tissue conducting water and nutrients up and down the trunk and branches. The xylem tissues function like a complex network of tubes, connecting the water-absorbing roots of the tree and the oxygen-breathing leaves of the tree's crown.[2] If you were to look at a cross section of a sugar maple, you would see, just under the flaking outer bark, the inner bark, or **phloem,** which conducts sugars from the leaves to the rest of the living cells of the tree. You would then see a layer of growing cells called the **vascular cambium,** which produces the xylem as it grows (creating rings of xylem as the tree grows), and then beyond that, the first ring of xylem, called the sapwood. The unique quality of the maple tree is that its sap can be accessed barely ¼ inch into the tree, yet because typically less than 10 percent of the tree's sap is being removed during each sugaring season, the tree still receives all of its necessary water and nutrients even as it is being tapped. (This is

1 "Sugar Maple," *The Newport Arboretum*, last modified May 2015; available at: http://newportarboretum.org/home/portfolio/sugar-maple/.

2 F. W. Went, "Plant Plumbing," in Nearing and Nearing, *The Maple Sugar Book*, 127.

also part of the reason why maple wood is so porous and adaptable for the decorative arts, an issue we'll come to in the later part of this chapter.)

Sugar maple trees can grow as tall as 90 feet, with their canopies (or crowns) spreading as wide as 80 feet. The trees, meanwhile, could be hundreds of years old, and as wide as 50 inches in diameter. When we built our facility on our Madava estate in 2010, we sadly had to cut down one old maple that an expert dated back to around the mid-1840s. We have many other maples that we believe are much older, including a few 40-inch-diameter trees that are unfortunately on their last leg of life. I can't help but be in awe of these trees, thinking of mankind's history that their lives have spanned. The age and density of these maple tree groves, in fact, was the thing that was most distinctive for arriving settlers to the American shores. In Europe, more than 50 percent of old-growth forests had been cut down as early as the Middle Ages—imagine the astonishment of the European settlers as they approached American shores to discover huge forests of immense density and in vast abundance. These trees predated any kind of human interference, and certainly predated the industry that Natives or settlers would produce.

NATIVE AMERICANS AND THE ORIGINS OF MAPLE SYRUP

The American landscape these Europeans encountered seemed utterly wild—yet the land was far from undeveloped, and these maple reserves were not untapped. By the time Europeans began to arrive in the eastern part of North America in the late 1400s, various Native groups had established extensive agricultural practices, with sophisticated technologies and traditions of tilling and working the land to produce food. While the colonists liked to think of their new homeland as a kind of Edenic plot just waiting to be cultivated, anthropologists have identified patterns that would suggest that Natives regularly cleared the forests and undergrowth by way of deliberate burning. Plots of forests were actually cleared and defined through this process for easier crop management, leaving others pristine for hunting and scavenging. While burning woodlands might seem today to be an act of destruction, this proved to be an effective method for various tribes to create diverse habitats, both for cultivation and for preservation.

Native tribes of the Northeast, including the Iroquois of upstate New York, the Mohegan of Connecticut, the Algonquin of Ontario and Quebec, and the Micmac (Mi'kmaq) of New Brunswick, relied on creating tools for extensive agriculture to supplement the naturally plentiful wild fruit-bearing trees throughout the region. Carefully arranged interplantings of corn, squash, and beans, the "three sisters" staples of the regional diet, could be found in almost every community, oriented from east to west and formed in rows set about 3 feet apart across the hills. The mixture of these plants showed a sophisticated understanding of natural science: the bean plants converted nitrogen from the air into fuel for the corn plants, which would in turn offer a natural trellis for the beans to climb. The low-growing squash would cover the ground area between the rows of corn, preventing weeds or other errant seedlings from taking root and protecting the soil beneath them. And around these carefully plotted landscapes, especially those in the Adirondacks, there were dense thickets of trees, offering a natural supply of sap and hiding between them a regular supply of wild walnuts, berries, and greens, perfect for foraging and supplementing the Native diet.

In all of these communities spread across the Northeast, the presence of the maple tree was extraordinarily significant. Much of what we know about Native American culture and maple sugaring is muddled in myth or filtered through the accounts of European

As painted by Paul Kane in 1846, this portrait of an Ojibwe village at Sault Ste. Marie depicts an early gathering of native maple producers of the Ojibwe tribe.

colonists who documented the sugaring experience back to the mid-1500s. We have our first accounts of North American maple trees from the French navigator Jacques Cartier in 1540, as he and the French Franciscan priest André Thévet were exploring the region adjacent to the St. Lawrence River. Accounts from settlers of the period give varying levels of credit to the Native Americans who introduced them to maple sap, expressing skepticism as to whether the Natives actually possessed the technology and know-how for turning the sap into sugar. Yet many have also noted the preexisting innovations of each tribe's mastery of agriculture, and their deep knowledge of the syrup's tradition—the language to describe the syrup existed well in advance. The Algonquin called it *sinzibuckwud*, "drawn from wood"; the Cree called the tree *sisibaskwatattik* and its syrup *sisibaskwat*. The Ojibwe referred to the tree as *ninautik*, "our own tree," a staking of a claim if there ever was one. It is likely that Native communities first discovered the secret of the maple trees from watching the surrounding animals burrow into the trees to access their sap. A broken branch, a trickle of sap, a late winter icicle that

proved surprisingly sweet on the tongue—these were the likely motivations of the first maple appreciators. And so, somewhat unsurprisingly, the method for securing their sap could only have developed from a community who paid close attention to the forests.

Whatever each tribe's explanation might provide as the source, knowledge of the sweetness of the maple trees was well documented in oral tradition and storytelling—people would look with great anticipation to the Abenaki, the "sugar moon" (usually occurring during the first full moon of April or May), a day when families would gather and dance the "sugar dance" in thankfulness for the forest's generosity. (This would be the second sugar dance of the season; the first likely took place at the first tapping of the trees, a call to bring on warmer weather and to encourage the sap to flow.) The running of the maple sap was widely considered a signal of spring, a moment to celebrate the changing of the seasons and the rejuvenation of the nurturing world. The Anishinabek tribes would actually move down from their winter lodges to camp directly underneath the maple trees in early spring, so they could be ready for the first drips of sap directly from the trees. This anticipation of the season resembles the Crown Maple woods crew spending all day in the forests as the short but inevitably sweet maple season approaches.

The beginning of each year's sugaring season was long anticipated. Though women were traditionally responsible for agricultural work, tribesmen would often set aside time during the maple season to work the trees and collect the precious sap. In the middle of February, the tribe's sugar tapper would hack into a nearby maple until the blade would be wet with sap. From there, the edges of the gash in the tree would be cleaned with a knife and awl. To create an ad hoc channel for the sap to flow, a birch or sumac twig would be split and scraped out to form a gutter, then it would be wedged into place at the

The origin stories for maple syrup—which vary with each tribe—mix earthly miracles and divine forces, often incorporating a Creator figure such as Nanabozho (Ojibwe tradition), Glooscap (the Wabanaki), or Wisakedjak (Cree). It seems only appropriate that the story of maple syrup would require a divine explanation—how else could you explain the tree's annual gift of sweet water?

№ 1

One Iroquois legend starts with an unconscious axe swing: Woksis, the leader of the tribe, killed a deer for the following day's meal, and then threw his axe into the trunk of a maple tree. Overnight, the sap from the gash in the tree dripped into his wife's cooking pot, and seeing it full of what she thought was water, she proceeded to simmer the venison in the pot. Soon she saw that the meat had become coated in a thick, brown syrup, and she became fearful of her husband's distaste. Upon seeing the meal, he initially scolded her, but once he took a bite of the sweetly barbecued meat, he could not help but smile with delight.[1]

№ 2

The Ottawa and Chippewa version of the story suggests that the hero Nanabozho was traveling across the land when he came upon a village that appeared abandoned. He kept looking and soon found the people lying underneath the maples, their mouths wide open, waiting to drink the syrup trickling from the trees. Disgusted at the laziness of the villagers, Nanabozho filled the trees with a lake's worth of water, diluting the syrup. From then on the people would have to boil the sap to obtain their sugar; no matter how natural the source, the work would still have to be done to transform it into something spectacular.[2]

1 Falk, *Culinary History of the Finger Lakes*, 27–29.

2 Pflüg, *Ritual and Myth in Odawa Revitalization*, 104.

№ 3

The Lenape believed that the maple tree was the most beautiful tree in existence. One night, bugs crawled into the maple tree's bark, and the maple tree began to itch. The tree was much too large to scratch its own itch, so it called out to the forest for help. The beaver replied, "I can help you, but if I scratch you with my teeth, I will probably kill you." The mouse said, "I can dig into your roots, but I may kill them, and so you." The bear said, "I have big claws to scratch down your bark, but that will tear you up." Then a woodpecker flew by. "I can help you," she said, "for though my beak is sharp, I cannot dig all the way into your bark." All the woodpeckers of the forest started pecking at the tree, and soon the bugs were gone and the maple tree was delighted. A few years after that itchy night, there was very little rain in the forest, and the creeks and rivers dried up. The thirsty animals did not know what to do, but then the maple called out to them again. "You animals helped me so when I was in need—call the woodpeckers again." The woodpeckers came, and they pecked deep into the maple's bark until the sap began to flow. The sap of the maple tree saved the animals, and each year when the other foods in the forest went missing, there was the maple to call upon, even in the very dead of wintertime.[3]

3 Adapted from Red Hawk, "The Story of the Maple Tree."

ax cut to direct the sap into a bucket or *mocuck,* a basket made from woven strips of birch bark and sealed with pine resin. The sap collected would hardly be the sweet syrup we are able to prepare today—if enjoyed raw, it might barely register as more than a slightly sweet sugar-water, but plenty of Natives and early settlers enjoyed it without boiling it down, and incorporated it into almost every meal. Behold, America's first condiment.

The sap would be cooked in clay pots, in which stones that had been heated in a hot fire would be dropped directly into the sap to bring it to a boil until only thin sweet syrup remained. Alternatively, the sap would be left in its container overnight during a freeze; the majority of the water in the sap would rise to the surface, and the ice could be broken off to enjoy the greatly purified sugar liquid underneath. From there, the sap could be cooked down further until it crystallized into maple sugar and could be pressed into wooden molds to be shaped into decorative cakes or blocks for easy transportation. There was no wrong way to enjoy the fruits of the maple tree: Early settlers noted that Native Americans might drink it straightaway like water, mix it with dried corn or wheat into a porridge, or use it to cook meat or fish.

Maple was considered a blessed food, because of its restorative powers and its reliable generosity from year to year. For Native Americans of the region, sweet flavors were hard to come by prior to the boiling of maple syrup. While honey and wild berries were available, they were nothing compared to the intense sugar rush of the maple syrup. Due to the quick supply of caloric energy that the maple syrup would provide, many Native Americans felt it was a strength-booster. In his 1653 text *The Complete Herbal,* the English botanist Nicholas Culpeper noted that the consumption of maple syrup was "excellent good [and may] open obstructions of the liver and the spleen,

At left, this 1908 photograph shows the traditional Ojibwe method of making mocucks *(birch baskets) to collect maple sap. Above, a 1724 illustration showing how the cooking of the sap would have been done in clay pots.*

and easeth pain of the sides thence proceeding."[3] Other botanists documented that the maple bark was used with herbs to make medicinal pastes and salves. (The efficacy of these treatments may have had more to do with the specific herbs used for each remedy, especially those containing menthol, eucalyptus, and aloe, but the moist bark of the maple tree was ideal for such mixtures.)

Medicinal effects aside, the tree itself was revered for being so bountiful in its gifts—not only the prized syrup, but also the wood of the trees. Tribes throughout the maple regions would use fallen trees to make bowls, paddles, ladles, oars, and furniture, creating more stable

---

3 Culpeper's, *The Complete Herbal,* 179.

shelters and tools for everyday use without significantly depleting the bounty of sugar trees. These trees were considered, among many different tribes, to be a gift of the gods, plentiful and naturally provided; even settlers of the period had to acknowledge that the food was a "kind of manna."[4] During the yearly maple syrup ceremony, the Seneca tribe would address the maple with this humble prayer, burning tobacco in a sacrificial fire as the priest would speak:

> O partake of this incense, You the forests!
> We implore you to continue as before,
> The flowing waters of the maple.
> It is the will of the Creator
> That a certain tree should flow such water.
> Now may no accidents occur
> To children roaming in the forests.
> Now this day is yours
> May you enjoy it,—this day.[5]

THE ARRIVAL OF THE SUGAR-LOVING SETTLER

The bounty of the maple tree, and the value of its sugar, was a central part of the Native American experience. And so it is no wonder that its introduction to European settlers was a huge success. The first settlers to the maple regions of northeastern America arrived in 1497 with John Cabot, yet most of the settlements in the region were built between 1600 and 1670 by a combination of English and French colonists. Our first written documentation of maple sugaring in North America comes by way of the 1557 account by André Thévet, a French monk traveling with Jacques Cartier, who said upon cutting into a maple tree they found "a juice, which was

found to taste as good and as delicious, as the fine wine of Orleans or Beaune."[6] The settlers carefully observed and documented the processes by which Native Americans throughout the Northeast collected and "distilled" the juice from the maple trees, down to the very size of the tap and the yield of the syrup. A 1672 account from Nicolas Denys, a French aristocrat and one of the leading colonizers of the early Canadian landscape, speaks specifically to the tapping method of the Micmacs:

> A gash is made about a half a foot deep, a little hollowed in the middle to receive the water. . . . Below the gash, 5 or 6 inches, there is made a hole with a drill or gimlet, which penetrates to the middle of the gash where the water collects. There is inserted a quill, or two end to end if one is not long enough . . . in 2 or 3 hours it will yield 3 to 4 pots of the liquid.[7]

The ingenuity of the early tapping process was something that settlers knew to observe closely. The tribes of the region had a deep awareness of which trees to tap, when they would yield sap, how deeply to cut into the tree, and how to enjoy the maple juice. How fortunate, then, that in each settlement, Native Americans demonstrated to the arriving settlers the bounty of the land and the plentiful syrup that awaited them within the trees.

The process of concentrating the trees' sap into syrup fascinated these traders, missionaries, and early settlers, who documented the techniques used by the Native peoples they encountered. By then colonists had already developed a taste for sugar—sugar had been available in Western Europe since the Crusades, after Christian soldiers discovered the white crystallized sugar in lands occupied by their Turkish enemies. The

---

4 Nearing and Nearing, *The Maple Sugar Book*, 34.

5 Parker, *The Code of Handsome Lake*, 101.

6 Thévet, *Les Singularitez de la France*, 17.

7 Denys, *Histoire Naturelle*, vol. 2, xx.

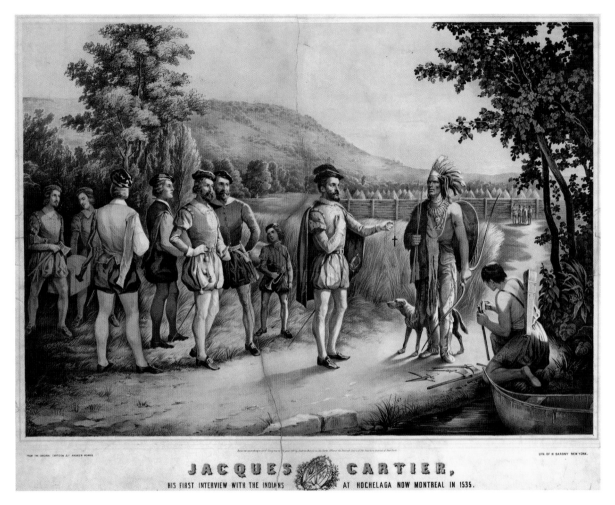

JACQUES CARTIER,

HIS FIRST INTERVIEW WITH THE INDIANS AT HOCHELAGA NOW MONTREAL IN 1535.

In this lithograph by Napoleon Sarony, we see Jacques Cartier in his first interview with the Indians at Hochelaga (now Montreal) in 1535. From the original cartoon by Andrew Morris.

cultivation of sugarcane for sweetener came almost simultaneously with the first waves of colonization of the Americas—in 1493 Columbus brought sugarcane plantings from the Spanish-ruled Canary Islands to the island of Santo Domingo, laying the groundwork for the first sugar colonies. The British colony of Barbados began its sugar production in the early 1640s, followed a few decades later by more plantations in Jamaica. The rise of the sugar industry was swift, responding to the incessant sweet tooth of the European market. It was also brutal, dependent on the labor of enslaved people, most of whom were brought from Africa by force to produce this most valuable commodity. Sugar had become a kitchen staple in England by the mid-eighteenth century. Its neutral flavor was incorporated into everything from specialty baked goods to afternoon tea.

Yet for those Europeans colonizing the northeast coast, the natural sugar of the maple tree was a symbol of burgeoning independence and self-reliance. In a land where food scarcity was a daily threat, tapping a maple tree would provide food in the early spring before crops would be available. It felt like a uniquely American enterprise, one that would take on even greater significance during the Revolutionary War—for the first (but far from last) time, the maple held an inherent political promise, that "those who have trees will not neglect the making of maple sugar, which is not only the most wholesome and pleasant sweetening, but being the product of our own country, will ever have the preference by every true American."[8] Details on the practice of producing maple syrup were even included in tracts sent to potential settlers who might set up new homesteads in Canada and the United States. An 1833 pamphlet produced in Dublin put the promise of the maple industry right up front, a beacon of potential success for the new arrivals:

A branch of rural economy and comfort, peculiar to North America, is necessary to be noticed for the information of the emigrant, which is the manufacture of maple sugar. The settler should examine his farm, and where he can get from 200–500 or more maple trees together, and most convenient, that should be reserved for a sugary.[9]

Yet first the colonist had to adopt the love of the syrup that the Native Americans promoted so freely. Seeing that the Natives used the syrup more than salt to season meat, they began to acquire the syrup themselves; settlers would buy baskets filled with maple sugar, what they termed "golden mocucks" from local tribes, and take them home to their new communities to experiment. Watching the Native American tradition of burying a pot of syrup-soaked beans in a fire pit to cook, settlers hung their iron pots over fires to simmer the first batches of New England–style baked beans, loaded up with slabs of pork fatback and cups of sweet syrup. It would've taken days for them to cook down the volume necessary to actually bottle the syrup, so what might have been cooked was a single day's haul from just one or two maple trees. Yet it was enough to season the foods of this new American landscape, and to add a sweet salve to these unfamiliar dishes.

The use of iron or copper kettles was a huge step forward for distilling the maple sap into syrup, and undoubtedly this was an advancement that colonists were happy to adopt. Additionally, the Native American method of cutting wide gashes into the tree to release the sap seemed a waste of potential sap. "It cannot be too often recommended to the sugar-makers, not to tap their trees with an axe, but to use a half-inch auger, which is a very useful tool to every farmer, and to plug up the hole

---

8 Lafitau, *Moeurs des Sauvages Ameriquains*, vol. 2, 155.

9 Found in Evans, *The Emigrant's Directory and Guide to Obtain Lands and Effect a Settlement in the Canadas*, 105.

at the end of the season."[10] Soon spouts were made from metal, stone, and other materials to insert into the trees. These new spouts would require only a small hole to be cut into the tree's trunk, less than half an inch in diameter, and would allow the spout to catch the entirety of the sap produced from the tree. However, to develop containers for the sap, settlers began to pull down other parts of the forest. Ash, basswood, and pine trees that might have fallen during earlier parts of the winter and fall would be hollowed out into troughs and then placed under the tree's spout to create a channel of troughs through which the sap could flow. Once the blacksmith trade began in greater force as more and more European colonists arrived, metal buckets were held on spikes that hung from each tree below its spout.

The full buckets could easily be transported to ad hoc sugar shacks that were built within the sugarbushes for the duration of the sugaring season. These were barely more than lean-tos, designed primarily to shelter boiler apparatuses from the wind and snow and to direct the steam out of the sugarhouse in great white smoky clouds. The actual cooking of the syrup was far from an exact science at the time, and recipes from the period are fairly inexact, with instructions ranging from "boil until it is done" to "boil as long as it can and not burn." Additionally, cooking times widely varied, depending on the amount of sap procured—a day's haul of syrup could be taken home the same day it was tapped, or it might be a commitment of many hours alone in the woods tending to the fire. The knowledge of what exactly they were cooking *for* was ambiguous. Colonists hoped it might resemble something from a past breakfast table—perhaps molasses, a by-product of processing sugar cane into sugar, or sorghum syrup, made from sorghum grass, or even coarsely granulated sugar. But most relied on

Though this photograph was taken in 1925, the early twentieth-century method of turning sap into syrup had remained mostly unchanged since the previous century.

This illustration from a 1916 issue of Harper's Weekly *shows the romantically rustic yet grueling work involved in the outdoor sugaring season.*

10 Rush, *An Account of the Sugar Maple-Tree of the United States*, 74.

Anno quinto

Georgii III. Regis.

C A P. XII.

An Act for granting and applying certain Stamp Duties, and other Duties, in the *British* Colonies and Plantations in *America*, towards further defraying the Expences of defending, protecting, and securing the same; and for amending such Parts of the several Acts of Parliament relating to the Trade and Revenues of the said Colonies and Plantations, as direct the Manner of determining and recovering the Penalties and Forfeitures therein mentioned.

WHEREAS by an Act made in the last Session of Parliament, several Duties were granted, continued, and appropriated, towards defraying the Expences of defending, protecting, and securing, the British Colonies and Plantations in America: And whereas it is just and necessary, that Provision be made for raising a further Revenue within Your Majesty's Dominions in America, towards defraying the said Expences: We, Your Majesty's most dutiful and loyal Subjects, the Commons of Great Britain in Parliament assembled, have

The Sugar Act of 1764 was only the first step in the Stamp Act of 1765, the notice of which was printed in the newspaper shown here. The Act consisted of a series of duties leveraged on colonists for their enjoyment of British-imported goods, included sugar made in the British-owned sugar plantations in the Caribbean. The sugar duties moved even more consumers toward the wild maple sugar— as we advanced toward independence, an independent sugar source became even more important.

their taste buds to identify the right sweetness, texture, and overall mapleness in the final product. It was the taste of the maple, after all, that made one fall in love with it.

THE EARLY MAPLE INDUSTRY

Prior to the nineteenth century, the maple industry in the United States was largely confined to backyard operations, on a scale that would be comparable to an urban beekeeper of today. This was partly due to the quick perishability of the maple product itself: In order to keep the sweetener beyond a short window of time, the sap would have to be boiled all the way down to sugar consistency, then left to dry and harden in cakes. While this would require no small amount of labor on the part of the person producing it, it would often leave farmers with huge stores of sugar for their personal use. By the time of the Revolutionary War, three out of four families in the American colonies owned their own farms, and for those farms in the maple-growing regions, that meant maple sugar would be used to season everything, including daily helpings of fresh milk and bread. Yet trade of maple sugar was primarily limited to within the colonies themselves, so maple would be traded with other Northeast-produced goods such as furs, fish, whale oil, and timber. Much of this trading took place within small communities; while the maple sugar could be pressed into bricks and transported, the syrup was more difficult to move, and would either be sold in large wooden barrels or in small metal tins that might easily pop open and release the syrup. In the pre-Revolutionary era, the maple sugar and syrup would often be passed over at markets in favor of the finer imported sugars from the West Indies (some of which would be processed into rum and then exported out again to Europe, Africa, and beyond). The volume of the maple sugaring industry paled in comparison to that of the sugar market: Of the millions of Africans captured and forced into slavery, many had been sent to work in the sugar-production colonies, raising and processing cane sugar to meet the insatiable demand of consumers.

Given its constant placement next to imported sugar, it's no wonder that maple syrup became the center of the first locavore movement in the Americas—the syrup was a local product, born first in the colonies and completely self-sustained. The consumption of West Indies–grown sugar was essential to colonists, but the passage of the Sugar Act in 1764, which raised import taxes for all cane sugar sources coming from non-British colonies, was squeezing them for even more revenue.[11] The colonists disdained tea, coffee, and other British-imported products as tariffs grew higher and higher; the question of what to do about America's unsustainable sugar addiction was at the fore. An article in the *New York Gazette* suggested a more local substitution, maple syrup:

> If some Man would build him a sugar-House, and provide a set of Boilers, and other Utensils, as they have in the West-Indies, I am persuaded he would find his Account in it, beyond what those in the West Indies can do. . . . All this charge might be subtracted from the Gentleman's account, who uses Maple trees, instead of cane, except the expence [*sic*] of tapping the trees, and gathering the sap, which is as nothing to compare with the other. . . . Trees fit for this business, are very plenty in the uncultivated Wilderness between Connecticut and Hudson's River, also in the Northern Borders of this Province: And could the one half of them be used I suppose they would more than furnish all the British Colonies upon the Continent with Sugar.[12]

---

11 Sugar Act of 1764, accessed July 5, 2015; available at: http://ahp.gatech.edu/sugar_act_bp_1764.html.

12 "Indian Method to Make as Good Sugar as the Islands Afford," *New York Gazette*, 1764.

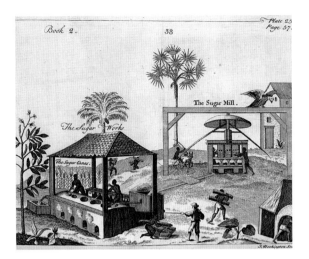

As depicted in this 1748 illustration, the elaborate sugar plantations built throughout Jamaica, Barbados, and the Caribbean could satisfy the early American demand for sugar, mostly through the use of enslaved labor.

How could colonists justify supporting foreign-provided sugar, when there was plenty of sustainable sugar right in their woods? Imagining maple syrup as an industry would mean having an emancipated sugar source, free from British control and developed by America's independent producers. Calls to develop maple into a standalone sugar trade rang out across the colonies for the next decade, and though sugar remained on the black market, many colonists began to nurture the wild maples into more organized and managed sugarbushes in the hopes of tapping an inherently American resource.

Throughout all of this, there was also the fundamental moral quandary of consuming cane sugar: not only did its trade profit from the insatiable appetite and high duties colonists would have to pay, but it also relied wholly on the enslavement of Africans forced to migrate to the West Indian cane plantations. Even with an increase in production, maple producers of the late eighteenth and early nineteenth century could

As painted by Thomas Sully in 1813, Benjamin Rush was a passionate abolitionist and advocate for goods produced without the aid of an enslaved workforce. His promotion of maple syrup in the years leading up to the Civil War led to the food's peak period of popularity.

not compete with the scale of cane sugar production, especially as it expanded into the American South. The Louisiana Purchase had opened up a burgeoning sugar industry, both on the mainland and, in 1849, in the American colony of Hawaii. Even with the British gone, sugar was going to be no small part of the American economy. People were also quick to disdain the brown color and unusual flavor of maple sugar, especially when compared to the highly refined, pure white, and neutral-tasting cane sugar to which they had become accustomed. An 1850 guide for farmers noted, "The sugar, in a brown state, has a peculiar flavor, very acceptable to those accustomed to it, though perhaps to some others objectionable."[13] The more comparable maple sugar could be made to cane sugar, the better; at the New York State Agricultural Fair of 1844, the committee deciding the prizewinning maple sugar sample based its acclaim mostly on its resemblance to cane sugar. "The whole coloring matter is extracted, and the peculiar flavor of maple sugar is completely eradicated, leaving the sugar fully equal to the double refined cane loaf sugar."[14]

Yet maple sugar was undoubtedly superior to sugar in its lack of reliance on African enslavement. Quakers were among the first of the colonist population to write about the link between slavery and the sugar trade, urging people to boycott sugar and choose alternative sugars instead. (This was part of the motivation for developing sugar from non-cane sources. Promotion of sugar made from beets first began in earnest in the United States during the Quaker Reformation in 1750. The desire to have access to slavery-free goods led to the creation of Free Produce societies, which bear a striking resemblance to today's community cooperative markets, that only supplied goods that were conflict- and slavery-free.)

13 Blake, *The Farmer's Every-Day Book*, 435.

14 Allen, *The American Farm Book*, 221.

The debates surrounding the compromised state of sugar were expressed in passionate diatribes from both politicians and civilians alike. William Cowper's 1788 poem "The Negro's Complaint" bemoaned the very existence of sugar, and the pain its harvest inflicted on the enslaved:

> Why did all-creating Nature
> Make the Plant for which we toil?
> Sighs must fan it, Tears must water,
> Sweat of ours must drench the soil.
> Think, ye Masters, Iron-hearted,
> Lolling at your jovial Boards,
> Think how many Backs have smarted,
> For the sweets your Cane affords![15]

In *Uncle Tom's Cabin*, Harriet Beecher Stowe even made a subtle reference to maple as the preferable choice to sugar during a visit to the homestead of the virtuous Miss Ophelia, St. Clare's abolitionist cousin. In it, the absence of slavery is signaled by the very presence of maple trees and a pervasive sense of order and respectability throughout the Vermont homestead:

> Whoever has travelled in the New England States will remember, in some cool village, the large farmhouse, with its clean-swept grassy yard, shaded by the dense and massive foliage of the sugar maple; and remember the air of order and stillness, of perpetuity and unchanging repose, that seemed to breathe over the whole place. Nothing lost, or out of order; not a picket loose in the fence, not a particle of litter in the turfy yard, with its clumps of lilac bushes growing up under the windows.[16]

Thomas Jefferson was deeply invested in the future of maple syrup, and he made a concerted effort to spread the word about its potential. This sketch from Lewis Miller's "Sketchbook of Landscapes in the State of Virginia," circa 1853, details the types of maple tree studies that early Virginian botanists would have performed.

---

15 Cowper, "The Negro's Complaint."

16 Stowe, *Uncle Tom's Cabin*, 226.

But sentiment was not enough to position maple as the moral choice in slave-owning America—the direct appeal from abolitionist to politician was crucial. The abolitionist Benjamin Rush (1746–1813) was central to the advancement of maple sugar over cane sugar during the period between the Revolutionary War and the Civil War. A prominent physician and politician in Philadelphia, he kept a close correspondence with Thomas Jefferson, and regularly wrote the then–secretary of state about his desire to undercut the cane sugar industry and promote maple sugar in its stead. He passionately pled his case for preserving and defending the sugar maples as a point of liberated commerce and production, citing its excellence in flavor—ideal for sweetening, as well as producing molasses, vinegar, and beer—and most importantly, an acceptable source of food for those protesting the institution of slavery. "I cannot help contemplating a Sugar Maple Tree with a species of affection and even veneration; for I have persuaded myself to behold in it the happy means of rendering the commerce and slavery of our African brethren in the sugar islands, as unnecessary as it has always been inhuman and unjust."[17]

Compared to the vile reputation of cane sugar, maple sugar was an "innocent" food, and other abolitionists agreed—Robert B. Thomas's 1803 *Farmer's Almanack* declared that maple sugar was "more pleasant and patriotic than that ground by the hand of slavery, and boiled down by the heat of misery," and that consumers should "feast not on the toil, pain, and misery of the wretched." In 1840's *Walton Vermont Register and Farmer's Almanac,* tasting notes for syrup are discussed as if they require a moral compass. "Sugar made at home must possess sweeter flavor to an independent American of the north, than that which is mingled with the groans

and tears of slavery."[18] Jefferson took up the cause himself, joining Rush's society for promoting the manufacture of sugar from the maple tree—after all, he himself had set down his own plot of sugar maples at Monticello in 1791.[19] Jefferson urged American farmers to increase their production to supply the American market and beyond. If maple became a reliable export, it could put the sugar producers out of business entirely. In 1790, syrup was sold at half the price of sugarcane, and maple forests of the period were not at risk to pests or disease in the same way sugar plantations were. (Considering bulk commodity prices of the late eighteenth century, a pound of imported cane sugar cost $0.21, about $5.50 today, whereas a pound of maple sugar cost about $0.10, about $2.25 today.)[20] Jefferson doubled down on his pledge during a 1791 trip with James Madison to Vermont, the newest state in the union, where he urged farmers and landowners to plant orchards of maples just as they would apple trees. "I have never seen a reason why every farmer should not have a sugar orchard, as well as an apple orchard," he wrote. Jefferson spoke frequently and at length about his preference for maple syrup. In the new whaling port of Hudson, New York in 1791, Jefferson urged the founder of the town's distillery to find a substitute for molasses, and encouraged some of the most prominent landholders in Bennington, Vermont, to approach the development of maple sugarbushes in the same way that they had built their orchards. His advice was broadcast in the *Vermont Gazette,* and one Bennington acquaintance, Joseph Fay, resolved "to

---

17 Rush, *An Account of the Sugar Maple-Tree of the United States,* 76.

18 Nearing and Nearing, *Maple Sugar Book*, 19.

19 "The Trees of Monticello," accessed July 1, 2015; available at: http://www.monticello.org/site/house-and-gardens/trees-monticello.

20 Berry, *Western Prices before 1861*, 568.

plant an orchard in regular form next spring, in hopes to encourage others in the same laudable undertaking."[21]

So why, given that maple had the upper hand politically and economically, did it not manage to overtake the popularity of cane sugar? Certainly the abolitionist arguments did slightly lessen the sale of slave-grown sugar, especially during the Civil War, but ultimately it became a question of volume and transportation. Maple trees require a very specific terroir to flourish, a rich yet moist soil with a prolonged spring to bring the sap down, and transplanting became a challenge. Efforts to bring the trees to mapleless parts of Europe and the American colonies were undertaken, and some strains of the sap-producing maple tree took root, but even those carefully transplanted saplings did not flourish into the "large plantations" Jefferson had anticipated. Today at Monticello you can see the last of the remaining saplings on the West Lawn of Jefferson's estate. Whether it was a result of improper planting technique, or inadequate tapping, it remains unclear; needless to say, the saplings were never quite as successful as Jefferson's vineyards. Syrup remained something best retained by its maker, hard to distribute and quickly enjoyed. And yet the awareness of the maple syrup industry led to an increase of production in the North. With more intrepid sugarmakers throughout the Northeast putting taps into trees, each subsequent spring brought thousands of pounds of maple sugar and syrup to the region, making it a signature food item and American flavor.

21 "Sugar Maple," accessed July 1, 2015; available at: http://www.monticello.org/site/house-and-gardens/sugar-maple.

— 2 —

Maple's Big Boom and Bust: A Century of Maple Ups and Downs, 1860–1950

AS WE'VE ESTABLISHED, maple's position as a food of virtuous origin moved consumers, producers, and politicians alike to support its growth. The moral incentive to choose maple over other sugars made it a stable source of revenue for the American Northeast, and proved vital during the hard times of the Civil War (1861–65). And in 1860, maple experienced its peak production year, with 40 million pounds of sugar and 1.6 million gallons of syrup reported to the USDA. While the South was crippled by the loss of its slave-based economy and the unspeakable human casualties of the war years, the North was revitalized by the movement of formerly enslaved people northward to support the growth of new industries and new economies. Though the model of the southern plantation was no longer available, and much of the South and mid-Atlantic suffered through a deep agricultural depression in the later part of the nineteenth century, in other parts of the country this period was a great time to be an American farmer, and by extension a maple syrup producer. Farms spread across the country and into the western territories, and the work that came with farming was better rewarded financially than ever before.[22] In addition, more policies were put in place to encourage the consumption of American-made food products and to limit imports from other parts of the world. But this boom was not the prolonged sugar takeover the abolitionists had hoped for.

22 Cochrane, *The Development of American Agriculture*, 341–52.

E. MOSHER.

Sap-Spout.

No 26,858.   Patented Jan. 17, 1860.

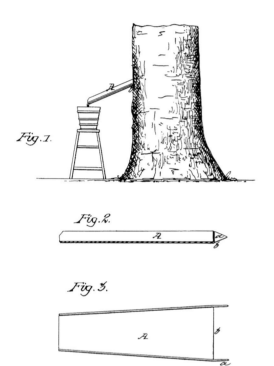

Eli Mosher's patent for the first metal spout ensured a tighter fit between tree and tap and thus greater sterility for the sap collected.

EXPANDING THE MAPLE PRODUCER'S MARKETPLACE

There were, of course, still challenges facing the American maple producer. For one, it was impossible to rely on income from a product that could only be made six weeks out of the year. Much as farmers and ranchers in other parts of the country would harvest different crops in seasonal rotation, many maple producers in New England have also traditionally been dairy farmers, especially throughout New York State and into southern Canada. The proliferation of farmers throughout the United States meant that a farmer could specialize in a few key crops but stagger them year-round, and the same wide swaths of hilly landscape ideal for growing maple trees worked well as grazing pasture throughout the year. The emergence of the dairy industry allowed maple producers to become far more secure in their yearly income; rather than relying on one short season for all the sugar their family could eat and sell, there was an opportunity to develop and hone the craft of sugaring while remaining profitable in the dairy business. The development of the transcontinental railroad in the latter half of the nineteenth century, and the creation of refrigerated railway cars in 1870, meant that farmers could transport milk and maple side by side into the Midwest and beyond. Maple syrup might still be a regional product, but it could now be nationally distributed, as could many other regional foods from the Northeast. This, of course, was entirely dependent on demand for maple across the country, which, as is evident from the early days of maple, took some time to develop.

ADVANCES IN MAPLE TECHNOLOGY

Most valuable to the booming production of maple syrup during this period was the emergence of newly efficient technology. Prior to the Civil War, the predominant technology for tapping the trees had remained fairly static—wooden spouts or spiles, accompanied by the use of augers (spiral drills) to create easy bore holes to access the sap, were hammered a few inches into the tree. A bucket was hung below to catch the sap. But this period of peak maple syrup demand led to a new focus on improving the basic sugaring method, with several key developments in the technology of tapping and evaporating. In 1860, Eli Mosher patented the first metal spout, which progressed from a wider end nearer to the tree to a narrower, tapered end as the spout entered the collecting bucket, and with a sharpened edge so it could be driven directly into the tree and still maintain a tight seal against the bark.[23] In 1875, the first metal sap collection buckets were introduced, making the collection of the sap more sterile than ever before. The aim of these maple innovators was to not only improve the methods of collecting the sap from the trees, but also to find ways to make the maple syrup industry run more efficiently for a range of producers, large and small.

It's not surprising that much of the innovation of the period focused on the cooking process itself—specifically by moving from the midcentury multikettle method to a contained and sheltered sugarhouse (first introduced in the 1850s) and, most importantly, to an evaporator that would speed up the syrup boiling process. In 1858, D. M. Cook of Ohio patented the first evaporating pan, designed with curved channels to separate the maple into spaces of varying width and depth. Called "flame-fines," these channels divided the surface area of the pan to create a vertical wavelike path for the sap to travel.[24] This followed on the early innovations of settlers who knew to boil their syrup in flat-bottomed pans rather than in rounded kettles, to increase the overall surface area on which the sap would be exposed to heat.

---

23 Mosher, Improvements in Sap-Conductors.

24 Cook, Improvements in Pans for Evaporating Cane-Juice.

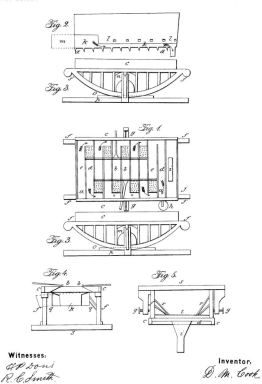

D. M. Cook's evaporator pan for cooking sap was a huge advance over the kettle-cooking methods of the past, improving the process with "flame-fines" to help channel the sap over a wide heated surface.

Improvements in maple technology spurred the growth of the maple producers in the late nineteenth century. Evaporator technology cut down the most demanding part of the syrup-making process, and allowed the syrup to finally become a cash commodity.

In 1864, David Ingalls added baffles to his evaporator pan, helping to create a channel for the boiling sap so it could be more easily and clearly separated from the finished syrup. Nearly three decades later, in 1890, George Wheeler introduced his patent for evaporating the water content from maple syrup using an enclosed flue pan with both an insulated cover and a drafted chimney to pull away steam without creating any further condensation.[25] In 1911, George H. Soule developed an evaporator with two pans and a metal arch or firebox to be installed underneath, decreasing the overall boiling time required to cook down the sap.[26] The advent of these new technologies was essential to meeting the postwar demand for maple—at the close of the century, maple syrup had become a huge cash commodity for producers throughout New England, and especially in Vermont, where by 1890 producers were refining 14 million pounds of

maple per year (about a quarter of the nation's supply). Of course, not all these advances in technology were perfect—in 1916, W. C. Brower invented metal tubing for sap-gathering, which, though durable, proved impractical during freezing winter nights.[27]

Developments in canning technology also helped push maple forward. During the Civil War, Union and Confederate soldiers received canned foods as part of their regular diets, but that was primarily limited to nutritional necessities on the battlefront, like canned fruit and preserved meats. Upon the conclusion of the war, many former soldiers began incorporating canned goods into their homefront meals, and by 1871 the U.S. canning industry was turning out more than 30 million cans of food per year, up from 5 million cans in 1860.[28] The ability to hot-pack maple syrup into tin cans immediately expanded its durability, and allowed the size of the maple product purchased to become smaller and easier for storage. This also marked the turning point at which syrup displaced sugar as the preferred form of syrup—by 1948, 97 percent of the total maple haul each year would be sold as syrup rather than sugar.[29] Yet with cane sugar rapidly becoming cheaper than maple, in both sugar and syrup form, this preference was to be somewhat short-lived.

ADULTERATIONS AND IMITATIONS

But while real maple producers were benefiting from new forms of technology, the threat of blended and imitation maple syrup was on the horizon. In 1887, Minnesota grocer P. J. Towle created a unique mixture—45 percent pure maple syrup, 55 percent cane sugar syrup—to produce the first-ever batch of Log Cabin

---

25 Wheeler, Process of Evaporating Maple-Sap or Other Fluids.

26 Soule, Maple-Sap Evaporator.

27 Brower, Sap-Collecting System.

28 Trager, *The Food Chronology*, 285.

29 Nearing and Nearing, *The Maple Sugar Book*, 195.

Syrup for retail. He priced this much lower than the pure maple syrup available on the market, and put it in a tin container shaped like a log cabin (the boyhood home of his hero, Abraham Lincoln).[30] Perhaps he was seizing on the residual anti-slavery sentiments surrounding maple syrup, or perhaps he was simply undercutting the more expensive retailers, but Log Cabin Syrup's distinct look and low price made it a popular choice for consumers. Other producers followed suit, making their own batch syrups with a mixture of sweeteners (sugar, molasses, and corn syrup, which had been in production since 1812) and fenugreek or hickory bark (to give off a maple flavor). These fake maplers were primarily storefront owners, getting directly to the consumer with their watered-down product before the real maple producers could do anything about it.

Trade magazines for maple producers were horrified at the notion that their syrup could be watered down and still marketed in the same nostalgic fashion. Similarly, an 1888 *New York Times* article called the maple adulteration movement "wholly counterfeit," and said, "While this rank and unnatural compound might deceive the inexperienced palate, the connoisseur would instantly miss the wild and delicate flavor and fragrance peculiar to the genuine article."[31] But this was an age of invention, and producers were trying to find a loophole through which they might capitalize on the popularity of an existing product while making something entirely their own. The magazine *Ohio Farmer* elaborated on this dilemma in an 1898 article by E. V. Bentley, stating that the whole matter might be resolved by "one single act by Congress, forbidding the sale of an imitation under the name of that which it is intended to imitate. Requiring all imitations, mixtures, and compounds . . . to be sold under a specific

This 1929 print ad was made and sold by the Log Cabin Syrup Company. What's notably still included in this advertisement is the word "maple," a label that would later be considered misleading given the lack of any real maple sap or syrup in the mix.

---

30 Trager, *The Food Chronology*, 326.

31 "Maple Sugar: Some Facts about the Trade and How the Article Is Adulterated," 8.

name of its own with a label giving the formula—ingredients, and proportions."[32] The question was not of imitation, but of transparency; no imitation syrup could claim to be 100 percent pure maple, but there was no barrier to giving themselves a new product name.

This question of advertising pure maple differently from that of its imitation competitors was at least partially resolved by the Pure Food and Drug Act of 1906, which required producers and sellers to label their products with a list of every ingredient included therein. The act was motivated by numerous incidents of egregious corner-cutting and additive use in the food industry. Just a few years prior, Upton Sinclair's *The Jungle* had exposed the horrific practices of the meatpacking industry (in which minced tripe would be dyed red and be sold as "deviled ham"), and the USDA had instituted a "poison squad" to test an array of American products for dangerous chemicals.[33] The concern was not only for the safety of the American consumer, but also for holding American producers to a new standard of production.

SUGAR-LOVING POLICIES AND PRICES

Yet for all the technological advances of the period, for all the stability that other industries and a few key laws had provided, maple still had one very real source of competition: cane sugar. What really ended maple's boom cycle of the late nineteenth century was the reemergence of cane sugar as a plentiful and accessible commodity. By 1884, the United States was consuming 38 pounds of sucrose per person per year, ahead of all major world consumers except the United Kingdom. In just three years, that sugar consumption had risen to 60.9 pounds per person.[34] The creation of the American consumer

The McKinley Tariff of 1890 gave a new batch of incentives to maple producers, leading more than 2,600 new people to file for sugar-making licenses in 1892. Yet as shown in this Boston Globe *political cartoon from May 1898, it also preceded the annexation of the Philippines, Cuba, Puerto Rico, Guam, and Hawaiian Islands, giving the United States unprecedented access to the islands' sugar plantations. (Here a waiter named McKinley serves up a menu from the U.S.'s new selection of food-producing territories.)*

market after the Civil War spurred extensive interest and access to sugar for the mainstream consumer, and halted the spread of the American maple industry before it could grow any further.

Price stabilization was a major factor in returning maple to its former obscurity: during the Civil War, duties on tea, coffee, and sugar were increased as a war effort to stimulate the economy, and the disruption of the activity on the sugar plantations in the South sent prices soaring. For a period sugar production was moved to the Hawaiian Islands, where there was plenty of cane sugar planted for harvest. This momentary disruption in the market left an opening for maple syrup, leading to its record year of production in 1860. But while maple had proven itself a worthy competitor to cane sugar for nearly twenty years, by 1880 maple sugar and cane sugar were approximately equal in price. Though the Pure Food

32 Bentley, "Adulterations and Imitations," 93, 11, 229.

33 Husband, *Daily Life in the Industrial United States, 1870-1900*, 155.

34 Mintz, *Sweetness and Power*, 188.

and Drug Act had bolstered the reputation of real maple syrup over its imitators, cane sugar was swiftly becoming cheaper than maple syrup—and more popular and widely distributed. The sustainable sugar beet industry began to become commercially viable by the 1870s, adding yet another competitor to the sweetener field, and one that could be produced at a greater volume and cheaper price than maple sugar and syrup.[35] Additionally, Americans had never really gotten over their preference for white sugar as the default sweetener: An 1893 letter to *Garden and Forest* magazine claimed that most city people did prefer the true taste of maple syrup, but that as white sugar became cheaper, maple was prized more as a distinct flavor than an everyday sweetener.[36]

Finally, while some of the laws of the period had bolstered the financial and marketing independence of the maple producers, there was still no true rollback of the availability of sugar. The McKinley Tariff of 1890 was enacted to protect domestic American manufacturers from foreign competition and, in doing so, generated revenue for the federal government. The tariff leveraged new duties on important goods such as wool, cotton, and certain metals, and offered a bounty to maple producers between 1891 and 1895 for two cents a pound for any high-quality maple sugars produced, and one and three-quarter cents a pound on lower-quality sugar. This was a huge incitement to aspiring maple producers, and more than 2,600 Vermont sugar makers took out license papers to make sugar in 1892.[37] Yet sugar was not subject to new duties under this bill, due perhaps to the significant United States stake in the sugar plantations in the Hawaiian Islands in place since the mid-1870s. (This is partially why, by 1885, cane sugar had dropped

to a lower price than that of maple sugar.) By the end of the Spanish-American War of 1898, the islands were officially annexed to the United States, and Spain had also ceded Puerto Rico, Guam, and the Philippines to the United States; they were all rich in sugar plantations and now part of the sugar economy. With the huge trove of sugar supplies available to the American market, sugar was now back to its pre–Civil War prominence. Maple producers looked upon the McKinley bill as a failure, saying, "The maple sugar bounty has no friends among Washington officers."[38] It took a long time for America to end its dependency on foreign sugar sources, but the wave of newly acquired sugar territories and the rise of the economically viable beet sugar industry meant that American sugar needs could be met in a refined, granulated state at last, and there was no incentive to promote maple sugar over all others. Cane sugar didn't need a moral platform to be appealing—it was a novelty, the product of American expansion and industry, and maple looked antiquated by comparison.[39] Moreover, Congress removed the tariff on foreign sugar in 1890, and instituted a bounty on sugar produced in the United States. In the following three years, only about $66,000 of that bounty went to maple sugar, a miniscule amount compared to that of the beet and cane sugar producers.[40]

Perhaps it was no surprise, given the limitations in product capacity. Maple had experienced record periods of production during the Civil War, as more New Englanders were encouraged to tap up their own maple stands as part of the war effort. But once wartime ended, the urgency fueling maple production dropped precipitously. From its peak of 40 million pounds of maple sugar in 1860, by 1870 production was down to

35 Kaufman, "Salvation in Sweetness?" 95.

36 Beahrs, *Twain's Feast*, 256.

37 Nearing and Nearing, *The Maple Sugar Book*, 64.

38 Hills, *Vermont Agricultural Report, 1893*, 108.

39 Woloson, *Refined Tastes*, 28–29.

40 Warner, *Sweet Stuff*, 165.

28 million pounds, by 1910 it was down to 14 million, and down to barely 2 million by 1930. Syrup was somewhat more stable, with a peak year in 1910 at 4 million gallons, but declining over the following decades down to 1.6 million gallons in 1949.[41] The problem was at least partially due to the trees: The method of making maple syrup was not easily scalable for mass production and cross-country distribution, and without clearly paved paths through the forests, sugarbushes still remained difficult to traverse without a sled. During World War I and World War II, maple experienced another brief rebound as worldwide sugar was scarce, but even then the appetite for white sugar did not entirely dissipate. (Per capita consumption of granulated white sugar in the United States in 1915 was double the level of what it was in 1880, partially due to the burgeoning carbonated soda industry.[42]) Maple consumption was not motivated so much by changing tastes but by a need to conserve the cane sugar supply. The 1917 United States Food Administration booklet "Seven Ways to Save Sugar" offered maple as a palliative for those cutting back on white sugar. "Can fruit without sugar. Use less sugar in tea and coffee. . . . Use honey, maple syrup and syrups, and other sweeteners. Cut out all desserts or other sweets that require sugar."[43] Cookbooks of the period, as well as those published during World War II, encouraged the use of maple syrup and sugar as a baking substitute for white sugar, but were more focused on limiting the amount of sugar used than eliminating it altogether. (Some cookbooks advocated simply skipping the frosting on the cake to cut back on the overall sugar needed.[44]) Maple prices held steady at $3.39 per gallon during

World War II (about $60 in today's dollars), still wildly out of reach for the struggling homefront American even as sugar was shipped overseas to support the troops. Consumers wary of maple's high prices continued to look for flavor substitutes. The Seattle-based Crescent Manufacturing Company struck gold in 1905 when company chemists developed the product Mapleine, an imitation maple flavor that many cash-strapped housewives used as a substitute during the Great Depression.[45] This flavoring was ideal for cooks and bakers, as they could still use conventional white sugar but get as much or as little maple flavor as they wanted (without ponying up for real syrup). The increasing availability of imitation syrups was always going to attract the most cost-concerned consumers—but real maple aficionados were out there, and many people could tell the difference between the artificial Mapleine and the truly distinct flavor of natural, pure maple syrup.

CHANGING OF THE MAPLE GUARD

Yet even as maple experienced these small booms and busts, more people were becoming committed to the study and maintenance of maple production and promotion. In 1888, Leader Evaporator Co. opened in Vermont and served as the dominant maple-equipment supplier to the new producers across the region, supplying metal taps and evaporators and lending guidance to those just entering the sugaring business. This came just as Vermont was establishing itself as America's maple capital, forming the Vermont Maple Sugar Makers Association in 1893, one of the oldest nongovernmental agricultural organizations in the country. The guidance of a formal association to determine rules and regulations for producing maple syrup made up for the lack of

41 Nearing and Nearing, *The Maple Sugar Book*, 228.

42 Trager, *The Food Chronology*, 412.

43 Eighmey, *Food Will Win the War*, 183.

44 "World War I Sugar Substitutes No Sacrifice Today."

45 "Crescent Manufacturing Company," last updated September 13, 2004; available at: http://www.historylink.org/index.cfm?DisplayPage=output.cfm&File_Id=2006.

federal coordination, and set standards for new producers that would clearly show that they were qualified to produce real maple syrup, no imitations allowed. In this sense, Vermont also became the only state to truly take on maple as its signature sweetener, with yearly celebrations surrounding the sugaring season and the resources to encourage local maple entrepreneurship. In 1904, the Cary Maple Sugar Company was incorporated in Vermont, making it the largest wholesale maple sugar company in the United States.

The early twentieth century is also the period in which we see the first generation of maple producers hand off the business to their children. The decades of trying to eke every drop out of a limited production line, and battling against competing sugar prices, had put some producers off the taste of continuing with their sugar groves. Some producers liquidated their orchards, selling the trees to mills demanding hardwood. Some were financially devastated after a 1938 hurricane destroyed many remaining maple groves.[46] Some simply felt that the work of keeping up the sugarbush wasn't worth the small amount of income they could create from local maple sales, especially when people could get imitation syrups at their local stores for a fraction of the price. But for those producers who passed their stands down to their children, it was an opportunity to bring the maple industry to its full technological heights. Producers began to consult in collaboration with each other, seeking out information on when each was seeing the first run start, determining what trees might be dying off or just ready to be tapped. The alliances within the region of maple producers created a powerful community of knowledgeable sugarmakers—quite similar, in essence, to the communal knowledge that Native Americans had shown with their early sugarmaking.

A NEWFOUND RESPECT FOR REGIONAL CUISINE

During the twentieth century, what also emerges is a deeper, richer appreciation of maple as a regional specialty, a food with a specific terroir, and a community that deeply understands its process and prestige. During the Works Progress Administration, the Federal Writers' Project commissioned the first series of *America Eats*, a collection of essays featuring regional cuisines, to put starving writers to work and to clearly document the culinary traditions around the country as they were practiced in the late 1930s. This was a period before fast food, when the refrigerator or "icebox" was still somewhat novel, and the arrival of regionally sourced fruits, like oranges from Florida or melons from Texas, still constituted a major event.[47] In his contribution to the series, titled "Vermont Sugaring-Off," the journalist Roaldus Richmond wrapped a blanket of nostalgia around the sugaring season, making the vista of Vermont in winter as majestic as the first appearance of maple sap:

> White mists rise from the snow-banked stream and fade in the early sun. Smoke plumes from the chimneys of farmhouses along the valley. . . . As the sun climbs the day grows warm. The snow patches soften and melt, the eaves drip, and in the sugar orchards sap tinkles into the pails. Farmers look at the weather and nod significantly. 'She's going to run today, boys, she'll sure run today.' It is the perfect sugaring day.[48]

This picturesque setting was not only to entice people to choose maple syrup with this gorgeous scenery in mind, but also to invite them to take a journey to the sugarhouse itself. As automobiles became more available

46 Whynott, *The Sugar Season*, 15.

47 Kurlansky, *The Food of a Younger Land*, 2.
48 Herd, *Maple Sugar*, 763–65.

across the country, the opportunity to participate in an early form of culinary tourism was finally available as a cheap, weekend form of regional entertainment. With changing accessibility and new opportunities for exploring and experiencing new places, it became more possible for the former snowbirds who had settled western and southern states to return home for a taste of their beloved maple syrup. The study of maple syrup was also more clearly formalized during this period: the University of Vermont and Cornell University opened research centers for maple syrup beginning in the 1940s, to better understand what was happening to the trees and sugaring seasons as they progressed. While maple syrup was still a niche product, it was something that the new generation of makers—and consumers—was taking very seriously.

— 3 —
The Renaissance of Forests and Maple Syrup Makers, 1970–Present

NEW TECHNOLOGIES

Though midcentury America found itself enchanted with consumer products made with newly scientific and artificial methods of processing, the new food technologies of the last fifty years not only made maple syrup more popular, but also more plentiful and of higher quality. With each decade of maple production, outmoded technologies were streamlined and replaced with tools that were both more durable and better suited to maple syrup as an industry rather than merely a hobby. In 1959, Nelson Griggs of Vermont patented the first plastic sap-gathering pipeline system, and it is impossible to overstate just how much this transformed the industry. Even with the advent of quality evaporators in the 1890s, maple production was still constrained by the sugarbush itself. Producers have not always had the resources to clear out and pave roads to make transportation from trees to sugarhouse easily accessible. With the addition of plastic tubing to create a network of pipelines throughout the forest, access to hundreds of acres at a time from a strategically placed collection house was possible. This system was uniquely designed to take advantage of the typically hilly, tree-crammed maple landscape; using gravity to drain the sap downhill toward a strategically placed collection house eliminated the need to gather individual buckets on a daily basis during the sugaring season. Finally, producers saw a major leap forward in the collecting process—one that people are now tinkering with even more, as pressurized vacuum systems are added to the tubing networks, expanding the efficiency with which maple sap is collected (and dramatically increasing the volume of sap that the vacuum system can provide).

The next major innovation in maple came in the 1970s with the introduction of reverse-osmosis machines. While evaporators had provided a significant advance over the multikettle boiling system of the early colonists, the challenge of removing the bulk of the water from sap remained the same. In order to process sap into syrup, one has to boil the sap to cook out the bulk of its water content, and to be able to increase the sugar concentration up to a minimum of 66° Brix. All maple producers know that maple hits a sweet spot where it contains exactly the right proportion of sugar to water, and that measurement for sugar concentration is called Brix, a unit for measuring the sugar density of the finished syrup. (See page 80 for much more on Brix and the science behind its determination.) Removing enough water to reach the desired Brix for maple syrup made with the old-fashioned multikettle system would have been a multiday process—and even with the improvements of the evaporator, this boiling down could take up to twenty-four hours to complete. With the introduction of the reverse-osmosis machine, maple producers were able to complete a preboiling removal of up to 90 percent of the water in the sap. It's no small surprise that this innovation for maple came in the same historical period as a water shortage crisis: the reverse-osmosis machine was developed in 1959 by graduate student Sidney Loeb as he was commencing his Ph.D. at UCLA. While researching methods of desalination, Loeb began to explore the filtration mechanisms involved by creating a membrane with a very thin skin surrounding a thick porous support layer. This created a kind of semipermeable filter through which water could move but salinity could be controlled. This discovery of the effect of manufactured reverse osmosis on water was immediately cheered by maple syrup producers. It

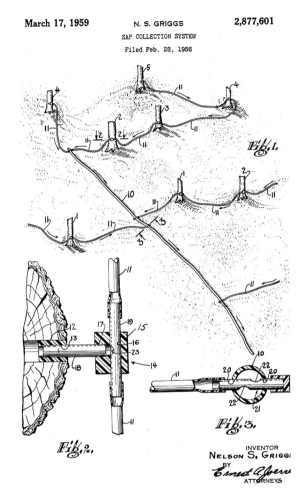

Nelson Griggs's patent for the first plastic sap-gathering pipeline was a breakthrough for maple producers to more effectively and efficiently collect sap.

would mean that, in the process of concentrating maple sap from its original 2 percent sugar to 8 percent sugar (a 75 percent reduction in the amount of water right off the bat), the initial run of syrup could be just ten gallons of sap rather than a full forty-three (a huge improvement on the Rule of 86; see page 81). This would also save an enormous amount of money when it came to fuel (especially important during the energy crisis of the 1970s.[49] Today, almost every major producer has an RO machine in their sugarhouse, and many producers do a 90 percent reduction of water right away. (Learn more about the RO machine on page 74.)[50]

NEW PRODUCERS IN THE NEW HUDSON VALLEY

Much of preserving the future of maple syrup depends not on the producers of the past, but on developing new farmers and new potential sugarmakers to pick up the business and continue to develop the region's rich agricultural heritage. Many people think of New York as just the city, but there are more than 36,000 farms throughout New York State—representing a $53.7 billion industry for the state and providing more than 200,000 jobs.[51] The area surrounding us in Dutchess County has some of the most beautiful naturally grown produce on the East Coast—apples, tomatoes, grapes, corn, cucumbers, and squash—and over the last decade, the farmers tending those crops have increasingly been former city mice rather than longtime farmers. The relationship between local agriculture and the dynamic culinary scene of New York City has never been stronger, and so intrepid young farmers and restaurateurs are looking to the Hudson River Valley for inspiration. Maybe it's a generational sense of distance from the natural world (much like what I observed when first looking for a vacation place), but it's also a desire to build a concrete relationship to your own food supply. In 2014, Governor Andrew Cuomo began a new initiative to support early-stage farmers with grant funds and loan forgiveness programs, a way to incentivize new farmers to start planting with a bit of help getting their start-up costs covered.[52]

Does this mean people are getting into the maple syrup business, though? I suppose it depends on if you count me as one of the "new, young" farmers out there. But I do believe that there are many potential farmers who are on the fence even as we speak—they may just not be farmers yet. Rarely are the crops a farmer's only source of income, and as in periods of farming past, maple syrup producers have almost always had a side gig or crop to nurture in the maple off-season. In a study conducted in 2007 among Hudson Valley farmers, many noted that they had a supplementary business in addition to their farming, or that the farming itself was a postretirement venture after concluding a more lucrative career off the farm.[53] And while more farmers may be flourishing in the Valley, they're not all able to make a living off their crops. In 2007, average annual sales per farm in Dutchess County were $68,300; average production costs in that same year were $88,800.[54] While dedicated maple producers would dislike the thought of being called "hobbyists," there is a question of how to entice people to open new food businesses on a scale that isn't simply a backyard production (as many of these very

49 Whynott, *The Sugar Season*, 59.

50 Cohen and Glater, "A Tribute to Sidney Loeb."

51 DiNapoli and Bleiwas, "The Role of Agriculture in the New York State Economy."

52 Press Office at Governor Andrew Cuomo, "Governor Cuomo Launches New Farmers Grant Fund to Support Agribusiness in New York."

53 Glynwood Center Inc., "The State of Agriculture in the Hudson River Valley," 28.

54 Ibid., 37.

small producers are), or to knowingly enter a business that tends to experience net loss from year to year. The twenty-first-century maple producer has much more on his mind than when the run might start—he may be thinking about how to clearly describe the terroir of his sugarbush on his packaging, or whether to set up a website and social media feed to get early orders going, or how to entice visitors to come see his facilities in action during the sugaring season. The interesting thing about many first-time farmers today, at least in my opinion, is that their relationship to food started with them being consumers—and questions about the food's source came much later.

Luckily, the first-time maple producer is not alone anymore. Resources like the exceptionally talented team at Cornell's Maple Research and Extension Program and the International Maple Syrup Institute are enormously helpful to those getting started in the maple business. As a producer here in the Hudson River Valley, I couldn't have survived our first few years without consulting with many of the small producers around me to see what they'd learned from their many years of experience. And as other producers have begun to taste Crown Maple syrup, they've come to me asking how they can improve their own practices. Every year, potential new sugarmakers are signing up for programs such as Cornell's annual Maple Camp, where more than two hundred people attend a three-day seminar to learn all about the growing, tapping, and processing systems used by major producers, and are encouraged to think strategically about marketing their own maple syrup and what retail might require of them.

ENSURING A SUSTAINABLE MAPLE SUPPLY

Most importantly, we all have an eye on what the challenges will be for ensuring maple's survival as a crop. Though there has been more of a deliberate effort to preserve and replenish the maple forests of the northeast corridor, there is a lingering concern over what climate change might do to the maple industry. While it's evident that climate change is having an impact on every part of the planet, we don't have conclusive evidence as to how exactly this will affect the health of the maple tree itself, or the length of our sugaring season. In retrospect, the poor sugaring season of a year like 2012 cannot be solely blamed on an early spring—we experienced high wind conditions that year, along with an overall warm winter with little to no snowpack, both of which contributed to a spike in maple syrup prices. Yet 2013 produced the greatest amount of maple syrup in the past ten years—3.5 million gallons, an amount not seen since World War II. Whether or not each year brings us a prolonged snowy season (as 2015 did), or an early thaw, we don't have preseason warning, but we do know that the temperatures for the sap to run will remain the same, and so we have to be ready when it comes. There are a million different things that might influence an unpredictable spring—cloud cover and wind patterns among them—and so all we can do is pay close attention to how the thaw proceeds and be ready when it does.

Maple producers also have to contend with two major competing fundamental issues: one, that we are simply not tapping enough of the available trees, and two, that we might not be developing maple syrup demand sufficiently to grow the industry to consume that syrup. In 2013, the U.S. maple syrup industry produced 3 million gallons of syrup, which was up 70 percent from its numbers in 2012. This seems impressive, but we had produced double that amount of syrup in 1860 (more than 6 million gallons). Surely if we used to consume 6 million gallons per year, and our population has boomed since that time, then maple syrup demand should be booming with it! Michael Farrell at Cornell has done extensive research into the current use of

American sugarbushes, and he's found that there is an enormous resource of untapped trees throughout the Northeast and upper Midwest. When considering all of the sugar and red maples of tappable size, less than 1 percent of the available resource is currently being used for syrup production. Vermont, the biggest producer of maple in the country, taps only about 5 percent of its size-appropriate trees and just over 25 percent of the available and accessible sugarbushes with sufficient density to warrant tapping. (By comparison, Quebec, which produces 80 percent of the world's supply of maple syrup, utilizes more than a third of its available trees.) There are nearly 190 million maple trees with sufficient density and accessibility available in the United States. If just 3 percent of these trees were tapped (the utilization rate in Vermont several years ago), this could translate into half a billion dollars in potential revenue, a seven-fold increase in profits over what the industry is making today.[55] Producers today are also getting a lot more syrup per tap, almost double the amount that they were pre-1970s, due to the dramatic improvements in the tubing and vacuum-powered collecting systems (see page 66 for more on this). Finally, the syrup made today may be better than ever in terms of quality, and large producers of our scale can afford to promote that quality difference more directly to the consumer than in the past.

We know that the production of maple syrup is increasing, and we know that demand is high—in the last few years, the demand for maple syrup has grown from 80 million pounds of consumption to around 120 million pounds worldwide.[56] So why aren't there multiple producers out there doing what we do to meet that demand? Partially because it's still a niche product—not nearly as readily available as white sugar or high-

fructose corn syrup—and partly because it's still a limited seasonal resource that has to be sold at a premium price to cover the costs of production. At maple's peak consumption rate, Americans were consuming 27 ounces of maple syrup per person per year. Today, that's down to 2.5 ounces per person—our appetites have clearly shifted in the wake of the processed food marketplace, where sugar is incorporated into almost every mass-produced food item. Of the eighty pounds of sweeteners Americans consume each year, maple represents less than 1 percent. Additionally, maple remains beloved regionally, but is only just starting to find a foothold beyond the maple-producing states—Americans living in maple-producing states consume six times more maple syrup than those in the rest of the country. It seems that even with a rise in appreciation for regional cuisine, it's mostly those who have already been bitten by the maple bug who are coming back for more. One of the biggest challenges maple is facing, and has always faced, is competition from other sweeteners that have broader industry and governmental support: While sugar still holds on to its substantial government subsidy, maple has none to speak of.

Another challenge is showing that maple quality does matter. For those who have never stepped foot in a sugarhouse, it's easy to ignore the complexity of the sugaring process, and thus easy to assume that the generic bottle on the store shelf is of the same quality as that from a single-origin producer. We're hoping to lead the way in showing that, just as there can be high-quality chocolate, honey, or olive oil, there is a range of quality levels out there in terms of maple syrup production. Part of the problem here has been the misperception of maple quality created by artificial syrups. True, the faux maple syrup still persists in the supermarket (Mrs. Butterworth's syrup, introduced in 1961, and Aunt Jemima syrup, introduced in 1966); they can't be

55 Pitcoff, "Boiling It Down."

56 Raspuzzi, "Maple Syrup Prices Jump."

marketed as "maple syrup," but instead as "pancake syrup." The word *maple* can't legitimately be introduced in the branding of these products, unless it's invoked as "maple-flavored."[57] Yet many of these pancake syrup manufacturers are still packaging their syrups in bottles that look uncannily like those of real maple producers, be they traditional clay jugs or slim glass bottles with screw-on tops. They're assuming that seeming like real maple syrup, and capitalizing on the nostalgia that real maple carries with it, might be even more important to the consumer than what they're actually eating.

In our modern supermarkets, consumers of all ages have begun to understand that if you can't identify the ingredients in your food, you probably shouldn't be eating it. Yes, these artificial foods are cheap, and that's always going to be important to the consumer, but you have to ask what's being sacrificed and subsidized to give you that unhealthy bottom line. Are we really being honest about the quality difference between a bottle of real maple syrup and a bottle of synthetic HFCS-based syrup—one advertising "100% pure maple syrup" and one with a laundry list of ingredients, including sodium hexametaphosphate, sodium benzoate, and phosphoric acid? (It thus seems ironic that in 2010, Log Cabin issued a press release that they would be removing high-fructose corn syrup from their product, making it the first ever "nationally distributed All Natural syrup."[58] Yet even the current bottle still can't claim to be all maple syrup—nope, it's still got brown rice syrup, xanthan gum, and "caramel color."[59]) Some of those ingredients

might be natural, but none of them are derived from maple sap.

But there's still plenty of hope for maple syrup support to turn around, and plenty of evidence that it is shifting already, at least in the mind of the consumer. Demand for maple syrup is growing more than 10 percent each year just in the United States, which is pretty good compared to other food items. We also know that the cost of production for maple producers is going down significantly as production methods become more efficient (especially among larger producers like ourselves). And finally, we can take heart that an increasing number of American consumers are incorporating more pure, natural foods into their diets. The last two decades have seen a resurgence of interest in the sweetener category— as consumers demand the ability to purchase different kinds of sweeteners such as agave nectar, stevia leaf, and evaporated cane juice—so too has awareness and interest increased in maple syrup. While it's not always possible to kick a sweet tooth completely to the curb (and some sweeteners are better than others; agave is higher in fructose than corn syrup), it's heartening to know that maple is gaining ground as one of the good sweeteners out there. (For more on maple's amazingly healthful chemical composition, see page 94.) Additionally, many of those adopting pure maple syrup as a sweetener are also interested in rebalancing their diets overall; while cane sugar is not made from animal products, some sugar is refined using bone char, a method of processing that would invalidate cane sugar for many vegans.[60] Similarly, those adopting a paleo diet would be inclined to pick up a bottle of real maple syrup over sugar because it's more naturally made, and for the most part has been enjoyed the same way throughout history. While these diets might seem to some like passing fads, there is a

---

57 None of the websites for Aunt Jemima, Mrs. Butterworth's, and Log Cabin syrups actually uses the term *maple* anywhere, as they cannot claim that they are 100 percent pure maple.

58 Pinnacle Foods Inc.

59 "Vt.: Log Cabin Syrup Not the Real Thing," September 9, 2010; available at: http://www.cbsnews.com/news/vt-log-cabin-syrup-not-the-real-deal/.

60 Yacoubou, "Is Your Sugar Vegan?", 2007.

deliberate thought process and consideration of ingredient sourcing in both—and quality maple syrup has earned a place in both the vegan and the paleo pantries. Finally, the consumer is becoming not only more knowledgeable and interested in ingredient sourcing, but also more inventive in using those ingredients in the kitchen: Traditionally, maple syrup has been limited to use as a pancake and waffle topping in the mind of the consumer. But quality ingredients demand broader uses and a bigger sense of creativity, and if we can change the consumer's view of maple from a breakfast condiment to one of the healthiest, most natural, and most sophisticated sweeteners, then the demand from the marketplace should grow rapidly.

The quintessential Dutchess County farm. Our neighbors in the Hudson River Valley are an invaluable part of our community—together we are all reimagining what a sustainable food industry can be.

And while many maple producers have some climate-driven fear over the future of production, the only thing to do is to continue developing our understanding of what these trees really need to survive. Looking at current projections from the USDA, it seems that maple may be one of the few indigenous American species that will endure for perhaps 150 to 200 years with no impact on its health.[61] There may be other elements that wipe it out before then—bugs, deer, disease—but it's unlikely that the demise of the sugar maple will be due to a total absence of winters. If anything, it might be what we've seen over the last few years—one year an early spring and a lousy season, and the next a long winter and a plentiful run. This is when we go back to the farmer's almanac, back to consulting with our peers in the maple industry, and back to paying close attention to the trees themselves—something we need to do anyway as responsible producers. Maple is perhaps the only truly naturally occuring American food, and having survived for more than four hundred years, we have to use twenty-first-century methods to ensure its survival for the next four hundred. But we also have to turn to the traditions of the past, to appreciate the ingenuity of all the sugarmakers before us and to really understand just how far we've come. In Part Two, as we look at what it takes to bring maple syrup to the marketplace, we'll consider the methodology that has driven this long history of sugaring, and the ways we can innovate to produce ever better, ever more delicious maple syrup today.

61 USDA, "Climate Change May Impact Maple Syrup Production."

PART TWO

The

SCIENCE OF GROWING, TAPPING, AND EVAPORATING SAP INTO SYRUP

W HEN YOU VISIT MADAVA FARMS, one of the first things you'll notice is the breathtaking beauty of the surrounding Hudson Valley— the gorgeous colors of the leaves, the fresh streams, the range in geography. These elements make our land unique, and in 2012, artist Sean Mellyn created a mixed-media mural that depicts this landscape (above). The mural shows our full sugaring operation amidst the sixty different species of wildlife that still call this land home. You can see our cabin adjacent to a pond, where we routinely see wild ducks and raccoons, and of course you can see our sugarhouse, over which hawks and bald eagles fly. What we do at Crown Maple takes place in a natural ecosystem: We live and die by the health of the trees and the length of the season, and there's not a lot we can do to control what each season's sugar run will yield. The particular challenge of the maple business is learning how, with the right technology and right team in hand, to give Mother Nature a little bit of a twenty-first-century boost.

This mural (above) by Sean Mellyn shows every part of our estate, and every part of what maple syrup means to us—the natural beauty of our woods, the wildlife on the farm, and the natural goodness of our maple syrup production process.

— 1 —

An In-Depth Look at the Trees

CARING FOR THE SUGARBUSH

It seems almost silly to break open a section on the science of maple syrup with notes on caring for the trees themselves. If you find yourself as lucky as me, to have thousands of thriving maple trees on your property, you will not have to deal with the responsibility of planting and nurturing maple saplings through their infancy. Finding an intact sugarbush indicates that the forest you're working with has all the right conditions for supporting maple trees: a bed of fertile soil that is cool, moist, and well drained; a forest that has a healthy ecosystem of other trees but enough clearance to allow new life in the undergrowth; and plenty of sunlight regardless of the season. A successful sugarbush will have deep, thorough irrigation and a built-in water supply near its roots (this is partially why you see so many sugarbushes alongside rocky streams). When nurtured properly, the trees will grow rapidly, half an inch or more in diameter every year. The trees are also fairly reliable when it comes to their forest neighbors: Birds and animals can happily perch in maple trees without damaging them.

Select insects can be more of a problem—the sugar maple borer in particular can do serious damage to the structure of a maple tree. (Though it's rare that a borer will prove fatal, an infestation will create a network of channels throughout the tree, weakening it and warping the grain.) Worse, where you find one tree affected by a borer attack, you're likely to find several that have already played host; sugar borers can live for up to two years, so their attack can be prolonged and fiercely devastating to your sugarbush. The best way to protect yourself against these critters is to watch for signs of infestation as soon as

The sugar maple borer is the bedbug of the sugarbush—if you find one, it's likely there are many more lurking in your woods, eating into your trees and weakening them over many years.

they start—wet discolorations on the bark, or dust where the critters have bored into the wood of the tree. If you are working with a sugarbush of similarly aged trees, you need to harvest all the trees as quickly as possible; for a mixed-age sugarbush, you can cull the matured trees only.[62] This may sound dramatic, but it requires about the same level of vigilance as you would see from any serious maple producer. It's generally true that borers are attracted to trees that are already weakened or diseased, so perhaps if a borer leads to a suffering tree, then it's not the worst thing to cut it down.[63]

There are also a few key animals and diseases to be aware of that might trouble a healthy maple grove. White-tailed deer love to snack on the seedlings, buds, and twigs of both red and sugar maples, which can jeopardize the maple's ability to spread its seed in the future; while they pose more of a long-term threat, and less of a threat to a large sugarbush like ours, they are something

62 Hoffard and Marshall, "How to Identify and Control the Sugar Maple Borer."

63 Waterworth, "Tree Borer Management."

many smaller producers need to be aware of if they want their forest to regenerate and spread naturally from year to year.[64] Additionally, funguslike diseases like anthracnose can occur over a long period of time in sugar maples, manifesting in the discoloration of leaves during the summer and fall seasons, but then quickly preventing the tree from either putting out new leaves or gaining in height or diameter. This is potentially devastating for sugar maples, as the broader and more lush the tree's crown, the more productive and sweeter the sap will be.[65] Awareness of all the potential threats to your trees, whether they come from pests, ice storms, drought, or loss of nutrients, is the best thing you can do to maintain the health of your sugarbush. Being out in the sugarbush may be the best medicine possible for both you and your trees.

To develop a healthy sugarbush, you can't have a monoculture environment where maples are the only trees that flourish—you need a sustained ecosystem of plant and animal diversity, one that you allow to grow wild but carefully monitor to ensure that the maple is getting what it needs to thrive. In fact, in most states a producer cannot get organic certification if he or she has harvested all the trees except the sugar maple, because that then creates an unnatural monoculture, and thus a nonorganic environment. Our sugarbush is a mix of sugar maples and red maples; both yield sap, though sap from the former has a higher sugar content than red maples. Red maple is known as "soft" maple (to distinguish its wood quality from that of the hardwood sugar maple), but both are frequently used to make furniture and decorative arts.[66] Red maple is actually more common in the eastern United States than sugar maple, and can grow faster in the same conditions. While our syrup

Other threats to the sugarbush's long-term health include infectious diseases such as verticillium wilt (shown here) and anthracnose, which can stunt a tree's further growth, and woodland neighbors such as the white-tailed deer, who snack on maple seedlings and thus stunt the natural regeneration of the sugarbush.

64 Curtis and Sullivan, "White-Tailed Deer," 2.

65 Douglas, "Anthracnose Diseases of Trees," 2.

66 Meier, "Differences Between Hard Maple and Soft Maple."

is made from sap that comes from both sugar maples and red maples, we do notice that our red maples stop giving good-quality sap about a week before the sugar maples. Typically if we are dealing with a portion of the sugarbush that is mostly red maple, we will stop producing from that area altogether once the trees start giving off what the maple industry calls "buddy" sap, produced very late in the season and with an inferior taste to the rest of the season's syrup. Where the reds are interspersed with sugars, we will selectively pull the taps from the reds while keeping the sugars on the line. While red maples will grow where the soil is either too wet or too dry to support the sugar maples, we prefer soil conditions that best support possible sugar maples: well drained yet moist, fertile with a diverse array of healthy micronutrients, yet loose enough that the tree's roots have room to spread out. Because we're an organic producer, we can't change the natural state of the soil. However, we find it doesn't really matter since the more natural the soil, the better it can support all our trees from season to season.

While there is information out there on how to plant a maple sugarbush from scratch, if you're hoping to be a producer within your lifetime, it really doesn't make much sense to be planting new trees—it can take up to forty years to see a maple tree grow to the size and circumference necessary for production, and even then there's no guarantee that every tree will produce sap worth tapping. Our sugarbush is so dense already that, if we do see a tree felled by a storm or some other natural disaster, it makes more sense for us to simply cull that tree and focus on keeping our remaining trees healthy than it does to start planting new saplings. One of the most common causes of losing maples in the woods are older, less stable trees falling over onto newer, healthier trees and inflicting serious damage. Culling the trees as they weaken, while opening up the canopy so the remaining

tree crowns can expand and produce more sugar per tree, is a better method of preserving the sugarbush.

As the maples grow, they produce a broad, rounded tree crown that can be two-thirds of the height of a tree (so for a one-hundred-foot tree, you may see a crown that is fifty to sixty feet wide). The larger and fuller the crown, the faster the growth of the tree, and the more sap the tree can produce. The crown also helps to partially cool and protect the forest floor during hotter months. (We chose Crown as the name of our company to reflect the importance of the tree's crown to maple production, but also to denote a royal quality to the product. Once suggested, I felt it was the perfect combination of two concepts in one name.) Maples are shade tolerant and can survive without too much direct sunlight, but they don't really flourish unless there is a decent amount of light reaching the forest floor through natural openings in the crown's leaf shade.[67] But too many crowns together mean too full a forest—if too many trees are located in the same small area, they develop narrower, spindly tops, and don't have a chance to grow fuller crowns or enough room to spread their roots. We have 100 to 120 trees per acre in our sugarbush, mostly sugar maples with a few red maples and other varietals mixed in, which is about as much tree concentration as the landscape can handle. Historically, sap yield and quality have been directly proportional to leaf area, so it is better to have a less crowded sugarbush with fewer, but far more full and lush, trees.[68]

There is ongoing research to assess the viability of tapping maple saplings with vacuum-extraction techniques, which suppose that the trees store their water in their roots rather than in their crowns.[69] Though

67 Denny and Siccama, "Sugar Maple (*Acer saccharum*) in the Hubbard Brook Forest."

68 Nearing and Nearing, *The Sugar Maple Book*, 81.

69 Brown, "Remaking Maple."

The larger and fuller the crown, the faster the trees can grow and the more sap each tree can produce.

this research is still in its nascent period, it could have tremendous implications for the future of maple sugaring, as it would mean producers could tap trees that were barely seven or eight years old, and were planted in neat, easily accessible rows in fields, rather than in dense acres of wild forest that have taken decades to mature and grow thicker. But given that it is in the best interest of the trees' health to have a forest of mixed-age trees, we don't see any reason to abandon the old guys in favor of younger trees at this time. This practice is experimental at best, and for those producers and foresters who have closely studied healthy and unmodified maple trees, we can't imagine that the trees will grow well after having their tops removed and their sap sucked dry. If these trees die, their syrup production will have been limited to one single sap season—and we're interested in keeping our trees healthier and happier for much, much longer than that.

THE NORTHEASTERN TERRAIN: CLIMATE, ELEVATION, AND SOIL

In order to nurture a healthy ecosystem within the sugarbush, one has to understand the unique challenges and opportunities of the northeastern terrain. We recently purchased an additional 4,400 acres in Vermont, and did an on-site inspection of the landscape in the middle of the rough 2015 winter. The new property is shaped much like a bowl, with dense clusters of tall trees throughout that reach upwards of seventy to a hundred feet. The scale of this land is ideal for a sugarbush—once

the trees are tapped and connected via vacuum tubing (see page 66), all of the sap from these trees will naturally flow down to one particular spot on the property, allowing gravity to play a natural and vital role in our collecting process. The very top of the elevation has some shorter and slightly more windblown trees, due to

This topographical map of our new Vermont property shows the huge array of elevations that the sugarbush offers—all ideal for creating a protected central bowl for collecting our sap. The red lines represent the property boundary. The black lines represent the actual or planned mainlines (e.g. wet/dry lines or conductor lines).

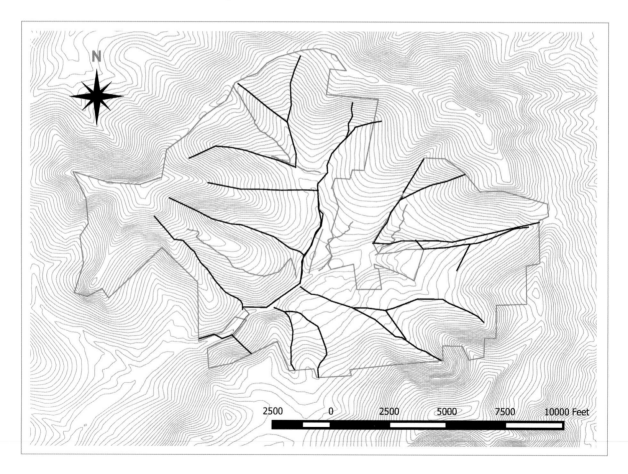

their hard mountaintop lives, but the trees down in the protected bowl of the sugarbush are tall and have large healthy crowns. What especially impressed us is that the sugarbush had a solid one and a half to four feet of snow covering its forest floor, which demonstrated that though the tree crowns were getting plenty of sun, the roots were still sheltered from thawing too quickly. This would mean a well-controlled environment for a sugaring season, and an additional 150,000 to 200,000 taps that we could place in just one property, making it one of the largest thriving contiguous sugarbushes in the United States. Finally, the most attractive part of this new property is its southern exposure. All experienced maple producers know that south-facing sugarbushes tend to get earlier and more frequent freeze-thaw cycles during the season—the early spring sun heats the forest directly during the day, and the cold temperatures come in at night when the sun is down. Northern-exposed sugarbushes might not get the necessary amount of sun or heat to kickstart the thaw on colder spring days. It will take some time to know exactly how big a difference this property's pitch and position will make in its sap production, but based on what we know about what healthy sugar maples need, we're very optimistic.

As we've discussed earlier, the northeastern U.S. climate is ideal for maple sugaring because of its cold overnight temperatures—32°F or below each evening—and its warmer daytime thaws that create the pressure differentials that assist the sap's movement in the tree. The biodiversity of the sugarbush and the composition of its soil are representative of the overall northeastern landscape—soil that is of medium-fine texture and thus well aerated, with plenty of nearby water sources and a wide array of forest life. To look at the sugarbush is also to look at the challenges that European settlers would have faced hoping for more easily maintained farmland—with such a dense array of trees and so many rocks to clear,

not every piece of the landscape would serve as ideal pasture. The soil in most sugarbushes tends to have a fairly balanced pH (ranging from 5.5 to 7.3), which partially results from maples that are growing in an organic, environment populated with other types of trees and plants. Sugar maples benefit from an environment with heavy leaf litter to help balance the pH of the soil and keep it rich with nutrients, and the maple will naturally spread its own seeds via the samaras throughout the forest.

Similarly, the elevation that would prove challenging for more conventional crops does not inhibit the growth of maple trees. In the northeastern United States, sugar maples can grow at elevations up to 2,500 feet. (In the warmer parts of the country, sugar maples have lower elevation limits of 3,000 feet and an upper limit of 5,500 feet, but those trees are most likely growing in conditions too difficult to reach to make tapping feasible.) Maples flourish in conditions that are the exact antithesis of pasture: complete foliage coverage of the forest floor and a regular bed of decomposing leaves, twigs, and branches within its soil. The natural stage of the northeastern forest bed is ideal for maple development because it acts as its own natural compost pile, creating a sodlike absorbent floor bed that retains water underneath a wide canopy of sunlight-absorbing leaves. The terrain of Dutchess County, where our estate is, has served as the landscape for pastoral retreats for vacationing New Yorkers (including the Astors, Vanderbilts, and of course FDR, whose estate was in Hyde Park, all arriving via the Hudson railroad line), and as a site for large-scale industry including brickyards and textile mills. The latter functions resulted in a significant amount of forest cleared, but much of the landscape has since regrown as more businesses have moved to the city and previously industrious farms have been abandoned. What we see today is somewhat similar to what we would've seen in early America: a mix of forest and grasslands with some pasture and hay-dense parcels.[70] We benefit from the natural biodiversity of our forest flavor and from the relatively predictable degrees of heat and precipitation—between 1971 and 2000, average temperatures for the sugaring season of January to April consistently began at around 22°F (-5.5°C) and concluded at around 47°F (8.3°C). The region received on average two to four inches of precipitation over the course of the season.[71]

The climate of the sugarbush region is the deciding factor in its sugaring success. Maple sugaring season depends upon a predictably long winter that promises enough snow on the ground to adequately water the trees, followed by a slow, wet spring with regularly thawing days and freezing-over nights. You know a good maple sugarbush climate by walking through it: a forest with squishy muddy trails, the type where your boots sink in a good three inches or more in the early spring, is ideal. During the sugaring season, it's the regular fluctuation between freezing overnight temperatures and slightly warm (42°F / 5.5°C or higher) days that creates the muddy trails, but also the right conditions for sap to flow. If those fluctuations cannot be counted upon, we have to find other ways to extract the sap from the trees. The ideal temperature will range from 40 to 50°F (4.4 to 10°C) during the day, and drop down to 25 to 30°F (-3.8 to -1.1°C) at night. Looking at the entire range of northeastern maple-growing regions, from New York up through to Quebec, you'll see that the whole region has this range of temperatures during the six-week sugaring season in the early spring. As you travel north in this maple corridor, the thawing period moves later within the spring, whereas ours is squarely in the late February to early April window. Most of the sugaring in this region

has concluded by early May at the very latest, though we can have an outlier warm or cold day that might wreak havoc on producers. (If we have a sudden extreme cold snap, it can take an extra two to three days for the trees to thaw after the fact; similarly, an unexpected warm spell early on can start and end the season earlier than we'd expected.) This is why true maple producers are weather fanatics, checking with three or four different weather apps, meteorologists, and farmer's almanacs for conflicting and confirming forecasts.

WHY THE SAP IS SWEET

When the sap first comes out of the tree, it's always a surprise to first-time tappers to see the results. For one, sap doesn't look like syrup at all—it doesn't look much like anything aside from water. And it wouldn't taste much sweeter, either—sap is only about 2 to 3 percent sucrose (as opposed to the 66 to 68 percent sucrose that you find in the finished syrup). But this shouldn't be a huge surprise—after all, what you're tasting is mostly water, with

It may look like these plastic sap-lines are full of just water—but sap pulled right out of the tree is mostly water; it's only about 2 to 3 percent sucrose.

70 Glynwood Center Inc., "The State of Agriculture in the Hudson River Valley," 3.

71 Bernhardt et al., "Climate and Air Quality of Dutchess County," 8.

the natural plant sugars that have been produced during the tree's photosynthetic processes.

In the summertime, a sugar maple tree's sap production is brewing, but not yet accessible. Water will be moving from the roots as it's gathered from the soil, along with other minerals, and rise up through the tree into the branches. This is where it will meet the leaves and undergo photosynthesis, adding sugar—energy—to the water to create sap. This is partially why the size of a tree's crown is so important: The more leaves the maple produces during its leaf-bearing seasons, the more sugar it can produce and store over time. The pores in the crown's leaves open and allow carbon dioxide to enter the leaf, evaporating some water and pulling more water up from the xylem to compensate. (See page 16 for more on the tree's internal structure.) This process is called "transpiration," and is a key part of the photosynthetic process. Once the sun goes down and photosynthesis concludes, the xylem does not need to pump as much water up to the crown and the water can return back down and be circulated throughout the tree.

The sugar in the sap stream is from carbohydrates stored in both the living ray parenchyma and the fiber cells within the tree's symplast, a cellular network that forms the outer layer of the tree's xylem. (Think of it as the tough rubber casing of the xylem's tubular structure.) The sugar is mobilized in late winter as temperatures change and is exuded into the xylem itself to move up and down the tree's trunk to fuel the leaf production of the tree (hence the "buddy" flavor that we detect in syrups produced near the very end of the season). Most of the carbohydrates in the rays are actually stored as starch grains, and an enzyme released into the xylem throughout late winter converts the starch to sucrose and mobilizes it in the xylem.[72]

The xylem sap is primarily composed of sucrose, but also contains large amounts of protein peptides, phytochemicals, amino acids, and other organic compounds that influence maple's unique flavor profile. (No one has actually quantified all the different flavor compounds present in maple syrup—there may be upwards of three hundred different flavor molecules, which vary from region to region.[73] For more on the health benefits and chemical composition of maple syrup, see page 94.) Despite this mystery, the distinctive maple flavor is variously attributable to the organic constituents of the sap and is amplified by heating. Variations in sugar composition change the flavor of each tree's sap, which is why maple syrup tastes different from syrup from other trees or plants. While many trees produce a sweet sap—and some producers have made delicious syrups from birch, walnut, hickory, sycamore, and butternut trees—only maple and palm tree sap has been able to be developed into commercially profitable sugar.

WHY AND WHEN THE SAP FLOWS

From what we've known historically about maple sap, our knowledge of the magic sap-producing season has been fairly serendipitous: An axe thrown into a tree yields a gush of maple water, and it seems like the right moment to tap. But sap flow is all about changes in external atmospheric temperature and the internal pressure within the tree, and how the two are interrelated. It also explains why sugar maples tend to produce so much sap in the sloppy springs of the northeastern United States.

Early in springtime, and especially in the northeast regions where maple trees tend to flourish, nighttime temperatures drop below freezing despite slightly warmer temperatures during the day. During the daytime's

72 Osnas, "Maple Syrup Mechanics."

73 "URI Scientist Discovers 54 Beneficial Compounds in Pure Maple Syrup." University of Rhode Island press release, March 20, 2011.

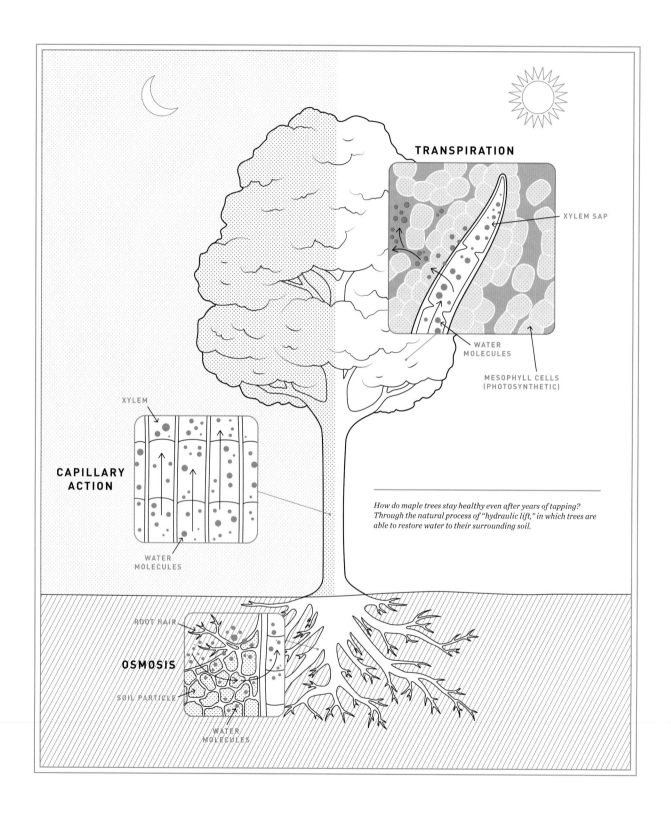

TRANSPIRATION

XYLEM SAP

WATER
MOLECULES

MESOPHYLL CELLS
(PHOTOSYNTHETIC)

XYLEM

CAPILLARY
ACTION

WATER
MOLECULES

*How do maple trees stay healthy even after years of tapping?
Through the natural process of "hydraulic lift," in which trees are
able to restore water to their surrounding soil.*

ROOT HAIR

OSMOSIS

SOIL PARTICLE

WATER
MOLECULES

warmer temperatures, positive pressure develops within the tree, causing the sap to move out of the tree through whatever exit it can find (such as the taphole). As the trees freeze at night, air and other gases within the tree shrink in size, creating a natural suction within the tree (negative pressure) that pulls water into the tree, and replenishes the sap for the following day of warmer temperatures. As they heat up again in the daytime, those same gases expand and create pressure differentials within the tree, pushing the sap within the tree once more. In the early part of the sugaring season, the sap that flows is the sap within the tree limbs and trunk, while the roots are still frozen—hence, we have small runs of sap, but very pure and clean sap (this is where we'll often collect the sap that will become our Golden syrup). Once the roots thaw out, the sap flows much more freely, and the entire working system in the tree is taking in moisture and pushing the sap to the exterior sections of the tree. The interior of the tree functions like a giant pump that, as the season progresses, pushes the sap out of the tree.

This is why the signature northeastern cycle of warm days and cool nights in early springtime is so key to the "sap season": It creates that natural push and pull that allows the sap to move to a place of negative pressure (outside of the tree, where our vacuum tubing system is happy to pull it away). This is partially why it's so crucial that we get our taps in at exactly the right moment before sugaring season—the sap is seeking out the point of least resistance in the tree as the daily temperature moves across the freezing line each morning. The alternation of vacuum drawing sap up toward the crowns and gravity pulling down toward the taphole each day creates a pumplike action that, if interrupted by coming across a new tap, can direct the sap right out of the tree. (This is where our vacuum pump systems come in, and prove so valuable: By creating not only a place for the sap to exit the tree, but also a compelling negative pressure to pull

it out, we can extract nearly three times the sap that we would without it.)

A healthy maple tree will continue to produce sap throughout its entire life, regardless of whether or not it has been tapped. If the right number of taps are set in the right-sized tree (see page 62), tapping does not damage the tree, or remove so much sap that it cannot continue to regenerate and flourish each year. Sustainable tapping procedures remove barely 10 percent (or less) of the tree's sugar and aim to in no way jeopardize the tree's survival. In addition, there's reason to believe that sustainably tapped maples not only retain all their necessary moisture and nutrients to continue thriving during tapping, but also return much of their residual water to the surrounding forest. In 1993, former Cornell professor Todd E. Dawson discovered that sugar maples participate in what is called "hydraulic lift": a natural phenomenon in which trees draw up water through their deepest roots during the day, then release large amounts of that water back into the surrounding soil via shallow roots overnight.[74] This is an important discovery in understanding how maple sugarbushes maintain their health after the sugaring season has ended and the tree is beginning to "bud out" once more. Rather than surrounding plants closing off a tree's ability to get adequate nourishment, the tree ends up nurturing the surrounding plants with its excess water. The tree pulls up what water it needs as it undergoes the transpiration process, then after freezing some of its water in the xylem, releases the remainder back into the soil. We always knew maple could be a sustainable resource, but we didn't know it was a *sustaining* resource as well. And knowing that the tree's production of sap, and that sap's desire to exit the tree, is all part of its natural life cycle makes us even keener to have our taps ready for the sugaring season.

---

74 Dawson, "Hydraulic Lift and Water Use by Plants," 566.

— 2 —

Tapping the Sap

PUTTING IN THE TAPS: DIFFERENT TYPES, DELIBERATE TIMING

When we know the sap is beginning to unfreeze and move around within the tree, we're already two or three weeks too late to get our taps in. At Crown Maple, we make a point of getting our taps into the trees starting in the first week of January and finishing by February 1, while the sugarbush is still freezing cold. This may be the most uncomfortable part of the season for our intrepid woods team, as they do the tough work of going into the sugarbush, both on our main Madava property and our three additional properties (one in Dutchess County, one in Putnam County, one in Westchester County), and making 50,000 new tapholes over the space of about a month. (We'll be adding our new Vermont property to this part of the process soon, making it more than 120,000 taps in 2016, and up to 250,000 taps by 2018.) January may seem like it's too early to be tapping for sap, especially since the moment you tap you open up the tree to a host of potential microorganisms. However, if hit with the periodic early spring and quick-thawing winter, we might find ourselves faced with the first non-freezing days in early February. If we tap too late, we might miss the first days of production, and since we only have twenty-five to thirty production days in a season, we don't want to miss a single one.

It took the first few years of our operation to really get a feel for the right kind of tapping process. A big misconception by those outside the maple community is that sugar maples can't always handle being tapped for syrup year in and year out. This belief is based on very old methods of tapping that would never be used by

Though the next chapter will detail our process for making syrup, many maple producers are still using the same methods of their predecessors—from tree to tap, bucket to bottle, there are only so many ways to tap for sap.

Getting taps in takes precision, endurance, and as good a head start as the season will allow.

modern-day producers. One of the big risk factors to the tree's health introduced by earlier maple producers was a misunderstanding of how to access sap—there is no need whatsoever to gash open a long hole in the tree to insert a tiny spile, especially when it only takes a small-diameter tap to access the sap. Deep gashes or regularly tapping one spot on the tree without ever moving the taphole can cause the tree to become physically weakened, increasing the likelihood that come the next year's sugaring season, the tree may have already collapsed during the winter. If tapped properly, maples experience none of these problems, and might even be able to handle more than one tap at a time: Producers can tap a maple tree and retain New York State organic certification once the trunk reaches at least nine inches in diameter, which usually takes about forty years to achieve. (Some researchers are experimenting with tapping saplings instead of matured trees, but the science of that process is still being developed—see page 54.) If we're working with a tree that is a minimum of fifteen inches in diameter, we may set two taps in the tree, ideally on opposite sides of the trunk. We put in three taps only if the tree is over twenty-five inches in diameter and in good health, and if the taps can easily be spread out on the trunk. But knowing exactly how to properly tap the tree is just as important as how many taps you can actually put in—in the first year or two of our production, we had to retrain members of our woods crew in drilling a clean hole, but by year three we had it down to a very efficient science.

To tap a tree, we begin by using a drill with a $\frac{5}{16}$-inch bit to create a very small hole in the trunk, barely an inch and a half deep, which is the right amount to access the xylem and capture the sap as it pushes its way out of the tree. Each tapper will put a new hole into every tree every year to avoid weakening or overstressing the wood, and never directly above or below the previous year's tap. (The old holes close up anyway during the intervening

HOW TO TAP: THE TRADITIONAL WAY

While our method of making maple syrup is more high-tech than this, we wanted to show you the traditional method from bucket to bottle, as many of the same rules apply to both methods. Generally the sap starts to flow between mid-February and mid-March. The exact time of year depends upon where you live and weather conditions.

1 ***Select your tree.*** Find a maple tree that is 9 inches in diameter (or 15 inches if you plan to use two taps instead of one).

2 ***Tap your tree.*** The tap hole should be at a height that is convenient for you and allows easy collection. The size of the drill bit depends on the type of spile you are using; most spiles require either a 7/16 or 5/16 bit. Drill a hole 2 to 2 1/2 inches deep (deeper than what's needed with a vacuum, see page 63. Wrap a piece of tape around the drill bit 2 1/2 inches from the tip as a guide.) Drill at a slight upward angle to facilitate downward flow of sap.

3 ***Insert the spile.*** Insert the spile into the loop on the hook (with the hook facing outward), and then insert the spile into the tap hole. Gently tap the spile into the tree with a hammer.

4 ***Hang the bucket and attach lid.*** Hang the bucket by inserting the hook into the hole on the rim of the bucket. Attach the lid by inserting the metal wire into the double holes on the spile.

Congratulations, you successfully tapped your first maple tree!

5 ***Fill your bucket.*** Sap flows when daytime temperatures rise above freezing (32°F / 0°C) and nighttime temperatures fall below freezing. The rising temperature creates pressure in the tree generating the sap flow. This is basically a transfer of the sap from the tree above the ground and the root system below the ground.

6 ***Boiling your sap.*** To make your sap into syrup, you must boil out the excess water. Fill a large pot three quarters full with sap. Place the pot onto the heat source. Once the sap starts to boil down to one quarter or half the depth of the pot, add more sap, but try to maintain the boil. The boiling sap will take on a golden color. Once the sap has mostly boiled down, but still has a very fluid texture, continue to boil the sap until it takes on a consistency of syrup. One way to check for this is to dip a spoon into the pot. The syrup will "stick" to the spoon as it runs off.

7 ***Filter your syrup.*** A small amount of sediment will be present in your syrup. A coffee filter is suitable to filter a small amount of sap at a time. After letting the syrup cool, pour a small amount into a coffee filter, collect the top ends of the filter into a bunch, and press the syrup through the filter into a clean container.

8 ***Bottle your syrup.*** Using a sterilized bottle and cap, pour the sediment-free syrup into the bottle and refrigerate. Your refrigerated syrup should be used within 2 months. Syrup can also be frozen (in a freezer safe container) to extend shelf life.

spring and summer, and you can note where the previous tap was by a small scar on the tree's bark.) What we usually do is go to the tree itself, assess the placement of the previous year's hole, place a new hole in a different spot on the trunk, and use a piece of our plastic tubing — the "dropline"—to connect the spout with the lateral line (see below for the description of our tubing system). We purchase disposable taps made from nontoxic (food-grade) plastic—this is a big shift from the older industry standard of metal taps, which were first introduced in 1860. The plastic taps also ensure an airtight fit of the tubing to the tap. We've found that with tens of thousands of trees to tap, plastic taps are easier and more sanitary to simply replace to guarantee a clean tap year-round. (Metal taps require sterilization.)

The tapping season is a concerted effort to cover the full expanse of our sugarbushes all in one go, and is one of the last opportunities to make repairs prior to the beginning of the sap season. The moment of tapping is when we feel like the sugaring season really begins, and it's the time of year when excitement really starts to build at Crown Maple. Once the taps go in, everyone is anxiously watching the weather reports to see when the first flow will happen, and when our vacuum tubing will start to gather the first sap of the season.

THE SAP LINE SYSTEM, ALL UNDER VACUUM

When I think about how producers used to function without a vacuum-powered sap line system, it makes my head spin. Perhaps it's not such a challenge for small producers with all their trees in one compact area—if you have a maximum of twenty to fifty trees, I can see how a bucket system might be feasible, and some hobbyist-sized producers hang plastic pouches on their trees to collect the sap. But even a fairly small producer can have two hundred taps in their trees, which can be distributed over many acres of forest—at that scale or larger, bucket systems simply aren't sensible. For our properties, we need a system that allows us to access our thousands of acres and tens of thousands of tapped trees in an expedient manner, but not overtax the resources of our woods team. This is one of the reasons we are so reliant on our system of three hundred miles of tubing across our various properties to convey all the gallons of sap collected each day to our collection houses. Tubing systems, first implemented in the late 1950s, not only dramatically cut down on the physical and human resources required to produce maple syrup, but also allow us to keep much of our forest as we originally found it, with very little land cleared for tractor or truck access. It also means that we can maintain the health and viability of our trees as part of a network rather than on a tree-by-tree basis. For a producer of our scale and production capacity, the vacuum-powered sap line is an absolute necessity.

Our tubing system acts like a giant straw that allows the vacuum pumps to gently suck sap from trees that can be a mile or two away and move the sap all the way to the collection houses and sugarhouse. We use a network of nonreactive plastic polymer tubing that increases in size from the tree to larger and larger diameters until the sap ultimately reaches the sugarhouse. Closest to the tree is the **drop line**, which is $5/16$ inch in diameter (the thickness of a standard no. 2 pencil) and connects to the spout or tap at the tree. This size tubing allows us to use a fairly small tap ($5/16$ inch in diameter entering the tree), which may seem antithetical to pulling the sap from the tree as quickly as possible, but it works fine and its small diameter actually is our insurance that the tree will properly heal after tapping. The drop line connects to the **lateral line**, which is also $5/16$ inch and networks several (usually four to seven) trees together. Lateral lines run to the **branch line**, which networks several groups of trees together within the sugarbush, and each branch line connects to the **conductor line**, also known as the

main line. At times the conductor line actually consists of two separate lines: the wet line, which carries the sap to the collection house, and the dry line, which transfers vacuum to the end of the branch and lateral lines.

Why do we sometimes have two separate lines (the wet and dry lines) on our conductor or main lines? During a large sap run, a main line may become full of sap; if this occurs it is difficult to transfer the vacuum to the end of the branches and lateral lines. To solve this problem, we installed the wet and dry lines—which are parallel to each other. The sap will flow in the wet line, which runs below the dry line and is generally slightly smaller in diameter. (For example, some of our wet lines are 1¼ inches in diameter and the associated dry lines are 1½ inches in diameter. In areas where we are collecting from large numbers of taps—say, fifty to sixty thousand—the pipes may reach 4 inches in diameter.) To better understand the reason for a dry line, consider trying to pour water from a can: If there is only one hole, the flow is slow and turbulent. However, if you put in a second hole allowing air into the can, the liquid will pour much more quickly. This is the same concept as the wet and dry lines: Without the dry line, the wet line will become full and we will have low vacuum at the end of the lines. By adding a dry line, we provide the ability for the vacuum to reach the end of the main line and ultimately the ends of the branch lines and laterals.

The pumps that we use to create vacuum may be the most expensive part of our woods system, but they are potentially the highest return-on-capital part of our program as well. There are plenty of producers who only use natural—that is, gravity-based—vacuum systems rather than boosting vacuum with pumps. Natural vacuum systems rely entirely on the pitch of the land to maintain the pressure in the tubing and pull sap from uphill trees to downhill collection houses. The downside to the natural gravity vacuum, of course, is that it only works well once

The plastic tubing network in our woods allows us to keep our taps small but our sap volume high. (The clear tube you see in the top photograph is the lateral line, which connects the drop line of each tree to network several trees together to the branch line. Branch lines connect to conductor/main lines to convey sap to the collection house and vacuum to the end of each lateral line.)

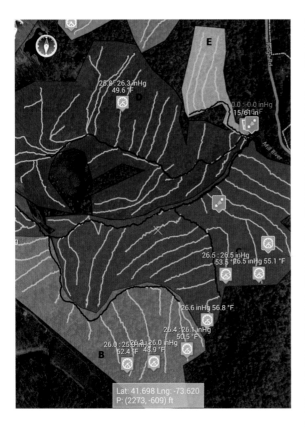

This is what it looks like when we are remotely monitoring the vacuum levels in our sap lines around the property—a huge advancement over having to head back into the woods and check every line connected to every tree. With twenty-first-century technology, we can go right to the cluster of woods where the vacuum pressure has dropped and repair any leaking or damaged lines right away.

the sap is generously flowing during the sugaring season. But an artificial vacuum system also uses vacuum pumps that can be turned on at the very first thaw of the sugaring season and left on 24/7, so not a drop of running sap is missed. But we're not pulling out any sap that isn't ready—sap flow is already headed out of the tree and toward the tap hole, as the internal pressure moving the sap increases to become greater than the atmospheric pressure outside the tree (due to the freeze-thaw cycle as previously discussed on page 57). What our vacuum-pumped system does is lower the pressure in the tube to even less than the pressure in the open air, creating a pull that speeds up the sap's exit from the tree to a place of lower pressure—again, like a person sucking on a straw to pull liquid from multiple places. Granted, this is a far more complex operation than the bucket-and-spile methods of producers past, and it requires a vacuum pump with a controller and release unit, which we maintain in each of our collection houses. In conjunction with our leak-free tubing system through each of our acres, the vacuum pumps can extract an extra quart to half gallon of sap each day, depending on that day's flow. That may not seem like a lot, but when you consider that each tree puts out about a gallon per day, that means an additional 25 to 50 percent more sap with the vacuum pumps than without them. As the technology for vacuum pump–assisted systems continues to improve, the gathering of sap will become more and more efficient and the costs per gallon will continue to decrease, making maple syrup affordable to a wider array of consumers. It's a huge benefit not only to producers of our size, but to the entire industry as well.

It does occasionally happen that the pressure in our vacuum system falters and we have to track down potential leaks or damaged tubes in order to rectify the problem. Through pressure sensors that we've placed through our woods system, we've created a way to remotely track the vacuum levels around the property. (I can actually track the readings from the sensors on my cell phone, as can everyone on our woods crew.) We have to be extremely vigilant about our vacuum pressure, as a drop can significantly hurt our sap flow and subsequent production. High vacuum is critical to extracting the maximum amount of sap from the trees during the peak part of the sugaring season. While a perfect vacuum seal is 30 inches of mercury, we've found that with great care we can maintain a vacuum of 27 inches of mercury in our woods system. More importantly, if we see the vacuum on one of our lines drop below the 25 to 27 range, we can pinpoint exactly which part of the tubing might be compromised down to the specific cluster of trees. This is enormously helpful to our woods crew, who are constantly walking the lines in the forest during the sap season, checking that they haven't been damaged by squirrels, coyotes, or other woodland varmints with curiosity and sharp teeth. For these repairs, there's no more efficient way to do that than to go out into the sugarbush and repair it ourselves—but our system for monitoring these leaks has become a lot more efficient and is a big time saver.

When each year's sugaring season is done, usually around early to mid-April, we pull our taps while the vacuum is still on, to ensure that we clean out whatever remaining sap might be left in the lines. We can then use the rest of the spring and summer season to inspect lines and assess which ones are in need of replacement. We typically replace our lateral tubing every ten years, and our drop tubing every three to four years. Each new piece of line will help us run clean sap from day one without any complications.

FROM COLLECTION TANKS TO SUGARHOUSE

During our sugaring season, we're in the woods before dawn, checking the lines to see that everything is working as it should be, and we may be in the woods all day, perhaps during the entire course of the day's sap run. It's grueling, exhausting work, but the woods are like our kitchen garden—we want to see it in action, as our product comes out of the ground and into our collection tanks. As the day of sap run progresses, we'll see sap from more than 23,000 tapped trees circulate into our four holding tanks. Add to that an additional 27,000 taps from our three peripheral facilities, and now an additional 150,000 taps on our new Vermont property, and you're looking at upwards of 200,000 gallons of sap accumulating per day, all monitored remotely and pumped here and there via our vacuum network. Not bad for a piece of sugaring technology that's barely half a century old.

At our Madava estate, our sap accumulates in three collection houses and is pumped to our main collection house. As soon as we have a few thousand gallons of sap in this house, we turn on the high-pressure pumps and start pushing sap one mile up the hill to the sugarhouse located four hundred feet higher in elevation. At the end of each day, usually at about 7 or 8 P.M., the sap collected during the day's run has made its way from the trees in the forest all the way to our main sugarhouse facility. Away from Madava, we have field crews actively managing our remote sites. At these sites, the sap is collected in the same manner as at Madava, but we begin the sap-to-syrup processing right in the collection houses, where we remove 75 to 90 percent of the water with on-site reverse-osmosis machines (see page 74 for more on the RO process). This concentrated sap is trucked to the main collection house at Madava, and unloaded usually by 11 P.M. (or by early morning if coming from our Vermont property) to complete its evaporation overnight.

During sugaring season, we start our evaporators late in the evening and process our sap into syrup in the early-morning hours, sometimes not concluding a run

We can see more than 200,000 gallons of freshly tapped sap come into our collection house each day—so we get extra large collection barrels (that can hold more than 9,300 gallons apiece) to meet the demand.

— 3 —
From Sap to Syrup: Filtering and Evaporating

I T TAKES FORTY TO FIFTY GALLONS OF SAP to make a gallon of pure maple syrup, and we want to start our sap-to-syrup process the same day the sap is collected, to keep it as fresh as possible. We have four stainless-steel collection tanks in our sugarhouse, each of which can be filled to the brim with nine thousand gallons of sap. But we'll start processing our sap long before all four tanks are filled. Once we have at least six thousand gallons of sap in our tanks, we begin the process of refining and boiling down the sap into syrup, which takes just about five hours, depending on the day. That is a dramatic improvement over what previous generations of maple producers might have done—for them it might take five hours just to collect the sap from buckets and transport them to the sugarhouse. From there, it could take them an additional twenty-four hours just to boil one day's run of sap into a few gallons of maple syrup. So while our process is still very much part of the Slow Food movement, our improved technology has sped things up quite a bit. Most importantly, our new technology has vastly improved the *quality* of the maple syrup—a twenty-first-century route to a timeless food resource.

A beautiful sugarbush is only part of the requirement for an exceptional batch of maple syrup. If the quality of a great maple syrup were dependent solely on the quality of the trees, syrup from the colonial days would taste quite similar to what we're producing today. But earlier maple producers didn't have the purification and filtration techniques we've developed today. The microbes in the sap convert the sucrose into invert sugars, which then multiply as the sap is cooked into a deeper and richer maple syrup. Invert sugar is formed naturally

until 2 A.M. Because the warmer daytime hours are when we need to be out monitoring the sap flow, it makes sense to process our sap into syrup overnight, to ensure that every hour is used even when the sap has frozen up in the trees once more. It's our standard to process the sap the same day it is gathered, so we'll spend the entire day of warm weather (9 A.M. until about 6 P.M.) collecting sap to process right away. Toward the end of the sugaring season, when there is an increased risk of temperatures not staying below freezing overnight, sap left out too long might build up yeast and other bioactivity if exposed to too-warm temperatures. The vast majority of our sugaring days involve processing the sap as soon as it's been transferred to our main sugarhouse. There it will be poured into a second round of clean stainless-steel tanks that sit just adjacent to the heart of our filtering and evaporating process: our DAF (Dissolved Air Flotation) and our RO machines.

during the boiling because at around 60°C (140°F), the sucrose molecules react with water molecules in a hydrogenation reaction. The water molecule is added to the sucrose molecule and, in the process, the sucrose molecule is split into two separate molecules that introduce two other simple sugars: fructose and glucose. The balance of the concentrations of the three sugars (sucrose, fructose, and glucose) in the maple syrup helps determine the smoothness of its mouthfeel. Each sugar crystallizes at different temperatures and produces crystals of different sizes under the same conditions, which can in turn disrupt the formation of crystals by the other sugars. We do cook some of our sap past its syrup stage, drying it out as it cooks over a higher temperature and eventually becoming a granular maple sugar, similar to how the early settlers would have enjoyed maple in their time. This works beautifully as a white or brown sugar substitute, and can be swapped one-for-one in baking and other recipes that call for granulated sugar.

All of this maple sugar development, however, is contingent upon our making the syrup as clean and shelf-stable as possible. As the sap comes out of the tree and into contact with the plastic tubing system, it develops naturally occurring microorganisms (yeast, fungi, and bacteria) that can compromise the color, flavor, and quality of the finished maple syrup. Having some of these microorganisms is perfectly normal in maple sap, and their increased presence in the tree over the course of the season partially explains why the later-season sap produces darker and richer syrup. For safety and product shelf-life, and to eliminate off flavors that would compromise the quality of the final syrup, however, the sap's bacteria needs to be killed or filtered out over the course of filtration, evaporation, and boiling into syrup. Our system at Crown Maple thus requires several different levels of filtration to remove large and small debris, bacteria, cellulose, and microorganisms, to produce the

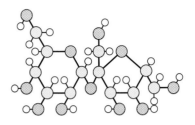

SUCROSE MOLECULE

GLUCOSE MOLECULE

FRUCTOSE MOLECULE

○ HYDROGEN
○ CARBON
◉ OXYGEN

Sap is only 2 to 3 percent sucrose when first collected, but our goal is to both bring the amount of sucrose up and bring out two more types of sugar, fructose and glucose. As you can see from these three molecules, it's all about forcing the water and sucrose together in a hydrogenation reaction to create more sugars and bring the overall composition of the syrup together.

finest and cleanest maple syrup possible. But in order to do this, we have to submit the sap to three very distinct steps of processing, each with its own rounds of filtration: a round of dissolved air flotation (DAF) to remove water-insoluble materials, exposure to UV light to kill off micro-organisms that might develop bacteria, and final filtering prior to our reverse-osmosis machine, which removes up to 90 percent of the water in the sap.

THE DAF (DISSOLVED AIR FLOTATION)

We consider the DAF the tool that sets us apart within the industry: a peerless method of clearing bacteria, yeast, and other water-insoluble debris from the sap before it ever meets the main RO machine or the evaporator. Dissolved air flotation is a technology that was originally designed for use in drinking-water filtration systems. Raw sap or partially concentrated sap from our remote locations first enters the DAF through a series of bag prefilters, each sized at 25 microns (a micron is one-millionth of a meter). These prefilters are located in filter housings the sap will pass through as it flows into the DAF tank (which can hold up to 2,000 gallons at a time, and through which we process about 3,600 gallons per hour). Pressurized air is forced into the sap through an apparatus at the bottom of the tank and the microbubbles float tiny debris, bacteria, yeast, and other unwanted particulates to the surface. On a timed basis, a skimmer arm runs across the top of the tank and pushes the unwanted materials off the top of the liquid to a discharge tank.[75] When the sap exits the DAF after about thirty minutes it is ready for its final concentration and evaporation.

When we first started considering the use of a DAF in our sugar operation, it was initially with a borrowed DAF that we had mounted on a trailer outside of our sugarhouse for temporary use. We pulled samples of our sap from those initial DAF runs and transferred them to petri dishes to see the difference between DAF-processed sap and sap not processed through a DAF. The results couldn't have been starker or more convincing: The samples that had not gone through the DAF looked moldy after a week, whereas the DAF-treated sap looked as clean as it had the day we processed it. This is a far more effective means of removing bacteria and debris from sap than simply straining before processing in the RO, and we here at Crown Maple were the first to see the potential of this technology for maple syrup production. The water-insoluble materials in maple sap—microorganisms and bacteria—would ultimately reduce the efficacy of the filters, not to mention gunking up our main RO and evaporator as we processed the sap. When we first started producing maple syrup, we did not have the DAF on hand, and every part of our equipment required more frequent and more intensive cleaning. This is extremely important for a producer of our size—we already clean our equipment after every batch of syrup, but by using a DAF, we remove infinitely more debris at the very beginning of the process, allowing cleanup to be more efficient and less time-consuming.

The DAF also enables us to make cleaner, purer late-season Dark and Very Dark syrups with richer flavors but without the bad aftertaste that typically accompanies late-season syrups. As the days get warmer, more and more bacteria are naturally introduced into the sap. Typically a maple producer would pass a threshold of sap viability when he or she experienced more days of warm weather than not, and spotted sap that was producing a much darker and headier maple syrup. The darker the

---

75 "Komline-Sanderson—Dissolved Air Flotation."

Treating our sap in the DAF (Dissolved Air Flotation) System allows us to remove a large amount of water-insoluble contaminants from the very beginning of our production process, resulting in vastly cleaner, purer syrup (especially during late-season tapping).

DISSOLVED AIR FLOTATION

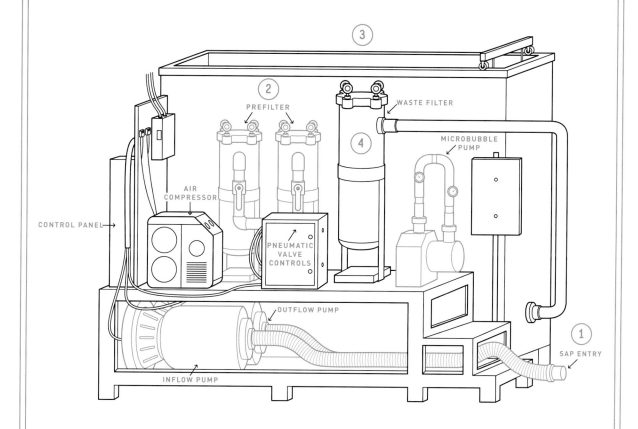

CONTROL PANEL

AIR COMPRESSOR

PREFILTER

PNEUMATIC VALVE CONTROLS

WASTE FILTER

MICROBUBBLE PUMP

OUTFLOW PUMP

INFLOW PUMP

SAP ENTRY

1 Sap Entry: Raw sap enters the DAF from 9,300 gallon holding tanks.

2 Prefilter: Sap is filtered through 25-micron filter bags prior to entering our 2,000 gallon DAF tank.

3 Sap tank: Sap flows through the gallon tanks at a rate of approximately 6,000 gallons per hour, with an average skim cycle of 20 minutes.

4 Waste Filter: Skimmed contaminates and sap are collected and filtered through a 3-micron reclamation filter.

syrup, the more bacteria is developing in the sap, and the more producers would have to discard because it couldn't be boiled to a level of taste or purity acceptable to the typical maple consumer. (This type of syrup was previously labeled as grade B, because it was considered less desirable than the lighter, more delicate syrups. Today it's labeled as Dark and Very Dark syrup, which is intensely maple flavored and quite delicious if it can be produced with a high level of purity and quality.) With a DAF adding a level of deeply thorough filtration right at the beginning of the sap's processing, our later-season runs of syrup make very high quality batches of Dark and Very Dark syrup. We were astonished at our first tastes of the post-DAF dark syrups—we had removed the bad things that would have made for a low-quality syrup, yet kept all the wonderful complex flavors of the maple itself.

UV STERILIZATION

After going through the DAF machine, the sap is then exposed to a series of tubes that are flooded with germicidal ultraviolet light. Our UV sterilization method is comprised of a stainless-steel cylinder with an inner quartz cylinder, around which twenty-four low-pressure UV lamps are placed. After going through the DAF machine, the sap flows in a thin stream within the narrow space between the quartz and stainless cylinders, where it gets a brief but intense dosage of UV light. It is important that the sap flows in a narrow thin stream across the UV light, so the light can penetrate and sterilize the sap completely as it passes through to the RO.

While we were able to filter out most of the micro, water-insoluble debris in the DAF machine, the UV light provides a method of killing the potential microorganisms on a cellular level so they don't reproduce after leaving the DAF and before entering the evaporator. Germicidal ultraviolet works by breaking apart the chemical bonds in the nucleic acids of microorganisms.

Without their nucleic acids, microorganisms are no longer able to live on to reproduce, and thus we can effectively consider the remaining sap 98 percent bacteria-free. This is enough to kill bacterial microorganisms and effectively sterilize and pasteurize the sap before it goes to the RO machine for the next stage of filtration and the most significant stage of its water removal. The UV sterilization system at Crown Maple can treat approximately 150 gallons of sap per minute, and takes about fifteen minutes to completely process the run of sap that has just gone through the DAF.[76] While the bulk of the sap's bacteria have been eliminated after its time in the DAF, the UV acts as our insurance against any contaminants reemerging before the evaporator. It's one of our filtration stages that ensures that our syrup is as pure as possible, and it's now fairly standard throughout the maple industry.

REVERSE-OSMOSIS FILTRATION

After the DAF process is complete, we transfer the sap via a series of prefilters (to make sure we capture any smaller particles not yet captured by the DAF) to our main reverse-osmosis filtration machine, set up just across the room from the DAF. As we mentioned earlier, the RO represents the biggest shift in maple technology in the twentieth century: It's the best means to remove water from the sap before it encounters the evaporator. Most medium- to large-scale maple producers use RO machines that remove at least 75 percent of the water from the sap, leaving the rest to be dealt with in the evaporator. Our main RO located in our sugarhouse is able to remove up to 90 percent of the water, which allows us to produce a concentrated sap that moves through the evaporator quicker, using far less energy. Because of the

76 "Liquid Sugar UV Disinfection Systems."

size of our RO, we can process up to nine thousand gallons of sap per hour.

As with the DAF, RO technology was originally developed for water purification, to remove different kinds of molecules and ions, as well as bacteria, by forcing it through a semipermeable membrane. Osmosis is the process by which all cell-based life on earth functions, the movement of molecules from the outside of a cell's semipermeable membrane to its interior, where the molecule is concentrated and used to fuel the cell's functions. Reverse osmosis is, as the name suggests, the reverse of that process: Reverse osmosis blocks the molecule from passing through the semipermeable membrane and lets the other molecules through, concentrating the desired molecule on the "outside" of the membrane. In water filtration and desalination, the pure water is let through the membrane and the detritus, microorganisms, and salts are blocked and concentrated on the "outside" of the membrane, allowing for easier disposal of the thickened, unwanted sludge of concentrated contaminants. In our process, the "unwanted" product is the water, and what remains on the "inside" of the membrane is what we want to carry forward—a concentrated sap rich with minerals and flavonoids, with most of its residual water removed well before it needs to be boiled.

There are two sides of our main RO machine, which we call "A" and "B." Each side can run by itself and process its own batch of sap at a rate of approximately 4,500 gallons per hour. First, the sap passes through a 5-micron prefilter designed to remove any remaining detritus and microorganisms remaining after the UV light treatment (which, if we had not already removed them, might clog up the main membranes of the RO). The RO itself contains a semipermeable membrane that is designed to let only water molecules through. The sugars and flavonoids are concentrated "outside" the membrane, and purified water flows through and out into a separate container. The resulting sap left behind has a sugar concentrate of about 16 to 20° Brix (see page 81). It's not syrup yet, but it's much more concentrated than it was before, and is now ready to be boiled down further in the final evaporator stage.

But what happened to all that permeated water that we removed from the sap? This is where the truly powerful environmental kickback happens: The water removed from the sap during its time in the RO is now a pure water molecule, highly purified and hugely valuable to our operations. We can use that water—and we might have well over 100,000 total gallons of permeated water on a big day—for any number of things: to clean our equipment at the end of the day or to wash out our collection tanks. After the entire day's run is processed and our equipment is cleaned, we overflow the remaining water back to the forest and distribute it into retention ponds, where it can be absorbed back into the sugarbush. Not only is this good business sense—not a drop of even our "waste" water is wasted—but it also reinforces the commitment we all feel to the landscapes we tap, to keeping them healthy and sustainable for many more decades and sugaring seasons to come.

There have been so many innovations in the maple syrup industry, but I'm thankful that I'm producing maple syrup now, in a post-RO world. Why is it so valuable to us, given that maple producers had been making maple syrup without RO machines for almost three hundred years? Primarily because 90 percent of the sap's excess water has been removed from the syrup before it has to go through the evaporator, saving us substantial energy costs. It also brings the sap much closer to its final desired Brix before entering the evaporator. This cuts down enormously on the time and labor it would otherwise require if we were using the evaporator alone. Additionally, if boiling is the only way you can remove water from your sap, you run the risk of making processing mistakes when your maple syrup has to sit over heat for a prolonged period of time. When a maple producer is working with an RO, he's free not only to escape a nine-plus-hour slog sitting over a boiling pot of sap, but also to produce much more maple syrup at a much higher quality than his sugaring forefathers. That's something that any serious producer can embrace, and the RO serves as a lifeline for anyone who has a sizable sugarbush.

Finally, an RO is a very contained piece of equipment, allowing for fast concentration of a huge volume of sap, so it requires deliberate care and careful maintenance after every sap run. After each day's run, we're able to effectively clean the RO with a combination of permeate water and food-grade soap. At the end of each sap season, we thoroughly clean the RO's eighteen membranes with a mild solution of food-grade citric acid, a completely organic cleaning treatment, which makes sure the membranes are not fouled up.

After using the DAF, the UV light, and the RO, we have clean, highly concentrated sap. But we still have to go through the final stage of production: the boiling off of water to increase the sap's sugar content and officially turn it into syrup. That takes the evaporator in its three distinct stages: the steam-away, the flue pan, and the finishing pan.

Medium to large maple producers everywhere rely on reverse-osmosis machines such as this one to remove large amounts of water from their sap, leaving behind a concentrated liquid that needs far less boiling off to turn into finished syrup.

REVERSE-OSMOSIS FILTRATION

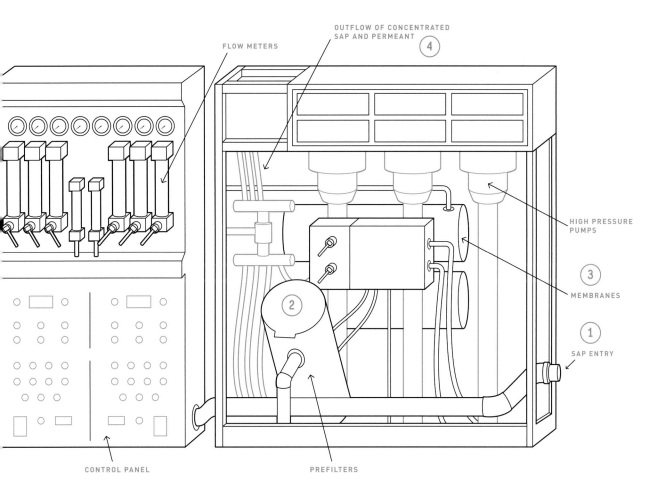

FLOW METERS

OUTFLOW OF CONCENTRATED
SAP AND PERMEANT
④

HIGH PRESSURE
PUMPS

③

MEMBRANES

①

SAP ENTRY

②

CONTROL PANEL

PREFILTERS

1 Sap Entry: The sap flows into the RO machine at approximately 2° Brix.

2 Prefilter: Sap flows through a 5-micron prefilter.

3 Membranes: Sap is concentrated up to 20° Brix by eliminating 90 percent of its water, using high pressure and membranes with a pore size of 0.0001 micron. The flow rate of the sap through the RO can be up to 9,000 gallons per hour.

4 Outflow of Concentrated Sap and Permeate: The now-concentrated sap is transferred to a holding tank in preparation of the final boil in the evaporator (see page 79). The permeate (membrane-filtered water) is stored in a 9,300 gallon tank and used to clean equipment at the end of the production day.

ENTERING THE EVAPORATOR: THE STEAM-AWAY AND FLUE PAN

The ROs do us a huge service in removing up to 90 percent of the unwanted water from the sap. Prior to the 1970s, the entirety of the water removal process would have taken place during the evaporating and boiling stage, a process that would have taken hours upon hours of work, peeling off half of one's wallpaper in that time. In our sugarhouse, it takes only twenty to thirty minutes for two thousand gallons of sap to circulate through the DAF, then only about fifteen minutes for the sap to go through the nine membranes of the RO machine. But we still need that final boil to evaporate out the remaining water and to ensure that our syrup has come up to the right amount of sugar density and richness in flavor and color. The evaporator is the final stage of our syrup-making process, and is built upon the simple gravity-driven concept of processing the sap into syrup over heat so it gains in density. As water evaporates out of the concentrated sap, it becomes heavier—as it becomes heavier, it moves from the steam-away (where it is about 20 to 25° Brix) to the flue pan (where it exits at about 55° Brix) to its final destination in the finishing pan (where it achieves its final sugar density of 66 to 68° Brix). This may sound complicated, but when you look at the illustration of the machine as a whole (opposite), you can see how gravity still drives this part of the sugaring process. The evaporator has been a crucial piece of equipment in the syrup-making process since the peak of the industry in the late nineteenth century, and remains remarkably unchanged in its structure; we are still relying on the same basic fluid mechanics that producers used a hundred years ago. And while the industry is continuing to develop ever more sophisticated evaporators, it's a highly efficient system as-is.

Maple producers use many different types of evaporators—some might be very small, some very large, some using direct heat from burning wood (as was historically done), others using natural gas, propane, or fuel oil. There is presently a growing trend among larger producers to use steam evaporators instead of direct heat from a flame, but ours uses both redirected steam heat and fuel oil. The evaporators we work with at Crown Maple are called "three-stage" direct heat evaporators and are designed to be as fast and energy efficient as possible. Ours are also the largest size (six feet by eighteen feet) used in the industry, due to our scale as a big producer.

Maple sap already has built into it one of the most powerful resources possible: water, which can be transformed into steam, and then recycled back into the machine to preheat the sap before it undergoes further cooking. The **steam-away** captures excess heat via heat exchange coils from the steam coming off the flue pan, the main workhorse of the evaporator. The concentrated sap first enters the evaporator via the steam-away chamber, and is injected with air drawn into the steam-away by an external high-pressure fan unit. The bubbles created in the aerated concentrate increase the surface area of the sap, and as the bubbles break at the surface of the sap, more water vapor is released. The steam-away process has also preheated the sap with steam, which in turn increases the evaporation rate. The combination of the aeration and preheating with steam uses waste heat from the flue pan with no additional energy, but increases the sugar content from 20° Brix up to around 25° Brix. If you were looking at a traditional evaporator of early maple sugaring days, you would see the steam released from the evaporator similar to how a chimney would release smoke from a fireplace—channeling it out and away into the air—without taking advantage of this savings. Certainly that would make sense in an outdoor

The evaporator is where the final evaporation of the sap happens, heating it in three unique spaces: the steam-away, the flue pan, and the finishing pan, where it reaches its final syrup state.

EVAPORATOR

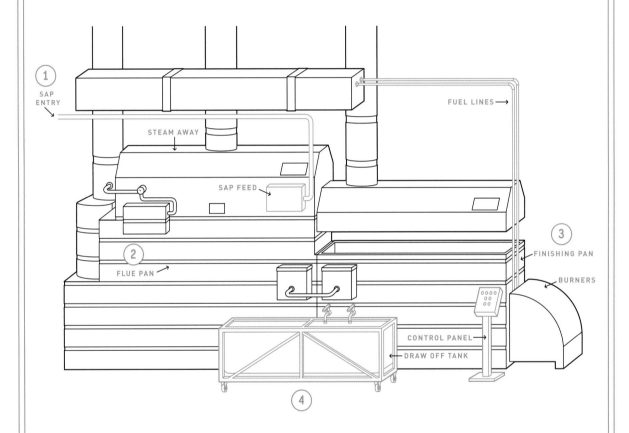

1 SAP ENTRY

FUEL LINES

STEAM AWAY

SAP FEED

3

FINISHING PAN

2 FLUE PAN

BURNERS

CONTROL PANEL

DRAW OFF TANK

4

1 Sap Entry: The concentrated sap flows into the steam away, which is the first stage of the evaporation process.

2 Flue Pan: The majority of the evaporation process takes place in the flue pan. Brix will increase from approximately 25 to 50° Brix during the flue pan boil.

3 Finishing Pan: The final boil of concentrated sap to the finished syrup (bringing it to 66 to 68° Brix) takes place in the finishing or syrup pan.

4 Draw-Off Tank: The maple syrup flows off the finishing pan, mixed with diatomaceous earth (DE), and filtered into a barrel for storage prior to bottling.

sugar shack of the late nineteenth century—but by using a steam away as part of our evaporator, all of that valuable vapor can be put back into the machine to make it even more efficient.

The **flue pan** is where the big boil of the syrup happens—the part of our operation that bears the most resemblance to the outdoor sugar shacks of earlier generations. At that time, a producer would remove the majority of the larger, more visible detritus and scum from the sap by hand (or with a hand skimmer), build a fire under an enormous pot of maple sap, and boil it down into syrup. And while today's machinery is more complicated and efficient and most modern producers add similar filtration and pretreatment steps to the process, the heart of maple syrup manufacturing is still the boil. At Crown Maple, the concentrated maple sap flows into the evaporator at the steam-away unit, but the main action happens once it makes its way to the flue pan. The flue pan consists of a small valley, with dips and peaks, which increase the surface area of the pan to provide maximum heat transfer to the concentrated sap. The sap is boiled in the flue pan to a temperature of 214 to 217°F. Then, the concentrated sap will flow through the flue pan due to a gradient created by the density and shallower depth in the pan. As the pan fills, the warmer liquids naturally move forward in the pan, allowing cooler, less dense sap to flow toward a lower point, where the liquid is shallower. As long as we have colder, less dense sap flowing into the flue pan from the steam-away, we will have this temperature gradient and sap will move through the flue pan toward the finishing pan. As the sap boils and evaporates, steam is created, which is then captured to preheat the sap in the steam-away.

Upon leaving the flue pan, our concentrated sap is well on its way to reaching its finished sugar content of 66 to 68° Brix—at this point it is about 55 percent sugar (a Brix of 55°), very, very close to where we want it to be when we can assess its grade and quality. But we still need to go through the final stage of boiling, in the finishing pan.

THE FINISHING PAN, WHERE THE BEST BRIX HAPPENS

The final stage for refining the syrup occurs in the **finishing pan**. The interior of the finishing pan is lined with racewaylike troughs, creating a zigzag path for the syrup to move through as it further evaporates and becomes denser and heavier. Why would we do this? Rather than having a single flat pan in which newly arrived sap and nearly finished syrup are intermingling, these zigzag runways allow us to isolate the sap into smaller batches almost by specific gravity while still giving it the same hot surface area to work through. These segregated batches of syrup allow for some retention time so the syrup only leaves the evaporator at the perfect specific gravity (density) and Brix level.

All maple producers know that maple hits a sweet spot where it is exactly the right proportion of sugar to water. We call the unit of measurement for sugar concentration the Brix—a unit for measuring the sugar density of the finished syrup. The Brix scale is a system of measurement developed in the early 1800s by scientists Karl Balling and Adolf Brix, working on behalf of the brewing industry to assess the amount of wort (sugar-filled liquid to be made into alcohol) in their beer and whiskey by determining a liquid's density in relation to the dissolved solids in these two beverages. While wort doesn't behave exactly the same as sucrose, in general the degree Brix is equivalent to the total percentage of dissolved sugar in water—the critical quantity we're concerned with as we cook the sap down into syrup. The goal is to concentrate the syrup down to 66 to 68° Brix, which corresponds to 66 to 68 percent sugar—but the great mystery in assessing the day's first batch of syrup is knowing at exactly which temperature (and after how much cooking time) the syrup has reached 66° Brix.

This assessment of perfect syrup sugar content was once strictly calculated by the Jones "Rule of 86," a rough formula to assess how many gallons of sap will be required to produce a certain number of finished gallons of maple syrup. As developed by C. H. Jones, a scientist and professor at the University of Vermont, in 1946, the rule dictated that if you divided the number 86 by the basic sugar content of sap, you will get a prediction of how much sap is needed to produce a gallon of syrup (and, within that formula, how much water needs to be boiled off to produce 1 gallon of syrup). Based on this rule, assuming a 2° Brix level in the sap, it would take 43 gallons of sap to produce 1 gallon of syrup. While this is a perfectly good guideline to anticipate a day's production, maple producers no longer live by this rule. Today, we abide by a rule that's a bit more specific, a rule of 88.2 rather than 86, resulting in a slightly more conservative estimate of how much syrup we can make (about half a gallon less) but a much more accurate measurement for producers of all sizes.[77]

As we mentioned earlier, pure straight-out-of-the-tree sap generally has a Brix level (sugar content level) of 2 percent. To calculate how much water needs to be boiled out of the sap to achieve our desired finished Brix of 66°, we use the updated version of the Brix rule: S (the initial volume of sap or concentrated sap required to produce 1 gallon of maple syrup) equals 88.2 divided by X (the Brix degree of the starting sap upon entering the boiling process) minus 0.32, or $S = 88.2/X - 0.32$. The water needed to be boiled off would be the final S number calculated, minus 1. So assuming a 2° Brix (X = 2 percent) of the starting sap, we see that S = 43.78 gallons of sap to produce 1 gallon of finished

Compare this image of cooked syrup from the finishing pan to the image on page 70 of the sap in the collection house. A total transformation.

syrup, and the water needed to boil off would be 42.78 gallons.

The calculation allows us to better plan our production schedules. We know that finished syrup needs to leave the evaporator at a sugar density of 66 to 68° Brix, both an industry standard determined by the FDA and a level of sugar that we've learned, through tasting experiences, creates the right proportion of sugar to water. Too high a Brix and you're dealing with a more crystallized sugar experience, too little and your syrup may be too subtle or watery, and it may ferment and go bad. Sugar content from the trees changes on a daily basis and our raw sap can range from about 1.8° Brix to 2.4° Brix. Using

77 Perkins and Isselhardt, "The 'Jones Rule of 86,' Revisited."

The science of syrup takes us back to chem class—we can use a refractometer to measure the grade of the syrup from the finishing pan and a hydrometer (seen above) to measure the sugar concentrates of the finished syrup.

the updated Jones Rule, we are able to determine the best running schedule for our RO to concentrate the sap and keep the evaporator timely, finishing syrup to the desired Brix count.

The concentrated sap leaves the flue pans and enters the finishing pan at approximately 55° Brix. The sap spends about five to ten minutes cooking over the finishing pan, but it's far from a standardized procedure. Our modulating draw-off valve on the finishing pan allows us to slow the final few percentage points of evaporation down so we can know exactly when our concentrated sap is hitting the 66° Brix sweet spot without overshooting and potentially ruining the batch. The temperature of a finished 66° Brix syrup will be about 216°F to 219°F, but that varies depending on surrounding barometric pressure. What we're really looking for is the correlation between a specific temperature and that ideal 66° Brix we're trying to achieve. Throughout the first run's journey over the finishing pan, we pull out a sample from the machine's modulating butterfly valve every few minutes and test its Brix with the use of a handheld refractometer. A tool developed for the wine and brewing industry, the refractometer can be used to measure the density of the concentrated sap to show us how close we are to achieving the right Brix in the syrup. We place a couple sample drops of the concentrated sap into our refractometer to ensure it reached our desired level of Brix, and that it can officially be called maple syrup according to our industry standards. (We can also use the more common hydrometer cup and thermometer to measure this, as both show us the relationship between our sugar concentration and our finishing temperature.)

Though we know for certain that the concentrated sap will rise the additional 10° Brix needed during its time on the finishing pan, you can also understand why it's ideal to have the steam-away as part of the evaporator, to act as the preheating mechanism of the evaporator:

216°F is an extremely high temperature, and if the sap were cold, or even room temperature, it would take hours longer to bring it up to the necessary temperature to boil out the bulk of the water. But by boiling off most of the water in the evaporator, and then using the steam to heat the concentrated sap as it heads toward the finishing pan, we can know with a good degree of certainty when our sap has nearly become syrup.

FINAL FILTERING AND BARREL-PACKING

Once we know the syrup is finished, we want to put it through even more thorough filtration before it can be hot-packed into our barrels. Our final stage of filtration is twofold: As each batch of finished syrup rests in the draw-off pan just beyond the finishing pan, we stir in a specific amount of food-grade diatomaceous earth (DE). Diatomaceous earth is the fossilized remains of diatoms, which are unicellular phytoplankton organisms. The shells are covered in tiny pores that trap microorganisms and other contaminants, like a fine sieve. While it has a number of uses in food-grade applications (and is a completely organic substance, safe for consumption and for use in organic food products), DE's importance here is as a kind of internal filtration system for the nearly finished maple syrup. By adding DE directly into the draw-off pan, we add an extra level of cellular-level filtration and precision to purifying our syrup. (While we only use food-grade DE in our sugarhouse, as do all other maple producers, DE can be sold for all kinds of industrial uses. It's important that you find the appropriate kind of DE to use in your own sugarhouse, so seek out reputable vendors online who have worked extensively with other maple producers.)

Once the DE has been sufficiently mixed into our syrup, we then put the syrup through a filter press, in which the DE acts as the filtration system. The DE extracts minerals that are naturally present in the syrup—during

Finished barrels full of syrup get a chance to cool down in our sugarhouse—otherwise the syrup in the barrel might keep cooking and become a completely different grade.

the evaporation process, these minerals are concentrated and hardened into a substance called niter, or sugar sand. The DE-charged filter press will remove the sand, and what we're left with is our final, purer-than-pure syrup. From there we pack the still-hot syrup into stainless-steel barrels, then move the barrels into a cooler part of our sugarhouse to stop the cooking process. If the syrup is not cooled quickly enough after packing into barrels, it can continue to cook in the barrel for an extra day or two. This can dramatically change its final grade—and assessing the syrup's true grade is the next big step in our process.

— 4 —

From Barrel to Bottle

DETERMINING THE SYRUP'S GRADE

The syrup is off the evaporator, and we know it has the right level of Brix . . . but what exactly did we produce? Even before it's bottled and stored, we have to assess the quality of the syrup and assign it a distinctive grade. We get more into the details and evolution of the maple grading system in Part Three (page 96), but apart from the industry's standards, we have our own clear standards to meet. As each batch of syrup comes off the evaporator, we pull a small sample into a glass jar to do an initial assessment of its grade. We couldn't possibly have made this assessment before now, and we couldn't do it by looking at the sap or monitoring the temperature of the woods that day, or even tasting this initial batch. No, the grade of maple syrup is based on a standardized color from the USDA, which is then supported by our second system of assessing each batch by flavor and quality. To assess the grade by color, we hold up a small box of four small bottles of syrup in a row that reflects the four grades of syrup as approved by the USDA. Before we can label and date each barrel, we have to first stop and acknowledge exactly what grade we've produced—and there's no way to know that before checking its color to see what classification it should receive, if it should be deemed Golden, Amber, Dark, or Very Dark. It's entirely unpredictable which trees are going to yield which color or in what volume before this final stage, and every season results in a different volume of each syrup.

That said, we use the same methods that farmers do—as we assess the strength of each crop, we stop and write down exactly when we harvested it, and what results we discovered. So as the syrup is hot-packed into

We use the USDA-approved guidelines for the various grades of maple syrup to check each batch and barrel, and conduct deliberate taste tests to assess the grade and quality of every potential bottle.

our stainless-steel barrels, we note every barrel with a grade assessment, date, and any other details we can capture (weather conditions, tree conditions, and so on). We'll also do a very quick taste test before the barrel packing, just to confirm that there isn't anything wildly off or worrisome about the taste of each batch. These barrels can each hold up to fifty-five gallons of maple syrup, and as they've been hot-packed in bacteria-free stainless steel, the barrels can be set aside for several months (or even two to three years) before they need to be retested and bottled for purchase.

TASTING, BOTTLING, AND STORING

Once we've captured the entire run of sap in barrels, we can finally sit down for my favorite part of the sugar-making process: the taste testing. We allow two to three weeks' time to pass between when we first hot-pack the syrup in barrels and when we sit down to taste it, to allow the syrup to develop and deepen in both flavor and complexity. We assemble a team of three taste testers—not because any of us are underdeveloped in our maple tasting ability, but because we have to compare notes in assessing what works and what doesn't about each batch. We know from our previous color grading that, upon packing into barrels, a particular batch might have been in the Dark, Robust category, but upon tasting we see that the color has deepened to something more appropriate to the Very Dark, Strong category. This may be because, if we haven't adequately cooled the syrup before it goes into the barrels, it may continue to cook in the barrel as it cools. We can't simply assume that the syrup post-boiling is going to be the exact same syrup to go into our bottles. The only way to really know is to do a tasting. We individually test and sample the syrup when the barrel is one-quarter full, and again when it's topped off (so we can compare the early part of the batch's syrup with the later part—we won't assign a truly final sugar count and color grade until we get ready for bottling). We do another taste test usually the day or morning before bottling, and then one more after the final bottle is sealed later that day, just in case the temperature and time in the bottles has changed it.

When we sit down for our first tasting, we bring together a three-person panel to taste and assess each syrup. Typically it is our head of production, one of our in-house chefs (who also advises us on product development), and the head of our inventory control. We knew early on that we wanted to have people with very different priorities for the syrup involved in our tasting—three different sets of eyes to assess if a syrup's color was closer to Amber, Dark, or Very Dark, and three different palates to assess if there was anything off or unusual about a maple's flavor that would affect its bottling.

Even with the standard grading system, we know through the tasting of our syrups that there are very specific flavors for each grade of syrup. Golden syrup has a very light and delicate flavor, closer to vanilla bean or popcorn, but also with a very light saltiness that

brings to mind salted caramel or brown butter. Amber syrup has to be in that classic maple zone, tasting like the flavors of fall (gingerbread, pumpkin, roasted nuts) with a medium body and sweetness that makes it easily adaptable to baking. Dark is my favorite for use in coffee, because it's more concentrated in flavor and has a slightly nuttier, smokier finish (which also makes it great for pairing with cheese and dried fruit). Finally, the Very Dark syrup has the most intense, boldest flavor of all, which is partly why chefs and fine food producers enjoy working with it. This was the syrup that won us a 2015 Sofi Award from the Specialty Food Association. As we conduct our tasting, we're looking for the signature flavors of each grade as we've noticed them in previous batches, and also noting how much we think is being produced of each type of syrup.

Once we've assigned a nearly final grade and flavor designation on our bottles, we filter the syrup through one more filter press so it has a final straining before going into the bottles. We then pour each barrel into bottles—usually we can get more than five hundred twelve-ounce bottles per barrel, though it depends on the season and each day's run. Many large maple producers have automated their bottling process completely from barrel to shipping box, and we have automated the filling process for each of our bottles. But before we seal the bottle for good, we also want the ability to stop and assess our syrup's quality one last time, just in case it has deepened in flavor or color enough to change the grade of the syrup. We do one last tasting (again, with our three-person panel), and then seal each finished bottle with its cork and foil by hand.

CERTIFIED ORGANIC

"Organic certification" means that a food processing plant has had its ingredients, equipment, and method of producing evaluated by an outside agency. Our products are certified organic by the Northeast Organic Farming Association of New York (NOFA-NY Certified Organic, LLC), and are in turn accredited by the USDA, which accounts for the USDA logo on our branded products. Receiving certification means that the evaluating agency has concluded that the plant has not introduced any synthetic chemicals or artificial ingredients into its food, nor has it jeopardized the natural resources of the food in the process of making the food product. In order to be certified organic, a producer has to comply with standards of organic farming (keeping the soil free from prohibited chemicals like fertilizers or certain pesticides for a specific number of years); provide water and soil tests, as well as extensive written materials, to document a chemical-free source; and comply with regular inspections from outside agencies to show that it is a sustained organic producer.

You'd think that this would be a fairly easy standard for maple producers to meet—after all, you need nearly a half-century of growing maple trees to produce quality syrup, and so modern-day producers end up inheriting the farming traditions of the sugar producers that came before them. But there is a very big difference between "natural" and "organic," and while maple syrup is natural, it would be easy to produce a maple syrup that could not be called organic. "Organic" is defined not only by the ingredients used to make the food, but also the environment in which the sap is tapped and the syrup is made.[78] If a producer removes all the nonmaple trees from their sugarbush, the resulting monocultural sugarbush constitutes an inorganic growing environment, and so the resulting syrup can no longer be called "organic." Similarly, if nonorganic chemicals are used to treat the finished syrup, or used to clean the processing equipment, that too can prevent the producer from receiving an organic certification. If selling as much maple syrup at as low a production cost as possible is a producer's bottom line, there are plenty of nonorganic ways to go about doing it, but we tend to think that shortcuts often jeopardize the quality of the finished syrup.

---

[78] Holmes, "'Pure' Maple Syrup?" 68.

THE RIGHT PRICE—AND THE REAL VALUE— FOR QUALITY MAPLE SYRUP

How do you really assess the value of maple syrup, when retail prices can fluctuate so wildly and availability changes from year to year? Pure maple syrup can be sold at a premium, given that it comes from a limited resource and can only be made about six to eight weeks out of the year, but you also have to consider that many consumers are used to picking up the giant $3.99 bottle of imitation maple syrup at the grocery store, and often balk at the small bottles of pure maple selling for upwards of $12.

The price of maple syrup has risen more than 182 percent since 1980.[79] Given our ever-changing weather patterns over the last three decades, it's no surprise that maple prices have changed as well. During the notoriously terrible year of 2012, the nation's syrup run fell 32 percent short of the previous year's run. That change in available supply, combined with a strong Canadian dollar, caused American maple prices to increase, especially as retailers made big purchases to create maple syrup "reserves" in anticipation of future shortages. The 2014 run, meanwhile, was one of the best on record, and prices per pound of syrup ranged from $2.65 for Golden and Amber syrup to $2.55 for Dark and $2.50 for Very Dark.[80] (By comparison, in 2007 the price per pound was $4 or higher, depending on the state of origin, due to a shortage in supply that drove nationwide prices higher.)

Producers have always had to consider the fair price for their syrup in relation to where that syrup is being sold. A small bottle of your last run can retail for $10 at the farmers' market without complaint, especially because the people buying it from you probably have a great awareness of the work that went into that $10 bottle. But this local appreciation has also been one of the historical

Sometimes we've put our syrup through so many assessments and filters before bottling, it's easy to forget the handiwork that creates the magic of a freshly filled bottle of syrup.

shortcomings of maple, preventing it from gaining a stronger foothold in the sweetener category: The more specialized your audience's knowledge has to be, the less likely it is you can go mainstream. Maple has always been a regional specialty, a signature northeastern flavor, and this has been very positive in giving it a sustained appreciation in the regional food movement (and the agritourism business). But this does limit the impact that maple producers can have on the national food market, especially when it comes to retail placement.

Perhaps the biggest impediment to getting high-quality syrup out to the general public is a question of distribution. Small or medium-sized producers are not large enough to get placement in major grocery stores, because they do not have the marketing power or packaging capacity to deliver the volume of syrup necessary to meet nationwide grocery demand. Medium-sized to large retailers generally buy from high-volume syrup packers, who contract with smaller producers to buy a whole season's run of syrup. While this takes away a lot

79 Dmitrieva and Kolet, "Syrup shortage? Prices Are Soaring."

80 "Bulk Price per Pound."

of the guesswork for producers as to how they'll recoup the costs of production, it also means that they sell the syrup with a fair amount of anonymity—the label on the bottle of their syrup doesn't say "Small Guy Vermont Maple Syrup" on it, but instead carries a label from the distributor, "Large Maple Sales Syrup," with no details as to the process or terroir of the syrup itself on the packaging. It also means bottlers buy everything available—not only the very best syrups a producer makes, but also the lowest quality, not-very-good syrups. There is a saying among the wholesale commodity maple producers: "The first two-thirds of the sugaring season, I make syrup. The final third of the season, I make money." By this they mean that during the last part of the season they produce bad syrup that generates cash flow from bottlers. A few seasons ago, one producer told us that more than 40 percent of his production was not very good, due to a quick, warm spring in his area—but then the bottler bought all his product anyway. The syrup packer blends these various "quality" of syrups and then bottles, packages, and sells that syrup wholesale under its brand to supermarkets nationwide or labels as "Store Brand X Maple Syrup." The result is a more affordable maple syrup, sure, but of widely varying quality.

With any high-end artisanal food, there is a trade-off between quality and price. Though it is more expensive to produce and thus more expensive to buy, we believe that super-pure, high-quality maple syrup and sugar allow for a great expansion of the use of maple outside of pancakes. If you are preparing your favorite cocktail, or making a sophisticated kind of pastry, or whisking together a dressing that uses maple as the sweetener, you will notice a big difference between a high-quality syrup and a poorer-quality one made from blended syrups. In fact, we believe many of the proposed uses in the next chapter really rely on the use of a high-quality syrup, and may be compromised if made with a low-grade, blended syrup.

BEYOND BREAKFAST: BRINGING MAPLE TO THE TABLE

The market for spreading enthusiasm for maple syrup doesn't lie solely in the syrup, but rather in expanding awareness of the different applications for high-quality maple syrup. As you'll see in our recipes (starting on page 103), high-quality maple syrup can be incorporated into almost anything a creative chef can dream up. The very first step is being open-minded when shopping for ingredients—to get excited about maple, you have to think beyond pancakes, and beyond syrup in general.

In addition to maple syrup, we always knew we wanted to bring back some of the earlier styles of maple consumption to show off the versatility of the food itself. Having the opportunity to sample maple sugar or maple pearls (see page 122) gives you some proximity to what the early colonists might have tasted, and stirring a bit of bourbon-aged maple syrup into a cocktail brings a fresh awareness of the culinary uses for maple. Maple-made products—syrup, sugar, and any prepared food to which maple gives its signature flavor—should be a revelation to the person tasting it, a chance to see how the complexity of the maple itself creates a new flavor experience.

The ultimate goal is to give anyone who tries our syrup a deeper appreciation of what maple really is—a wild, heirloom resource that, if made with a great amount of care and technological ingenuity, can transform the way you experience sweetness, and the way you think about your food in general. Fully appreciating maple syrup requires a deep dive into so much history and science that it's easy to skip ahead and just appreciate it for flavor alone. But a good recipe leads to even greater curiosity—and as you'll see in Part Three, we've provided plenty of tasting opportunities to get people curious when they sit down to a dish made with our syrup. Sweet isn't even half the story.

COOKING
WITH MAPLE SYRUP

— 1 —

Maple Syrup as a Sugar Substitute

THE RECIPES THAT FOLLOW IN THIS SECTION are all Lydia's doing—yet as soon as we started tapping for syrup, I too began to realize the potential for incorporating maple syrup into almost everything I ate. Well, everything that needed a touch of sweetness . . . which, in the American diet, is almost everything. We've become so accustomed to adding sugar to everything— our tea, our oatmeal, our ketchup, our meatloaf—that actually tasting what natural sweetness is like can be a real shock. When I started substituting maple syrup and maple sugar for white sugar, suddenly the way I experienced sweetness completely changed.

It's a commonly held myth that the way we experience sweet flavors lies, quite literally, on the tips of our tongues. But in fact, our receptors for sweet flavors exist all over the mouth, throat, and esophagus, all places where taste buds can be found.[81] Each kind of sweet flavor functions differently in the mouth, as saccharin sets off one series of reactions and sucrose another.[82] The dominant sugar in maple syrup is sucrose, with small amounts of glucose and fructose that are introduced from the invert sugar produced during the boiling process. No matter how you shake it, maple syrup is still primarily sucrose, a plant-derived disaccharide made from glucose and fructose, and one that doesn't look so molecularly different from table sugar. Calorically, it's not much different either, registering about 210 calories per ¼ cup (80 g) compared to white sugar's 196 calories.

But the way we experience maple's flavor is dramatically different from how we experience that of white sugar; the amino acids in maple syrup, which develop as the sap flow increases and deepens throughout the season, amplify the organic flavor compounds of the sap, including vanillin (yes, the same molecule that delivers vanilla flavor), propionaldehyde (a naturally occurring compound that gives maple its flavor compatibility with bourbon and brandy), and strawberry furanone (a compound frequently used in making perfumes, for its floral, sweet scent).[83]

It's no surprise that the exact compounds responsible for maple's taste are still unknown, yet its distinct flavor is so uniquely different from any other sugar that it'd be impossible to mistake it for anything else. Perhaps it's because when you taste maple syrup, you're tasting the entire cooking process, the heating and caramelizing of the sap into syrup, and the effects of the tree's time during the sugar season. It's like a time capsule of where the plant has been; the depth of flavor changes with each season, and each winter produces a slightly different vintage and complexity of syrup. Really cold winters with cooler than normal sap seasons often lead to more amber syrup, with the hints of vanilla lasting longer into the season. An early, slightly warmer spring can lead to dark syrup with much stronger late-season flavor. Because we aim to make the purest maple syrup possible, what we're trying to do is release the deepest levels of flavor within the syrup—any syrup can be sweet (and most lower-quality syrups are), but lower-quality producers don't know how to filter out the bacteria, yeast, and other sugaring matter without creating a bland finish. When we look for complexity of flavor, those chalky, burnt, or residue-filled flavors that you get

---

81 Chen, *The Taste of Sweet*, 22.

82 Ibid., 25.

83 Ball, "The Chemical Composition of Maple Syrup," 1649.

This flavor wheel was developed by a team of agricultural specialists from Agriculture and Agri-Food Canada, in consultation with maple scientists from Center ACER, as a thorough glossary and guide for describing the taste of various maple syrups and maple products. From the detail and complexity of this wheel, you can see the range of maple flavor components that add up to that distinct maple taste and gustatory experience. (Source: Agriculture and Agri-Food Canada).

Nutritional Value of Various Sweeteners
Percentage of Recommended Daily Value (DV) per ¼ cup (60 ml)

	MAPLE SYRUP		HIGH FRUCTOSE CORN SYRUP		HONEY		BROWN SUGAR		WHITE SUGAR	
	¼ cup / 80 g		¼ cup / 78 g		¼ cup / 85 g		¼ cup / 55 g		¼ cup / 51 g	
	% DV	mg	% DV	mg	% DV	mg	% DV	mg	% DV	mg
RIBOFLAVIN	37	0.59	1	0.01	2	0.03	0	0.0	1	0.01
THIAMIN	1	0.01	0	0.0	0	0.0	0	0.0	0	0.0
MANGANESE	95	1.89	4	0.07	4	0.07	2	0.04	0	0.0
ZINC	6	0.58	0	0.02	2	0.19	0	0.02	0	0.0
MAGNESIUM	7	16.5	0	0.0	1	1.75	2	5.0	0	0.0
CALCIUM	5	58.0	0	0.0	0	5.0	4	45.8	0	0.48
IRON	1	0.09	0	0.02	3	0.36	3	0.39	0	0.03
SELENIUM	1	0.4 pg	1	0.55 pg	1	0.66 pg	1	65 pg	1	0.3
POTASSIUM	5	167	0	0.0	1	44.0	2	73.3	0	0.96
Calories	210		220		261		216		196	

SOURCE: USDA Nutrient Database and Canadian Nutrient File

NOTE: The values shown are the overall minimum values for the minerals and nutrients and the overall maximum values for the calories reported by the USDA Nutrient Database and the Canadian Nutrient File. The percent daily values (%DV) were calculated using the Health Canada recommended daily intake values for an average 2,000 calorie diet.

This grid, compiled via the USDA Nutrient Database and Canadian Nutrient File, compares the daily percentage of minerals and nutrients in maple syrup to a number of other popular sweeteners. As you can see, maple syrup is not only the lowest caloric sweetener available, but also has almost 20 times the amount of manganese and riboflavin as other sweeteners, making it even more nutrient-dense than honey.

with mediocre syrups don't make the grade. The flavors of maple syrup are so nuanced, in fact, that a research team from Agriculture and Agri-Food Canada developed a glossary of terms to describe the flavor of maple syrup. While you'd have to taste a million different maple syrups to truly experience the full range of maple flavors, this wheel isn't a bad place to start when you sit down with four of our bottles side by side. Do you taste more vanilla in one? More woodsmoke in another? Is one more sweet, spicy, or savory?

Certainly if we were judging on flavor alone, maple syrup would have no equal. But there's another strength that maple has among sugars: an unparalleled amount of naturally present nutrients and antioxidants. While it is sugar, it might be the most nutritionally sound sugar available.

As you can see from this chart, most sugars have almost zero nutrient value to them. Not surprisingly, given that sugars are first and foremost vehicles of simple carbohydrate energy, they can't be treated as a whole food providing balanced nutritional value the way fruits, vegetables, or proteins would. However, where maple syrup really stands out is in its amounts of riboflavin (a.k.a. vitamin B₂), and manganese. Vitamin B^2, like other B vitamins, plays an important role in our metabolic processes. Not only does it facilitate the absorption of good fats into the bloodstream, but it also protects necessary antioxidants from free radicals as we consume nutrient-rich foods. (This is why having a miso and maple dressing on your spinach salad, as you'll see on page 146, may be one of the most valuable ways to incorporate maple syrup into your diet!) Additionally, manganese is an essential enzyme in processing our most common dietary sources of cholesterol, carbohydrates, and protein. Our bones, blood, and metabolism all depend on a regular supply of manganese, and without it, we're at risk for osteoporosis and anemia, among other frightening ailments.[84] Maple syrup also delivers a nice amount of our daily zinc, magnesium, calcium, and potassium needs, keeping our immune system, heart, bones, and teeth all in order. (These are the same polyphenolic compounds that can be found in berries, tomatoes, tea, red wine, and flax seeds.) Maple syrup is a naturally gluten-free and vegan choice, and as long as you're enjoying 100 percent pure maple syrup, it is a completely natural, non-GMO food. While many of maple's nutrients can, of course, be found in many other natural foods, including soybeans, nuts, whole grains, and leafy green vegetables, the reality of our modern diet is that we're much more inclined to add a little extra sweetness to our diets than to swap out foods completely. So what would happen if, instead of cutting out sugar from our diets entirely, we decided to start using better sugars?

We know maple is one of the most complex and most nutritious sugar sources available today—but we also know that it's one of the most sustainable sources of sugar. By sustainable, I don't mean bottomless; when the tree is done giving up its sap for the season, it's done. We can't make it produce any more than it's willing to give—we live in its thrall, in whatever it wants to turn over in each season. And sugarmakers cannot afford to be a hasty bunch; remember, it takes at least forty years for a maple tree to be tappable! However, if we practice sustainable forestry, and selectively cut back dying or troubled trees, the forests can continue to produce collectable sap for hundreds of years, all the while remaining a safe haven for the many creatures that call the forest home. Our goal has always been to promote this amazing sugar source that is completely symbiotic with nature, and we have found an economically viable way to preserve the land from developers who would treat it as anything other than a beautiful landscape and natural resource. Maple producers are an example of how a patient food industry can be a more renewable, sustainable, and kinder industry—a more generous industry, with its eye on future rewards for generations to come, rather than instant profits.

So if you're choosing between cheap and nutrition-free white sugar or high-fructose corn syrup, and naturally sweet, naturally sustainable, and naturally rich in flavor maple syrup . . . why not go with the natural choice?

[84] Food and Nutrition Board of the Institute of Medicine, *Dietary Intakes for . . .*, "Manganese," 396.

— 2 —

Cooking Techniques for Maple Syrup

ALL ABOUT THE GRADES

As a sweetness delivery system, maple syrup couldn't be easier to incorporate into any number of dishes. But if you're only familiar with the one store-bought brand available to you, what we have at Crown Maple may look a bit unfamiliar, especially if you're used to the old grading system.

First developed in the early twentieth century, the maple syrup grading system was created to both establish a transparent standard for the industry (and the consumer) and determine a commercial value for syrup that would be true across all producers. Because each grade of syrup is harvested at a different point in the sugaring season, each has its own distinct color and flavor. For reasons that related more to retail preferences than to actual quality, the lighter colors were primarily sorted into grade A, and the darker colors into grade B. With today's processing techniques, formerly grade B syrups are not necessarily inferior to grade A, nor should grade A syrups be used solely for one thing and grade B syrups for another. If a graded maple syrup is offered for sale at all, it means that it has been designated acceptable for human consumption and that it meets labeling standards.

Fortunately, recent legislation has made the assessment of the meaning of each maple grade much, much simpler, and much more oriented to the results you know you can see and taste. In March 2015, the USDA Agricultural Marketing Service, following new guidelines developed by the International Maple Syrup Institute, revised the standards for classifying maple

syrup so they would be uniformly framed and referenced for all makers. This also makes it much easier for consumers as well. Rather than using letter grades that make sense only to maple insiders, you can now assess different types of syrup based on color and flavor.

GRADE A COLOR CLASSES	TASTE	LIGHT TRANSMITTANCE (% Tc)
U.S. Grade A Golden	Delicate	> 75.0
U.S. Grade A Amber	Rich	50.0–74.9
U.S. Grade A Dark	Robust	25.0–49.9
U.S. Grade A Very Dark	Strong	< 25.0

[85]

What does this actually mean for the kind of syrup you should use for each dish? Truly, it comes down to your personal preference. If you prefer a lighter, more traditional maple flavor, start with the Amber syrup. If you are cooking or baking with the syrup and want a more intense maple flavor, start with Dark. The very lightest grade, Golden, is the most delicate, and so it might be best for drizzling on top of something with mild flavor, using it more like a very light honey. Chefs have told us that they love working with the Dark and Very Dark syrups because they can stand up to stronger-flavored spices and meats, as well as hotter preparations like roasting and braising. And yes, you can braise with maple syrup.

MAPLE OVER HEAT

You can cook with maple syrup, just like you would with sugar, honey, molasses, or any other sweetener. Maple syrup or sugar can be substituted for just about any other kind of sugar, provided that you use the right ratio of substitution: 1 cup (240 ml) maple syrup can be swapped

85 USDA, "United States Standards for Grades of Maple Syrup."

NOTES FROM THE TASTING ROOM

GOLDEN COLOR/DELICATE TASTE:

- **AROMAS & FLAVORS:** *Although still light, Golden has a pleasant weight and depth, with a finish and flavors that linger. Popcorn and peanuts, roasted nuts, salted caramel, and brown butter are all highlighted in this syrup.*
- **USES:** *With its salted flavors and aromas, Golden syrup is an ideal partner for glazing proteins such as pork belly and bacon. Whiskey-based cocktails that call for additional fruit or other sweet components benefit from Golden in place of muddled sugar cubes. Also provides an excellent substitute for palm sugar in many Thai recipes.*

AMBER COLOR/RICH TASTE:

- **AROMAS & FLAVORS:** *Brings to mind the sights and smells of late fall and early winter. The aromas of gingerbread and roasted chestnut are present, with the flavors of rye, toffee, and freshly roasted ground coffee.*
- **USES:** *The depth and weight of Amber syrup demand to be paired with food that displays bolder flavors. Perfectly ideal for many baked breads, ginger cookies, and chocolate. If used for cocktail purposes, heavier spirits are called for—bourbons that have seen many years of barrel aging, or Scotch with a heavy smoke or peat. It's also a decadent topping to chocolate or vanilla ice cream.*

DARK COLOR/ROBUST TASTE:

- **AROMAS & FLAVORS:** *Shares a similar flavor and aroma character to the Amber syrup, but with more weight, depth, and concentration. The aromas of coffee and chocolate are present, along with flavors of brown sugar and toasted almond.*
- **USES:** *Dark syrup provides the ultimate replacement for typical sweeteners in coffee. The depth of flavor and richness that is added to a freshly brewed cup is unmatched by conventional granulated sugars or simple syrup. Can also be an interesting alternative to honey as a condiment for many hard and soft cheeses.*

VERY DARK COLOR/STRONG TASTE:

- **AROMAS & FLAVORS:** *The most robust maple syrup, Very Dark has exquisite depth of flavor and a bright finish. Due to its intensity, it is the preferred syrup among chefs, and is sometimes referred to as "cooking syrup." The maple flavor is very dominant, though hints of toffee and molasses can be detected.*
- **USES:** *Well-suited for cooking and baking, as its richness blends with and shines through even the boldest of food pairings. It works well with meat glazes, hearty bean dishes, root vegetables, and desserts.*

WHAT GOES WITH MAPLE SYRUP?

- **INGREDIENTS THAT ARE ALSO WILD AND WELL LOVED IN NEW ENGLAND AND MID-ATLANTIC CUISINE:** *walnuts, pecans, oats, corn, squash, apples, and stone fruits.*

- **NATURALLY SWEET VEGETABLES AND FRUITS:** *peaches, pears, sweet potatoes, carrots, and bananas.*

- **FOODS RICH IN UMAMI:** *mushrooms, cheese, pork (especially bacon), poultry, beef, and soy sauce.*

- **SPICY OR SMOKY FOODS:** *Maple can soften a strong cup of coffee or balance a dried chile pepper.*

- **STAY AWAY FROM:** *flavors that are too similar and possibly overwhelming—for example, dark brown sugar or molasses. You might set off a sugarbomb.*

out for 1 cup (200 g) white sugar, but you must reduce the overall liquid in the original recipe by ¼ cup (60 ml) to make up for the difference. If you are going to swap out maple syrup for sugar, though, beware of using too high a temperature when cooking—because the water in the maple syrup has not been completely cooked out, you'll want to carefully monitor the temperature of your recipe to prevent the syrup from burning. Too high a temperature, and you end up cooking out too much of the syrup's water. Yes, this is a bit like making a caramel, where you want to slowly heat up the syrup so it cooks down rather than putting it in direct contact with a hot surface. So a slow rise in temperature, rather than a fast boil, is your best bet when making a glaze or sauce with maple syrup. Or, if you're worried about boiling off too much liquid too quickly, make sure the other ingredients you're using to flavor your dish come in liquid form. For example, a little pomegranate juice mixed in with your maple syrup guarantees a more smoothly cooked glaze than just maple syrup alone.

Vis-à-vis baking, maple syrup and sugar behave very similarly to white and brown sugar, and have similar needs when it comes to storage. Once a bottle of maple syrup is opened, you immediately introduce the possibility of evaporation to the syrup. That's not so surprising, given that it's the syrup's water that would begin to evaporate away, leaving you with—ta da!—the hardened sugar itself. The best way to prevent this is to seal your bottle immediately after using and place it in the refrigerator to prevent excess crystallization and possible bacterial growth. (Maple sugar will also begin to lose moisture over time just as regular sugar would, so if it becomes hardened, treat it much like you would brown sugar: For immediate use, you can seal it in an airtight container with a slice of sandwich bread or a few slices of apple, or if it really hardens up, you can spoon it into a bowl and top with a damp paper towel for a 20-second

zap in the microwave.) If you do see crystallization on your syrup bottle—do not worry; your syrup is still good! Maple syrup is hygroscopic—meaning it attracts water—so if left exposed to air, the syrup will attract and absorb the moisture around it. So just wipe off the crystals, keep cooking, and open a new bottle when you've worked through the first one.

A NOTE ABOUT THE RECIPES

In the following recipes, we specify which type of maple syrup we've used to prepare each dish, noting its color and taste in parentheses. All of these maple notes are guidelines, not hard and fast rules—as you start cooking from our favorite recipes, and substituting maple syrup for sugar in your own recipes, learn which syrups you like best with which dishes. You may discover that you really like a Golden syrup for roasting chicken, or a Dark syrup for topping ice cream. Set up your own tasting room at home, with a few shot glasses out for each syrup, and see if you can tell the differences between them.

It really is okay to play with your food. We do it all the time.

— 3 —

Maple in a Minute

NCE WE STARTED USING MAPLE SYRUP as a substitute for sugar in our day-to-day meals, we found that the uses for maple were almost infinite. Because maple can go either sweet or savory, depending on the recipe it's used in and the grade of the syrup, you can quickly improvise to incorporate maple flavor into any number of delicious and unexpected recipes. Here are our "maple in a minute" guidelines, a great way to start playing with maple syrup in your daily meals. (These recipes can be used with any of our syrups, though some would be especially great with our bourbon barrel–aged maple syrup, for a smokier, more savory finish.)

SPICY HOT MAPLE SYRUP

For a dipping or drizzling sauce for almost anything, bring ½ cup (120 ml) maple syrup to a simmer in a nonstick saucepan. Add 4 to 5 dried ancho chiles, then remove from the heat and let steep for at least 30 minutes. Strain the syrup into a squeeze bottle and use to top almost any kind of food with spicy-sweet flavor. (You can also try this technique with fresh herbs—woody herbs like sage, rosemary, and thyme work best.) This syrup will keep for up to 2 weeks in the refrigerator.

MAPLE-ROASTED GRAPEFRUIT

Preheat the broiler, and line a baking sheet with foil. Slice off the rounded top and bottom of a halved grapefruit (so it will sit flat), and cut into the segments of the fruit so they are easy to scoop out later. Sprinkle the cut tops of the grapefruit with 1 tablespoon maple sugar. Broil the grapefruit for 3 to 5 minutes, until the tops are browned and caramelized. Enjoy warm.

WHIPPED MAPLE BUTTER

Perfect for pretty much anything breakfasty (pancakes, French toast, waffles), though I'm happy to eat it on just a piece of toast with some jam. Whip ¾ cup (1½ sticks/170 g) softened unsalted butter in a stand mixer fitted with a paddle until creamy; pour in ¼ cup (60 ml) maple syrup and ½ teaspoon ground cinnamon and beat until well combined. Refrigerate, covered, for up to 1 month, or freeze and keep for up to 3 months.

MAPLE BOURBON-GLAZED BACON

Prepare your breakfast bacon as desired, slightly undercooking it. Brush the slices with our bourbon barrel–aged maple syrup, then cook for a few more minutes, until crisp and candied.

MAPLE-BALSAMIC VINAIGRETTE

This vinaigrette is a staple in our house—we almost always have a jar in the refrigerator for use in both salads and in marinades. Put ½ cup (120 ml) balsamic vinegar, ¼ cup (60 ml) maple syrup, 2 teaspoons Dijon mustard, and salt and pepper to taste in a blender. Pulse to combine, then add 1 cup (240 ml) olive oil in a steady stream with the motor running. This recipe makes 2 cups (480 ml) of dressing, which will keep for up to 1 month in a sealable container in the refrigerator or on the countertop.

MAPLE-GLAZED CARROTS

This works well for almost any vegetable, but it's especially great with carrots. In a large skillet, combine 3 pounds (1.4 kg) sliced carrots, ¼ cup (60 ml) maple syrup, 2 tablespoons unsalted butter, ½ cup (120 ml) water, ½ teaspoon salt, and ¼ teaspoon ground black pepper. Boil, then reduce the heat and simmer for 12 to 15 minutes, until the carrots are tender and the glaze has set. Serves 4 to 6 as a side dish.

MAPLE-CHILI ROASTED CHICKPEAS

Put a bowl of these next to a crudité platter and some olives, and your party platter is complete. Preheat the oven to 375°F (190°C) and line a baking sheet with parchment paper. In a bowl, toss together 2 (15-ounce/425-g) cans drained chickpeas, 3 tablespoons olive oil, 1 teaspoon kosher salt, ½ teaspoon chili powder, and ¼ cup (35 g) pure maple sugar. Spread the chickpeas on the baking sheet and roast, stirring a few times, for 30 to 40 minutes, until the chickpeas are golden brown and crunchy. This will serve 4 to 6 people, depending on who gets access to the bowl. (If there are any left, once cooled completely they can be stored in an airtight container for up to 1 week.)

MAPLE-GOAT CHEESE CROSTINI

Stir 1 to 2 tablespoons maple syrup into 1 cup (115 g) crumbled soft goat cheese, and process in a food processor until smooth. Spread on toasted rounds of bread and garnish with slices of fresh fruit, or top with roasted kale, tomatoes, or summer squash. (Or if you want to make it even easier, just spread 1 teaspoon of your favorite goat cheese on either crackers or crostini, add garnishes, and drizzle with maple syrup.)

MAPLE-MINT ICED TEA

For a simple but refreshing summer tea, boil 2 cups (480 ml) water, then remove from the heat. Bruise several fresh mint leaves with a spoon, then add to the water with a few of your favorite tea bags and allow to steep for the proper time. Strain the steeped tea into a large pitcher. Stir in ¼ cup (60 ml) maple syrup and chill. Serve over ice and garnish with fresh mint.

MAPLE COFFEE OR MAPLE TEA

I love both maple syrup and maple sugar in my coffee in the morning. Try it in your coffee or tea instead of other sweeteners for a healthy and delightful difference.

MAPLE WHIPPED CREAM

Combine 1 cup (240 ml) cold heavy cream with 2 tablespoons maple syrup (or more, depending on your preferred sweetness) in a chilled mixing bowl, and whip until soft peaks form. This will keep in the refrigerator in a sealed container for up to 3 days.

MAPLE BANANA SPLITS

Halve a banana and lay it in a long dish alongside your favorite ice creams (slightly softer flavors work best here—pistachio, strawberry, peanut butter). Drizzle with maple syrup and dark chocolate sauce, and top with nuts, whipped cream, and a cherry.

BREAKFASTS AND BREADS

MAPLE GRANOLA AND YOGURT

BOWLS

PREP TIME: **10 MINUTES** | COOK TIME: **1½ HOURS**

This light and crunchy granola is so simple to make and so good for you—both the chia seeds and the flax meal are rich with omega-3 fats to help your heart and improve your digestion, and just one helping of granola gives you the rec-ommended daily amount of vitamin E, courtesy of the wheat germ. (The granola is also naturally vegan, with all the good coconut fats working for you where butter might work against you.) Maple syrup is always a go-to for my yogurt in the morning, but my girls will also eat it in the evening after dinner for a snack (though they do like to load it up with blueberries, strawberries, and raspber-ries in the morning). A great way to begin and end the day.

1 **MAKE THE GRANOLA:** Preheat the oven to 250°F (120°C); line a rimmed baking sheet with parchment paper.

2 In a medium bowl, toss together the oats, flax seeds, wheat germ, and chia seeds.

3 In a small saucepan, warm the maple syrup, coconut oil, and salt over medium heat until the coconut oil melts. Pour over the oat mixture and toss to combine.

4 Spread onto the prepared baking sheet antand crispy. Let the granola cool, then store in an airtight container for up to 1 month.

5 **TO ASSEMBLE THE BOWLS:** Place ½ cup (112 ml) yogurt in the bottom of a bowl and top with ¼ cup granola. Scatter ¼ cup fruit on top of the granola, drizzle with syrup, and serve immediately. (This recipe has enough yogurt and fruit for 8 bowls.)

MAKES ABOUT 7 CUPS
(595 G) GRANOLA

3½ cups *(310 g)* rolled oats

½ cup *(65 g)* ground flax seeds

½ cup *(60 g)* wheat germ

2 tablespoons chia seeds

1 cup *(240 ml)* Crown Maple syrup (Dark Color, Robust Taste), plus more to drizzle

½ cup *(120 ml)* coconut oil

¼ teaspoon kosher salt

1 *(32-ounce/960-ml)* container plain Greek yogurt

2 cups *(280 g)* fresh sliced fruit and berries of your choice

BAKED APPLE-ALMOND

OATMEAL

PREP TIME: **15 MINUTES** | COOK TIME: **25 MINUTES**

Oatmeal is a must in the morning for our girls, an easy and hot quick-fix on our way to school. My daughter Ava in particular always pours a little extra syrup on hers . . . I can't blame her, as I like to put maple syrup in everything (including my coffee). But imagine what a sad world it would be if you only got to experience maple syrup during a weekend pancake breakfast. Luckily, this oatmeal can be made on a lazy Sunday and then reheated in slices throughout the week. To store, slice the oatmeal into individually sized portions and refrigerate, then reheat in a hot skillet or in the microwave.

SERVES 6

2 tablespoons unsalted butter, plus more for greasing and serving

2 cups *(175 g)* rolled oats

½ cup *(45 g)* chopped almonds

1 teaspoon baking powder

1 teaspoon ground cinnamon

½ teaspoon kosher salt

¼ teaspoon ground allspice

¼ teaspoon freshly grated nutmeg

1 large Gala or Fuji apple, peeled, cored, and chopped into 1-inch *(2.5-cm)* chunks

1¾ cups *(420 ml)* unsweetened almond milk

⅓ cup *(75 ml)* Crown Maple syrup (Amber Color, Rich Taste), plus more for serving

1 large egg

2 teaspoons pure vanilla extract

1 tablespoon Crown Maple sugar

1 Preheat the oven to 375°F (190°C); generously butter an 8-inch (20-cm) square baking dish.

2 In a bowl, mix together the oats, the baking powder, cinnamon, salt, allspice, nutmeg, and half of the almonds.

3 Reserve about one quarter of the apples and stir the remaining apples into the oats mixture.

4 Melt the butter in a small saucepan set over medium heat, then remove from the heat and let cool slightly.

5 In another bowl, whisk together the almond milk, maple syrup, egg, melted butter, and vanilla until you have a smooth mixture.

6 Spread the oat-apple mixture in the bottom of the prepared baking dish. Slowly drizzle the milk mixture over the oats, and shake the baking dish slightly to allow the milk to soak through completely. Scatter the reserved apple and remaining almonds on top. Sprinkle with the maple sugar.

7 Bake for 25 minutes, until the top is nicely golden and the oat mixture has set. Remove from the oven and let cool for a few minutes before serving. If enjoying warm, serve in slices with a pat of butter and a drizzle of maple syrup on top.

GLAZED MAPLE-PECAN

SCONES

PREP TIME: **15 MINUTES** | COOK TIME: **15 MINUTES**

These scones are one of my favorite recipes we've ever made. When I go up to the sugarhouse café, I always make sure to put some scones aside to take back with me (to supplement my own little stash at home). There was a period where every coffee shop in America wanted to serve maple-glazed scones. But there is really no substitute for using real maple syrup in the mix. The dough for these wonderfully rich, crumbly scones freezes beautifully, so rather than get the basic store version, bake up a few whenever you have time to do so. Then you can have your own little stash ready to go.

1 MAKE THE SCONES: Preheat the oven to 375°F (190°C); line a baking sheet with parchment paper. Lightly dust a work surface with flour.

2 Spread the oats and pecans on the baking sheet and toast them until they are fragrant and lightly browned, 7 to 9 minutes. Let cool and remove to a bowl; reserve the parchment paper–lined baking sheet.

3 Increase the oven temperature to 450°F (230°C).

4 Whisk the milk, cream, egg, and maple syrup in a large measuring cup until incorporated; remove 1 tablespoon to a small bowl and reserve for glazing.

5 Place the flour, maple sugar, baking powder, and salt in a food processor fitted with the metal blade and process, with a few pulses, until combined. Add the cooled oats and nuts and pulse until combined. Scatter the pieces of cold butter evenly over the dry ingredients and process with 10 to 20 pulses until the mixture resembles coarse cornmeal.

6 Slowly pour the milk-maple mixture into the dry mixture, pulsing intermittently, until large clumps form and the dough comes together in a cohesive mass.

recipe continues

SERVES 4 TO 6

FOR THE SCONES:

1½ cups *(130 g)* rolled oats

½ cup *(50 g)* pecan halves, coarsely chopped

¼ cup *(60 ml)* whole milk

¼ cup *(60 ml)* heavy cream

1 large egg

¼ cup *(60 ml)* Crown Maple syrup (Very Dark Color, Strong Taste)

1½ cups *(190 g)* all-purpose flour

1 tablespoon Crown Maple sugar

2 teaspoons baking powder

½ teaspoon kosher salt

1¼ cups *(2½ sticks/285 g)* cold unsalted butter, cut into ¼-inch *(6-mm)* cubes

7   Turn the dough out onto a floured work surface and gently pat into a rectangle 1 inch (2.5 cm) thick. Using a chef's knife (or a round biscuit cutter), cut the dough into large scones and set on the parchment-lined baking sheet, spacing them about 2 inches (5 cm) apart.

8   Brush the tops of the scones with the reserved milk-maple mixture. Bake until golden brown, 12 to 14 minutes. Cool the scones on the baking sheet for 10 minutes, then remove the scones to a wire rack and cool to room temperature.

9   WHILE THE SCONES COOL, MAKE THE GLAZE: Whisk the maple syrup and confectioners' sugar together in a small bowl; drizzle the glaze over the cooled scones and let set for 5 minutes. (The scones may be kept in an airtight container for up to 1 week.)

FOR THE GLAZE:

3 tablespoons Crown Maple syrup (Amber Color, Rich Taste)

½ cup *(65 g)* confectioners' sugar

BANANA-WALNUT CRUMBLE
MUFFINS

PREP TIME: **10 MINUTES** | COOK TIME: **18 TO 20 MINUTES**

There always seem to be extra bananas at our house, and when Lydia first adapted this recipe from Clean Eating, *we finally knew what do with them. These muffins are naturally sweet, and the maple sugar in the crumb topping makes them extra delicious. All the parts of this recipe can be made a day ahead of baking; just refrigerate the ingredients, then let them come to room temperature and give them a fresh stir before baking. Make sure your bananas are really truly ripe before preparing—they'll bump up the muffins' natural sweetness.*

MAKES 12 MUFFINS

FOR THE CRUMB TOPPING:

¼ cup *(30 g)* finely chopped walnuts

3 tablespoons whole wheat flour

2 tablespoons Crown Maple sugar

½ teaspoon ground cinnamon

¼ teaspoon sea salt

2 tablespoons unsalted butter, at room temperature, cut into small pieces

FOR THE MUFFINS:

1 cup *(125 g)* whole wheat flour

1 cup *(150 g)* oat or wheat bran

1½ teaspoons baking powder

1 teaspoon baking soda

1 teaspoon ground cinnamon

¼ teaspoon sea salt

1 large egg

3 very ripe bananas, mashed *(about 1¼ cups /375 g)*

½ cup *(120 ml)* whole milk

¼ cup *(60 ml)* Crown Maple syrup (Amber Color, Rich Taste)

3 tablespoons vegetable oil

1 Preheat the oven to 350°F (175°C); grease a 12-cup muffin tin with butter, or line with paper liners.

2 MAKE THE CRUMB TOPPING: Put all the topping ingredients except the butter in a small bowl and stir to combine. Stir in the butter, mashing with a whisk and breaking up clumps with your fingers, until you have a moist crumbly mixture; set aside.

3 MAKE THE MUFFINS: In a large bowl, whisk together the flour, bran, baking powder, baking soda, cinnamon, and salt. Set aside.

4 In another large bowl, lightly beat the egg, then add the bananas and whisk until combined. Add the milk, maple syrup, and oil and whisk until combined.

5 Add the wet mixture to the dry mixture in large spoonfuls, stirring between batches until you have a smooth batter. Fill each muffin tin about three-quarters full and sprinkle the crumb topping over the top of each.

6 Bake the muffins until a toothpick inserted into the center of a muffin comes out with a few moist crumbs, 18 to 20 minutes. Let cool in the pan for 5 minutes, then transfer to a wire rack. Serve warm. (The muffins may be kept in an airtight container for up to 3 days.)

MAPLE-PECAN

STICKY BUNS

Sticky buns have been in Lydia's family ever since she can remember. Her father is an amazing bread maker and often treated the family to sticky buns on a Saturday morning. She especially loved the moment when he flipped the buns over, and the syrup and pecans would just run down the sides of the buns and back into the pan. She wanted to get every last drop of syrup, so she would use her sticky bun to wipe up all the syrup left in the pan. Now we make these buns for our girls, and I can see that they want to do the same thing Lydia did growing up.

1 MAKE THE DOUGH: In a large bowl of an electric mixer, dissolve the yeast and 1 teaspoon sugar in the warm water. Let stand until foamy, 5 to 10 minutes.

2 Add the remaining ⅓ cup (65 g) sugar, the water, eggs, butter, sour cream, vanilla, salt, and 1½ cups (190 g) flour to the bowl with the yeast. Beat at medium speed with a dough hook for 5 to 7 minutes, adding an additional ½ cup (65 g) flour at a time as necessary, until you have a soft but pliable dough (you'll know when the dough looks just a little less firm than raw pizza dough).

3 Turn out the dough onto a lightly floured surface. Clean and grease the bowl with additional butter. Knead the dough for 4 to 6 minutes, or until the dough feels soft and buttery, but not sticky. Place the dough in the greased bowl, turning to coat all sides. Cover with a slightly damp towel and let rise in a warm draft-free place until doubled in bulk, about 1½ hours.

4 Generously grease a 9 by 13-inch (23 by 33-cm) baking pan. Butter a 13-inch (33-cm) length of parchment paper; set aside.

recipe continues

MAKES 12 TO 15 ROLLS

FOR THE DOUGH:

1 tablespoon active dry yeast

1 teaspoon plus ⅓ cup *(65 g)* granulated sugar

¼ cup *(60 ml)* warm water (110°F/45°C)

2 large eggs, at room temperature

⅓ cup *(75 g)* unsalted butter, melted, plus more for greasing

½ cup *(120 ml)* sour cream, at room temperature

1 teaspoon vanilla extract

1 teaspoon fine sea salt

2½ to 3 cups *(320 g to 385 g)* all-purpose flour

5 MAKE THE MAPLE TOPPING: Combine the maple syrup, brown sugar, butter, and salt in a small bowl, and pour into the prepared pan. Sprinkle the bottom of the pan evenly with the pecans; set aside.

6 MAKE THE CINNAMON-NUT FILLING: Toast the pecans in a small skillet over medium heat for 3 minutes, stirring occasionally, until they are just fragrant. Transfer the toasted nuts to a small bowl to cool slightly, then add the brown sugar and cinnamon. Stir to combine, then set aside.

7 On a lightly floured surface, punch down and roll out the dough to a large pan-sized rectangle. Spread the top of the rectangle with butter, leaving a ½-inch (12-mm) margin on one of the long sides of the rectangle. Sprinkle the dough evenly with the cinnamon-nut filling. Beginning on the buttered long side, tightly roll the dough up and away from you, jelly-roll fashion. Pinch the seam to seal.

8 Cut the roll widthwise into 12 to 15 equal slices. Arrange the buns cut-side down in the prepared baking pan on top of the topping. Cover the top of the buns with the buttered parchment paper. Let the buns rise in a warm draft-free place until doubled in bulk, about 1 hour.

9 Preheat the oven to 375°F (190°C). Remove the paper on top and bake the buns for 30 minutes, or until golden brown. Let the buns stand in the pan for 1 minute; invert the baked buns onto a platter or a wire rack set over parchment paper.

10 Spoon any topping remaining in the pan over the buns. Let stand for 5 minutes, and serve warm. Store any remaining sticky buns in an airtight container up to 2 days.

FOR THE MAPLE TOPPING:

½ cup *(120 ml)* Crown Maple syrup (Amber Color, Rich Taste)

½ cup *(110 g)* packed light brown sugar

⅓ cup *(75 g)* unsalted butter, cut into small pieces

¼ teaspoon kosher salt

1 cup *(120 g)* chopped pecans

FOR THE CINNAMON-NUT FILLING:

½ cup *(65 g)* chopped pecans

⅔ cup *(145 g)* packed light brown sugar

1 teaspoon ground cinnamon

MAPLE SAUSAGE AND

POTATO HASH

PREP TIME: **15 MINUTES, PLUS 1 HOUR CHILLING** | COOK TIME: **1 HOUR**

Most of the breakfasts we've served up here are fairly light, and most mornings a bowl of oatmeal or a bit of yogurt and granola is more than enough to get me started. But when I have time, I want a hearty bowl of this gently sweetened savory hash. We make our hash with ground lamb, in part because the meat is so flavorful with the sage and maple mixed in, but you can use pork if you prefer. However you make it, it will make a very versatile sausage that you can enjoy in any number of recipes.

SERVES 4

FOR THE MAPLE SAUSAGE:

1 pound ground lamb or pork

3 tablespoons Crown Maple syrup (Very Dark Color, Strong Taste)

1 tablespoon chopped fresh sage

2 teaspoons kosher salt

1 teaspoon fennel seeds

1 garlic clove, chopped

1 teaspoon ground cayenne

A good hash is usually made with loose sausage, but if you want homemade links without any casings or fancy charcuterie-stuff, it's fairly easy to do. After mixing the meat, set a long piece of plastic wrap on your countertop. Place ¼ to ½ cup (55 to 115 g) meat in the center of the plastic wrap and shape it with your hands into a strip 6 inches (15 cm) long. Wrap the sides of the plastic wrap around the sausage and roll the ends to create a long tube of meat-filled plastic. (You want the plastic to create a shape kind of like a Christmas toy cracker, tightly wrapped in the middle with twisted ends.) Move your hands swiftly at the ends of the plastic to tighten and compress the sausage into a tube. Repeat with the remaining sausage meat until you have a series of "links," which you can then refrigerate for up to 3 days, or freeze for up to 3 months. Once you're ready to cook, remove a sausage from its plastic and cook it over medium-high heat with a splash of olive oil for about 10 minutes.

1 MAKE THE SAUSAGE: In a large bowl, mix the meat, maple syrup, sage, salt, fennel, garlic, and cayenne until well combined. Cover and refrigerate for at least 1 hour before cooking.

2 MAKE THE HASH: Preheat the oven to 400°F (205°C).

recipe continues

3   Toss the potatoes with the oil, salt, pepper, garlic, and sage in a large ovenproof dish. Roast the potatoes for 30 minutes, or until they are starting to brown but are not quite soft.

4   While the potatoes cook, prepare the onions: Melt the butter in a skillet over medium-high heat. When it foams up, add the onions and season with salt. Lower the heat slightly and cook the onions for about 30 minutes, stirring occasionally, until they are dark brown and thoroughly caramelized. Transfer the onions to a medium bowl.

5   Add the sausage to the now-empty pan and reduce the heat to medium. (If the pan seems dry, add an additional splash of oil.) Cook, stirring, until the sausage has lost most of its pink color, about 10 minutes. Transfer to the bowl with the onions, and pour off all but 1 tablespoon of the excess fat.

6   Remove the potatoes from the oven and stir in the cooked onions and sausage. Return to the oven for an additional 15 minutes to finish cooking and warm through together.

7   Prepare the eggs to your liking (our favorite is over-easy or poached, so you get runny yolks all over the hash). Scoop out warm bowlfuls of the hash, and top each with 1 or 2 eggs. Garnish with chopped herbs or Spicy Hot Maple Syrup, and serve warm.

FOR THE HASH:

3 cups *(425 g)* diced potatoes

3 tablespoons olive oil, plus more if needed

1 tablespoon kosher salt, plus more to taste

Freshly ground black pepper, to taste

2 large garlic cloves, minced

1½ tablespoons minced fresh sage

1 tablespoon unsalted butter

2 medium yellow onions, quartered and thinly sliced

Up to 8 large eggs (optional)

Chopped fresh herbs (parsley, basil, etc.), or Spicy Hot Maple Syrup (page 99), for serving

PUMPKIN

PANCAKES

PREP TIME: **7 MINUTES** | COOK TIME: **10 MINUTES**

Yes, maple syrup is good for much more than just pancakes—but we'd be remiss to give you a maple syrup book without at least one spectacular pancake recipe. I love waking up to the smell of these pancakes when my daughter Ava makes them on a Sunday morning. It's a great way to quickly gather everyone around the breakfast table.

Mixing pumpkin into a pancake batter gives you a slightly sweet, dense, and deliciously flavorful pancake, with a rich rustic flavor closer to the johnnycakes of yore. If you prefer lighter and fluffier pancakes, separate the eggs and beat the yolks with the yogurt, then beat the egg whites until you have stiff peaks and fold them into the batter.

1 Mix together the bran, flour, maple sugar, baking powder, salt, and spices in a large bowl. Set aside.

2 Beat together the pumpkin puree, yogurt, vanilla, maple syrup, and melted butter in a separate bowl.

3 Add the wet mixture to the dry mixture and stir together, then beat in each of the eggs until well combined. Add ¼ cup (60 ml) water to thin out the batter, and beat until smooth.

4 Heat a griddle or large skillet over high heat. Once hot, lightly grease the pan with butter.

5 Pour about ¼ cup (60 ml) of the batter per pancake, spreading each outward from its center like a crêpe. Leave space between the pancakes. Reduce the heat to medium, then cook on one side until you see bubbles on top and the edges are slightly browned, 3 to 5 minutes. Flip the pancakes and cook for an additional 2 to 4 minutes, until both sides are crisp and brown. Add a little oil or butter to the skillet for each new batch.

6 Serve immediately with extra maple syrup on the side.

SERVES 6

¾ cup *(115 g)* wheat or oat bran

1½ cups *(190 g)* all-purpose flour

2 tablespoons Crown Maple sugar

1 tablespoon baking powder

½ teaspoon kosher salt

¼ teaspoon ground cinnamon

¼ teaspoon ground ginger

¼ teaspoon ground cloves

⅔ cup *(165 ml)* canned pumpkin puree

1 cup *(240 ml)* nonfat yogurt or buttermilk

1 tablespoon vanilla extract

1 tablespoon Crown Maple syrup (Amber Color, Rich Taste)

2 tablespoons unsalted butter, melted, or vegetable oil, plus more for frying the pancakes

3 large eggs

MALTED

MULTIGRAIN BREAD

PREP TIME: 2½ HOURS, INCLUDING 2 HOURS RISING TIME | COOK TIME: 30 TO 35 MINUTES

Lydia says that she grew up spoiled, because her father always had homemade bread at the ready. But I think we're spoiled today, because she makes this bread with our syrup and it's beyond delicious. Toasted with a little butter or jam—it's perfect. While this recipe requires a lot of special ingredients, there's a unique alchemy in the way all these rough grains become soft and buttery in the finished bread. If you have kids who are reticent to try whole wheat bread, this power-packed recipe might be the game changer you need.

Rolled wheat flakes, rye flakes, and bran flakes (also known as coarse wheat bran; do not confuse with breakfast cereals such as Raisin Bran) are often enjoyed as hot cereals and are great natural baking ingredients. They can be found from brands such as Bob's Red Mill or Shiloh Farms, and you can purchase them from your local natural foods store or from online retailers. If you can't find wheat or rye flakes, you can substitute 2 cups (180 g) rolled oats.

1   In the bowl of a stand mixer fitted with the paddle attachment, mix the wheat flakes, rye flakes, butter, ⅓ cup (75 ml) of the maple syrup, and the hot water until well combined; let cool to room temperature.

2   Dissolve the yeast and remaining 1 teaspoon maple syrup with the warm water in a small bowl. Let stand until foamy, 5 to 10 minutes. Lightly flour a countertop for rolling out the dough. Clean and grease a large bowl; set aside.

3   Stir the yeast mixture into the wheat-flakes mixture. Add the milk powder, salt, bran flakes, wheat germ, and 1 cup (125 g) all-purpose flour. Beat at medium speed for 2 minutes, or until well combined. Stir in whole wheat flour, then all-purpose flour, alternating flours and adding ½ cup (65 g) at a time, until the dough becomes too thick to stir. Knead the dough

---

MAKES 2
(9-INCH/23-CM) LOAVES

(180 g) rolled oats.

1 cup *(90 g)* wheat flakes, plus more to sprinkle on top

1 cup *(90 g)* rye flakes, plus more to sprinkle on top

¼ cup *(1 stick / 55 g)* unsalted butter, cut into 4 pieces, plus more for greasing

⅓ cup *(75 ml)* plus 1 teaspoon Crown Maple syrup (Amber Color, Rich Taste)

2 cups *(480 ml)* hot water (200°F/90°C)

2 tablespoons active dry yeast

⅓ cup *(75 ml)* warm water (110°F/43°C)

1 cup *(85 g)* nonfat milk powder

1 tablespoon kosher salt

½ cup *(75 g)* bran flakes

½ cup *(55 g)* wheat germ

Up to 4 cups *(510 g)* all-purpose flour

1½ cups *(185 g)* whole wheat flour

1 large egg white

by hand, working ½ cup (65 g) of extra flour in as necessary, until the dough comes together in a mass that no longer sticks to the sides of the bowl.

4 Turn out the dough onto the floured surface. Knead the dough for 10 to 12 minutes or until it has become smooth and elastic (it will be very dense, but gradually the gluten will develop and make it into more of a dough texture). Place the dough in the greased bowl, turning to coat all sides. Cover with a slightly damp towel and let rise in a warm place, free from drafts, until doubled in bulk, about 1 hour.

5 Grease two 9 x 5-inch (23 by 12-cm) loaf pans or two 2-quart (2-L) casserole dishes; set aside.

6 Punch down the dough, and knead again for an additional 30 seconds. Divide the dough in half and shape into smooth loaves. Place in the prepared pans and cover each loaf with a dry towel. Let rise until doubled in bulk, about 1 hour. (If only one of the loaves has sufficiently risen after 1 hour, you can go ahead and bake that loaf and leave the second one to rise further.)

7 Preheat the oven to 375°F (190°C). Beat the egg white with 2 teaspoons water in a small bowl.

8 Brush the tops of the loaves with the egg white glaze and sprinkle with additional wheat or rye flakes. Slash the tops once lengthwise with a sharp knife, and bake for 30 to 35 minutes, or until the bread sounds hollow when the pans are tapped on the bottom. Remove from the pans and let cool on wire racks before slicing. (This bread can be kept in a bread box or wrapped in a paper bag and stored in a cool, dry place for up to 1 week.)

MAPLE-NECTARINE

GOOD

PREP TIME: **10 MINUTES** | COOK TIME: **45 MINUTES TO 1 HOUR**

If you're ever in need of a good laugh, read through a vintage cookbook's pastry section. There are more bizarre-sounding names for fruit-filled baked goods than you can imagine: slumps, buckles, grunts . . . . The list sounds like the onomatopoeia of what people do as they're eating. It takes a special kind of audacity to call a breakfast cake a "good," but that's exactly what this cake is. Where does this name come from? No one really knows, but this recipe is for a spiced but simple cake where the batter rises up around slices of seasoned fruit, almost resembling a clafouti or custard tart. Ripe nectarines with just a dusting of maple sugar work beautifully in this not-too-sweet, perfect-for-morning-coffee cake. (If eating cake for breakfast bugs you, swap in whole wheat flour . . . but it's never stopped me.)

MAKES I
(9-INCH/23-CM) CAKE

¾ cup *(1½ sticks/170 g)* unsalted butter, softened, plus more for greasing

1¼ cups *(180 g)* plus 2 teaspoons Crown Maple sugar

1 teaspoon almond extract

1½ cups *(190 g)* all-purpose flour

1½ teaspoons baking powder

½ teaspoon ground cardamom

¼ teaspoon kosher salt

3 large eggs, at room temperature

1 ripe nectarine, thinly sliced

Juice of ½ lemon

¼ teaspoon ground ginger

½ teaspoon ground cinnamon

1 Preheat the oven to 350°F (175°C). Grease a 9-inch (23-cm) springform pan with butter.

2 Cream the butter and 1¼ cups (180 g) maple sugar together in a stand mixer until fully incorporated and fluffy. Stir in the almond extract.

3 Whisk the flour, baking powder, cardamom, and salt together in a separate bowl.

4 Add the flour mixture to the mixer and blend until well combined. Add the eggs, one at a time, and beat until you have a smooth, moist batter.

5 Spread the batter evenly into the prepared pan. Arrange the nectarine slices on top of the batter in a pinwheel shape, and drizzle the lemon juice over them. Combine the remaining 2 teaspoons maple sugar with the ginger and cinnamon in a small bowl, then sprinkle over the top of the fruit.

6 Bake for 45 minutes to 1 hour, until a toothpick comes out clean. Serve warm or at room temperature. Once cooked, the cake can be covered with plastic wrap or tinfoil and kept on the countertop for up to 2 days.

MAPLE-CHESTNUT

CORNBREAD

PREP TIME: **10 MINUTES** | COOK TIME: **30 MINUTES**

This cakey cornbread is just a touch sweeter than traditional cornbread, so it's best as a side dish to a rich savory meal—we especially like it with our favorite chili (see page 127), as a great fall meal that's easy to prepare ahead of time. The chestnut flour really delivers a distinct texture and flavor that pairs well with maple syrup. I've definitely sneaked down to the kitchen and had a slice of this with a scoop of ice cream on top—but it's just as good for breakfast with a dollop of Greek yogurt and a side of fresh fruit.

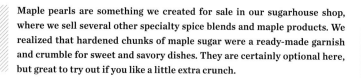

Maple pearls are something we created for sale in our sugarhouse shop, where we sell several other specialty spice blends and maple products. We realized that hardened chunks of maple sugar were a ready-made garnish and crumble for sweet and savory dishes. They are certainly optional here, but great to try out if you like a little extra crunch.

1   Preheat the oven to 350°F (175°C); grease a 9 x 13-inch (23 by 33-cm) baking pan.

2   Whisk the cornmeal, flours, baking powder, maple sugar, salt, and baking soda together in a large bowl. In a small bowl, whisk together the eggs, maple syrup, and buttermilk.

3   Fold the wet ingredients and maple pearls (if using) into the dry ingredients. Pour the batter into the prepared pan and spread in a thin layer. Bake for 30 minutes, until lightly golden and a knife inserted in the center comes out clean.

4   Let the cornbread cool for at least 15 minutes before cutting. Store any remaining cornbread well wrapped for up to 3 days.

MAKES ONE
9 BY 13-INCH (23 BY 33-CM)
PAN CORNBREAD;
ABOUT 15 SQUARES

Unsalted butter, for greasing

1 ½ cups *(210 g)* fine-ground yellow cornmeal

½ cup *(65 g)* all-purpose flour

1 cup *(130 g)* chestnut flour (available online, but you can also use coconut flour, almond flour, or hazelnut flour)

2 teaspoons baking powder

1 tablespoon Crown Maple sugar

¾ teaspoons kosher salt

¼ teaspoon baking soda

3 large eggs

½ cup *(120 ml)* Crown Maple syrup (Dark Color, Robust Taste)

¾ cup *(180 ml)* buttermilk

½ cup *(100 g)* Crown Maple pearls (optional; see Note)

CROWN MAPLE

MEAT, POULTRY, AND FISH

SIMMONS FAMILY

CHILI

PREP TIME: **5 MINUTES** | COOK TIME: **3½ HOURS**

This is a favorite family recipe of Danielle Simmons, my administrative assistant (and a very big Crown Maple fan as well). Her husband's family is from Louisiana, so he likes to make this chili with Tony Chachere's, a special Creole seasoning blend. Us northerners have used Cajun seasoning here, which adds a nice kick to this full-flavored chili. This makes a large pot of chili, but as with all excellent chilis, this one freezes beautifully, perfect for a day you need a hearty meal without a lot of prep time. (A good thing for Danielle's family, as they've just had their first child!)

A WORD ABOUT THE SEASONING: **We've deliberately left the amounts of salt, cumin, curry powder, and Cajun seasoning to your liking—taste as you cook the chili down, and increase the spices in ¼-teaspoon increments. Once you've figured out your preferred level of spice, note it for the next time you make a batch.**

1   Heat the oil in a very large (more than 5-quart/4.7-L) pot over high heat. Add the onion and cook until translucent, about 1 minute.

2   Add the garlic and chiles (and diced pepper, if using), and cook, stirring, until the garlic is fragrant, about 2 minutes. Reduce the heat to medium.

3   Add the chili powder, paprika, and cayenne and stir to coat. Add preliminary amounts of ¼ teaspoon each salt, cumin, curry powder, and Cajun seasoning and stir to coat the vegetables. (You can add more oil to the pan if needed, but this should be a very sticky spice and vegetable paste.)

4   Add the meat and mix it in really well to coat with the spices and vegetables. Cook for 10 to 12 minutes, stirring, until the meat has lost almost all of its pink color.

recipe continues

SERVES 10

2 teaspoons vegetable oil or bacon fat

1 large white or yellow onion, diced

4 large garlic cloves, minced

1 *(4½-ounce/127-g)* can chopped green chiles

½ Italian long green pepper, diced (optional)

2 tablespoons chili powder, plus more to taste

2 tablespoons ground smoked paprika, plus more to taste

Dash of ground cayenne

Kosher salt to taste

Ground cumin to taste

Curry powder to taste

Cajun seasoning to taste

5 pounds *(2.3 kg)* ground meat (a mix of beef, pork, and veal, at least 80% fat)

2 *(15½-ounce/439-g)* cans red kidney beans, with their liquid (optional)

8 cups *(2 L)* beef broth

6 whole allspice berries

5 Add the beans and broth, along with the allspice, liquid smoke, and syrup; you will have a thick mass of beans and meat in a somewhat thin but spice-laden broth. Stir and cook, uncovered, for about 3 hours, stirring and tasting every 45 minutes to add more spices, until the liquid reduces by almost a third and the chili is very thick. (If you don't have time to cook further, you can refrigerate the chili at this point and reheat when ready to serve. As it chills, the residual fat in the chili will float to the top, which makes it very easy to scoop off and discard at this point.)

6 Skim off the red fat at the top of the chili, and taste again and add more salt, cumin, curry powder, and Cajun seasoning as desired. Stir in the yogurt or cream cheese and continue to cook for an additional 15 minutes, until the mixture is complex in flavor. Adjust the spices once more, add black pepper to taste, and serve with desired toppings.

10 drops liquid smoke

6 tablespoons *(90 ml)* Crown Maple syrup (Dark Color, Robust Taste)

1 cup *(240 ml)* full-fat Greek yogurt or cream cheese, plus more to taste

Freshly ground black pepper to taste

Diced tomato, sour cream, chopped chives, and shredded cheddar cheese for toppings

MAPLE-CHILE FLANK STEAK

FAJITAS

PREP TIME: 45 MINUTES, INCLUDING 30 MINUTES MARINATING TIME | COOK TIME: 30 TO 35 MINUTES

Why add maple syrup to fajitas? It's all about balancing out spice with sweetness. Chipotle chiles, which are smoked dried jalapeños, are particularly great when amplified by sugar. Additionally, the marinade for this steak becomes even in flavor once it's cooked down; if you're worried about going too spicy, start with ½ teaspoon chile flakes, then taste and adjust the sauce as you reduce it. Don't forget to serve with some tortillas and rice on the side.

1 In a large measuring cup, whisk together the maple syrup, oil, chile flakes, garlic, lime juice, tequila, and salt and pepper. Put the steak in a sealable plastic bag; add the marinade, seal, and turn the steak over to coat. Let the steak marinate in the fridge for at least 30 minutes or up to 2 hours.

2 Brush the pepper and onion slices with oil, and season with salt and pepper. Remove the steak from the bag, reserving the marinade.

3 Heat a gas or charcoal grill for 10 minutes, or heat a cast-iron skillet over medium-high heat (if using a skillet, you may need more than one pan).

4 GRILL THE STEAK: Place the steak on the grill or in the skillet and cook for 15 minutes, turning once halfway through, for medium-rare doneness. Move the finished meat to a plate, cover with foil, and let rest.

5 GRILL THE VEGETABLES: Place the peppers and onion on the grill or skillet and cook for 10 to 15 minutes, until the onion is tender and the pepper skins are slightly blistered. Transfer to the plate with the steak.

6 Transfer the marinade into a small saucepan and boil over medium heat until slightly thickened into a sauce, about 3 minutes. Slice the steak against the grain and serve with the grilled vegetables. Fill warm tortillas with meat and vegetables, plus a drizzle of sauce and a handful of cilantro and scallions. Garnish each plate of fajitas with cheese, a dollop of sour cream, and some lettuce.

SERVES 4 TO 6

¼ cup *(60 ml)* Crown Maple syrup (Very Dark Color, Strong Taste)

¼ cup *(60 ml)* olive oil, plus more for brushing

1 tablespoon chipotle chile flakes

3 garlic cloves, minced

2 tablespoons fresh lime juice (from 1 lime)

2 tablespoons tequila

Kosher salt and freshly ground black pepper to taste

1½ pounds *(680 g)* flank steak

2 bell peppers (red, orange, or yellow), seeded and sliced thickly

1 large sweet onion, cut into thick slices

Warm flour tortillas, chopped fresh cilantro, and scallions for serving

Grated cheddar cheese, sour cream, and shredded lettuce for garnish

MAPLE

PULLED PORK

PREP TIME: **5 MINUTES** | COOK TIME: **3½ TO 4 HOURS**

Pork and maple are best friends on any plate—and not only when you add a drizzle of maple syrup to a side of crispy bacon. By rubbing a bit of pork shoulder in maple sugar, bourbon, and plenty of bright spices, what you get by the time the pork's done is a pot full of rich, complex sauce. Serve a big platter of this juicy pulled pork alongside plenty of thick bread, pickles, and a batch of coleslaw such as our Maple-Mustard Apple and Fennel Slaw (page 147). This is one of my favorite lunches, especially if I can serve it to our nieces and nephews when we're on vacation together.

1 Preheat the oven to 300°F (150°C). Place the pork in a deep Dutch oven or roasting pan.

2 Mix the bourbon, maple sugar, spices, and salt in a bowl and pour all over the pork, turning to coat. Cover the roasting pan with a lid or foil and bake for 3¼ to 4 hours, checking its internal temperature halfway through. (The finished pulled pork should have an internal temperature of 195 to 200°F / 90°C, and the texture will be right when the thermometer slides into the meat without resistance.)

3 Remove the pork from the oven, reserving the liquid, and transfer it to a cutting board. Let cool slightly, then shred the meat with two forks.

4 While the meat cools, cook down the remaining liquid in the Dutch oven over high heat for about 10 minutes, until it has slightly reduced and thickened. (If desired, whisk in the cornstarch to thicken.) Stir in the maple syrup and season with salt and black pepper to taste, then add the shredded meat and stir to coat with the sauce. Serve warm.

SERVES 4 TO 6

4 to 6 pounds *(1.8 to 2.7 kg)* boneless pork shoulder

½ cup (120 ml) good-quality bourbon

¼ cup *(35 g)* Crown Maple sugar

2 tablespoons freshly ground black pepper, plus more to taste

1 tablespoon crushed red pepper flakes

1 teaspoon ground ginger

1 teaspoon ground allspice

1 tablespoon kosher salt, plus more to taste

1 tablespoon cornstarch (optional)

¼ cup *(60 ml)* Crown Maple syrup (Dark Color, Robust Taste)

MAPLE-BRAISED

PORK CHOPS

AND PEACHES

PREP TIME: **10 MINUTES** | COOK TIME: **30 MINUTES**

Even though they're synonymous with southern agriculture, peaches are grown all over the Hudson River Valley (we have them growing at Madava!), and in early August you can find a dozen farms all over the region offering a chance to pick your own. If you can hold off on eating the entire bushel, you should set aside a few peaches for these delicious pork chops. The peaches release their juices into the pan and make a lush and savory sauce (and side dish) all at once.

SERVES 4

4 center-cut pork chops (1½ to 2 pounds/680 to 910 g total)

Kosher salt and freshly ground black pepper to taste

1 tablespoon olive oil

1 small onion, sliced

4 medium peaches, cut into wedges 1 inch (2.5 cm) thick

¼ cup (60 ml) dry white wine

¼ cup (60 ml) white wine vinegar

¼ cup (60 ml) Crown Maple syrup (Very Dark Color, Strong Taste)

½ cup (20 g) chopped fresh basil leaves

1   Pat the pork chops dry and season with salt and pepper.

2   Heat the oil in a cast-iron skillet over medium heat until hot. Add the pork and cook, turning halfway through, until the pork is browned on all sides, about 5 minutes. Transfer the pork chops to a plate.

3   Add the onion to the pan and cook, stirring occasionally, until it has begun to soften, about 5 minutes. Add the peaches to the pan. Pour the wine over the peaches and season with salt and pepper. Cover the pan and cook for 5 minutes. Flip the peach slices over, brush with some of the pan juices, and cook for 3 minutes longer, or until they have started to soften.

4   Whisk together the vinegar and maple syrup in a small bowl. Set aside.

5   Return the pork to the pan along with any juices accumulated on the plate. Pour the maple-vinegar mixture into the pan. Cook, turning the chops and peaches midway through, until the chops are cooked to an internal temperature of 145°F (63°C) and the peaches are thoroughly softened, 10 to 12 minutes.

6   Transfer the finished chops to serving plates, adding a large spoonful of peach slices to each plate. Cook the residual juices in the pan down for 1 to 2 minutes to thicken slightly. Drizzle the pork with the remaining pan sauce and sprinkle both pork and peaches with basil before serving.

MAPLE AND POMEGRANATE–

GLAZED HAM

PREP: **5 MINUTES** | COOK TIME: **1½ HOURS**

This dish is holiday-ready, but couldn't be easier to make for a regular week-night meal. The trick is finding a good ham for the cooking—you can adapt this to any number of different cuts of ham, but we especially like using an uncured ham, since it's much lower in preseasoning and nitrates and more adaptable for different kinds of glazing and cooking. (It also cooks far faster and at a lower temperature than a fully fresh ham.) Just don't skimp on the cooking-down time for the glaze—as it gets thicker, the flavors become deeper and richer. Lydia loves serving this with a side of mashed sweet potatoes (laced with some maple syrup, of course) and a platter of steamed green beans with toasted sliced almonds.

SERVES 4 TO 6

1 *(4- to 5-pound/1.8- to 2.3-kg)* uncured ham

3 cups *(720 ml)* pomegranate juice

1 cup plus 2 tablespoons *(270 ml)* Crown Maple syrup (Very Dark Color, Strong Taste)

1½ tablespoons dry mustard powder

¼ teaspoon ground cinnamon

¼ teaspoon ground cloves

¾ teaspoon kosher salt

1 Preheat the oven to 325°F (165°C).

2 Place the ham in a large roasting pan, add 1 cup (240 ml) water, and cover with foil. Roast for 45 minutes to 1 hour, until the center of the ham reaches a temperature of at least 135°F (57°C). Remove from the oven as soon as the meat reaches the target temperature.

3 Combine the pomegranate juice, maple syrup, mustard powder, cinnamon, cloves, and salt in a saucepan set over medium heat. Simmer the mixture for 15 to 20 minutes, until the glaze thickens enough to coat a rubber spatula.

4 Remove the foil from the ham and carefully spoon a little of the glaze over the whole ham. Return to the oven and roast for 15 to 20 minutes, stopping every 5 minutes to spoon additional glaze over the ham until it caramelizes and turns a dark golden brown. The internal temperature of the finished ham should register 140 to 145°F (60 to 62°C).

5 Remove the ham from the oven and brush with the glaze one last time. Let cool slightly and serve hot.

FENNEL AND CORIANDER–SPICED

MAPLE DUCK BREASTS

PREP TIME: **30 MINUTES** | COOK TIME: **20 MINUTES**

We already know that maple pairs perfectly with pork—in part because as pork cooks, it gives off so much of its fat and flavor. Duck responds exactly the same way—and once lacquered with a blend of fragrant spices and maple syrup, this is as decadent and flavorful a dish as any. Save the rendered duck fat for a side dish of roasted potatoes, which will come in handy for soaking up all the glorious juices on the plate.

SERVES 4

4 medium duck breasts *(about 6 ounces/170 g each)*

1 teaspoon kosher salt, plus more for seasoning

½ teaspoon fennel seeds

1 star anise pod

1 teaspoon coriander seeds

1 teaspoon whole black peppercorns

½ teaspoon crushed red pepper flakes (optional)

Grated zest of 1 medium orange

2 tablespoons unsalted butter or vegetable oil

¼ cup *(60 ml)* Crown Maple syrup (Dark Color, Robust Taste)

1 Lay the duck breasts skin-side up on a cutting board, and gently score the skin in a criss-cross pattern, being careful not to cut through the meat itself. Rub the salt gently over the skin and set aside for at least 30 minutes to come to room temperature.

2 Grind the fennel, star anise, coriander, peppercorns, and pepper flakes (if using) to a fine powder using a mortar and pestle or spice grinder. Transfer the spice mixture to a small bowl and stir in the orange zest. Rub the seasoned duck breasts with about 1 tablespoon of the spice rub (just to coat the skin).

3 Preheat the oven to 375°F (190°C).

4 Heat an ovenproof skillet or saucier over high heat for 1 minute. Add two duck breasts, skin-side down, to the hot pan. Cook for 5 to 7 minutes without moving, until you can feel the skin contract and easily pop off the surface when you try to lift up the breasts with a pair of tongs. (You will see much of the fat from the duck melt and render off as the skin crisps.) Remove the duck breasts to a plate and repeat with the remaining two breasts. Lower the heat to medium-low and pour off the rendered duck fat into a small heatproof sealable container. (Duck fat is a terrible thing to waste, so store yours in the freezer for up to 1 month, so it's available the next time you're in need of some breakfast hash browns.)

5 Add the butter to the pan and stir in the remaining spice mixture and the maple syrup to make a light sauce. Working two at a time, return the breasts to the pan and increase the heat slightly to medium. Cook the breasts for an additional 6 to 8 minutes for medium-rare doneness, or 130°F (54°C), spooning the maple-spice sauce over them as they cook. (If the breasts are not medium-rare after 8 minutes, transfer them to the oven and roast for an additional 5 minutes, or until they are medium-rare.)

6 Remove the duck to a cutting board, skin-side up, and continue cooking the remaining breasts. Let them rest on the cutting board for 2 minutes, then cut into thin slices and serve with the pan sauces on the side.

MAPLE TERIYAKI

CHICKEN

PREP TIME: **4 HOURS, 10 MINUTES, INCLUDING MARINATING TIME** | COOK TIME: **20 MINUTES**

I'm always amazed by people who rely on takeout for their daily meals. Sure, it's often delicious (and occasionally I miss it), but it's so much fresher to make your meals at home. Luckily, this sweet-and-savory take on Japanese teriyaki is an easy way to close the gap—not only is it much healthier than takeout, it's so easy to make that even our kids can help prep it. (The marinade is also great on beef or fish, or even on meatballs.)

SERVES 6

½ cup *(120 ml)* soy sauce

½ cup *(120 ml)* Crown Maple syrup (Very Dark Color, Strong Taste)

2 tablespoons plus 2 teaspoons semi-dry sherry

2 teaspoons sesame oil

1 tablespoon fresh lemon juice

2 teaspoons minced fresh garlic

2 teaspoons minced fresh ginger

½ teaspoon coarsely ground black pepper

6 boneless skinless chicken thighs *(about 3 pounds / 1.4 kg)*

2 medium sweet onions, peeled and cut into chunks

1 teaspoon cornstarch

1 Whisk together the soy sauce, maple syrup, 2 tablespoons sherry, the sesame oil, lemon juice, garlic, ginger, and black pepper with 2 tablespoons water in a small bowl.

2 Place the chicken in a resealable plastic bag or container and pour the marinade over the chicken; allow the chicken to marinate in the refrigerator for at least 4 hours, or overnight.

3 Preheat the oven to 400°F (205°C). Spray a 9 by 13-inch (23 by 33-cm) baking pan with nonstick spray and scatter the onions in the pan. Remove the chicken, reserving the marinade, and carefully place the chicken on top of the onions in the pan.

4 Bring the reserved marinade to a boil in a small saucepan. In a small bowl, mix the 2 teaspoons sherry and the cornstarch together with a fork or small spoon; pour a small amount of the hot marinade into the slurry and then add the mixture to the saucepan. Whisking constantly, bring the mixture back to a boil. Continue whisking constantly, for 1 to 2 minutes, until slightly thickened. Divide the glaze equally between two bowls.

5 Brush the chicken with half of the glaze. Bake the chicken, turning once, until a thermometer registers 180°F (82°C) in the thickest part of the meat, about 20 minutes.

6 Remove, baste the cooked chicken with the remaining glaze, and serve.

LYDIA'S FAVORITE

SALMON

PREP TIME: **2 MINUTES** | COOK TIME: **12 TO 15 MINUTES**

I never thought maple syrup could be paired with salmon, but after Lydia created this dish, it quickly became one of our family's favorite combinations. I can't think of a simpler yet more fresh and flavorful way to use maple syrup than in this glaze, which can be used for just about any kind of lean meat or seafood. If you're lucky enough to get fresh salmon during the summer, this is a great way to prepare it. It's perfect with a quick side dish of roasted potatoes and sautéed shredded Brussels sprouts.

1   Preheat the oven to 400°F (205°C). Place the salmon in a shallow baking dish and season with salt and pepper.

2   Whisk together the maple syrup, whiskey, mustard, and lemon juice in a small bowl. Spoon the sauce over the fish to coat.

3   Bake the salmon for 12 to 15 minutes, until the fish flakes slightly. Serve immediately.

SERVES 4

4 *(6-ounce/170-g)* pieces salmon fillet

Kosher salt and freshly ground black pepper to taste

3 to 4 tablespoons *(45 to 60 ml)* Crown Maple syrup (Amber Color, Rich Taste)

2 tablespoons good-quality whiskey

2 tablespoons stone-ground mustard

Juice of 1 lemon

CORNMEAL-FRIED

TROUT

WITH MAPLE-SAGE BUTTER

PREP TIME: **10 MINUTES** | COOK TIME: **30 MINUTES**

There's a prolific school of wild trout in one of the streams that runs through the Madava woods. While I don't fish in it, we do have a few neighbors who like to play catch-and-release off one of our bridges. In my mind there's nothing like trout fried in a well-seasoned cast-iron skillet with some bacon fat, and nothing like enjoying the fish with a little maple-sweetened butter. For Maddie, this meal reminds her of being in the log cabin for the first time with all of us. In fact, this might have been one of the first meals we enjoyed there.

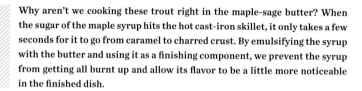

Why aren't we cooking these trout right in the maple-sage butter? When the sugar of the maple syrup hits the hot cast-iron skillet, it only takes a few seconds for it to go from caramel to charred crust. By emulsifying the syrup with the butter and using it as a finishing component, we prevent the syrup from getting all burnt up and allow its flavor to be a little more noticeable in the finished dish.

1 Finely chop 8 of the sage leaves. Mix the chopped sage with 2 tablespoons of the butter and the maple syrup in a small bowl. Set aside.

2 Pour the cornmeal into a shallow, rimmed plate or pie pan and whisk in the baking powder, salt, and pepper. In a second plate or pan, whisk the egg white with 2 teaspoons water. Pat the trout dry, then dip both sides of each fillet into the egg white mixture, letting the excess drip off. Dredge each fillet in the cornmeal mixture on both sides to coat and set aside.

3 In a large cast-iron skillet or sauté pan, cook the bacon over high heat until crisp, about 10 minutes. Set the bacon aside on a paper towel–lined plate to drain. Pour off all but 2 tablespoons bacon fat into a small dish for later use. Crumble the bacon into small pieces.

SERVES 4

16 fresh sage leaves (about 1 large bunch)

5 tablespoons *(70 g)* unsalted butter, softened

4 teaspoons Crown Maple syrup (Amber Color, Rich Taste)

¾ cup *(90 g)* stone-ground cornmeal (yellow or white)

1½ teaspoons baking powder

1 teaspoon kosher salt

Freshly ground black pepper to taste

1 large egg white

4 brook or rainbow trout fillets *(6 to 8 ounces/170 to 225 g each)*

6 slices thick-cut bacon

4   Reduce the heat to medium and add 2 tablespoons butter to the skillet.
Once the fat sizzles, add the fish to the skillet, as many fillets as will
comfortably fit and are easy to flip. Fry for 2 to 3 minutes on each side, until
crisp and lightly browned on the edges. Transfer each finished fillet to a plate
and spread about ½ tablespoon of the maple-sage butter on top so it melts
into the hot cornmeal crust; sprinkle lightly with salt. Cover the plate loosely
with foil until all of the fillets are cooked.

5   Add a little more bacon fat and the remaining 1 tablespoon butter to the
pan and fry the 8 remaining whole sage leaves until they are just crisp, about
1 minute. Serve the trout topped with the fried sage leaves and crumbled
bacon.

CROWN MAPLE

VEGETABLES AND GRAINS

SPICED MAPLE

CAULIFLOWER SALAD

PREP TIME: **5 MINUTES** | COOK TIME: **35 MINUTES**

One of Lydia's favorite cookbooks of the last decade has been Yotam Ottolenghi's Jerusalem. *She especially loves it for its creative approach to preparing vegetables. Ottolenghi often roasts his cruciferous veggies, and maple is a fantastic roasting medium: When whisked together with some olive oil and coarse salt, it brings out any vegetable's natural sweetness and best textures. This recipe was adapted from* Jerusalem, *and the simplicity of this salad's preparation belies how complex and layered its flavors, colors, and textures are, and it makes a great vegetarian main dish or a summer salad.*

SERVES 4

1 head cauliflower, broken into small florets *(1½ pounds/680 g)*

¼ cup (60 ml) olive oil

½ teaspoon kosher salt

Freshly ground black pepper to taste

3 teaspoons Crown Maple syrup (Amber Color, Rich Taste), plus more for drizzling

¼ teaspoon ground cinnamon

¼ teaspoon ground allspice

½ cup *(55 g)* chopped hazelnuts

¼ cup *(13 g)* whole flat-leaf parsley leaves

½ cup *(70 g)* pomegranate arils (from about ½ medium pomegranate)

2 tablespoons sherry vinegar

4 cups *(160 g)* mixed greens (spinach, mesclun, arugula)

1 Preheat the oven to 425°F (220°C). Line a baking sheet with parchment paper.

2 Toss the cauliflower with 3 tablespoons of the oil, the salt, and the pepper, 1 teaspoon of the maple syrup, the cinnamon, and the allspice in a large bowl. Spread on the prepared baking sheet and roast for 35 minutes, until the cauliflower is crisp and parts of it have browned. Transfer to a large bowl and set aside to cool.

3 While the cauliflower is roasting, heat a small skillet over medium heat. Add the hazelnuts to the pan and toast, shaking the skillet every so often, until they are fragrant, about 5 minutes.

4 Add the toasted hazelnuts to the cauliflower, along with the remaining 1 tablespoon oil, the parsley, and the pomegranate arils. Season with the vinegar and the remaining 2 teaspoons maple syrup, adjust the spices to taste, and stir to coat.

5 Spread the mixed greens to make a bed on a platter and top with the cauliflower mixture. Add a final drizzle of maple syrup and serve.

STRAWBERRY AND

SPINACH SALAD

WITH MISO-MAPLE DRESSING

PREP TIME: **10 MINUTES**

What exactly is the flavor of miso? Enjoyed by itself, the first reaction you might have is pure umami, but when blended with maple syrup and a light vinegar, it binds together a dressing that delivers a gentle, creamy sweetness without overwhelming other ingredients. (This may be because it's a complete protein source, with all the essential amino acids. It's also naturally high in antioxidants and vitamin B$_{12}$. Miso also can be very salty, so proceed with caution if adding additional salt.) Add a handful of spinach, some sliced strawberries, some candied nuts, and you've got a great colorful salad for lunch or dinner.

1   MAKE THE DRESSING: Combine all the ingredients in a clean jar with a lid. Seal the jar and shake the dressing until it is fully emulsified and creamy. Taste the dressing and season with salt and pepper to your liking, then set aside.

2   MAKE THE SALAD: Toast the almonds in a hot dry pan over medium heat until just fragrant, about 5 minutes. Sprinkle the maple sugar over the nuts. Remove the pan from heat and stir to coat while the nuts are still warm.

3   Put the spinach in a large bowl, then gently add the strawberries on top. Add the almonds, then drizzle half of the dressing over the top and toss to lightly coat. Add the remainder of the dressing just before serving, and garnish with the strips of Parmesan. (Any leftover dressing can be kept in the sealed container in the refrigerator for up to 1 week.)

SERVES 4

FOR THE DRESSING:

¼ cup *(60 ml)* olive oil

1 tablespoon white miso

1 tablespoon Crown Maple syrup (Amber Color, Rich Taste)

1 tablespoon white wine vinegar or rice wine vinegar

Kosher salt and freshly ground black pepper to taste

FOR THE SALAD:

1 cup *(93 g)* sliced almonds

1 tablespoon Crown Maple sugar

6 cups *(115 g)* baby spinach

1 cup *(165 g)* sliced strawberries

6 to 12 long strips shaved Parmesan cheese

MAPLE-MUSTARD APPLE AND

FENNEL SLAW

PREP TIME: 65 MINUTES, INCLUDING 30 MINUTES CHILL TIME

Fennel is my favorite secret salad ingredient—it takes the place of onion or celery and delivers a hint of sharp licorice flavor that jazzes up even the most traditional recipe. I love coleslaw in any form, but coleslaw made with fennel and apples, and in a slightly sweet, tangy dressing, is even better than the more traditional versions. You may want to use a darker grade of syrup than Golden, but don't overdo it; the very subtle flavor of maple here keeps all the other flavors in balance.

SERVES 4 TO 6

½ head Napa cabbage

Kosher salt to taste

1 fennel bulb

2 Golden Delicious apples, sliced

½ teaspoon fennel seeds

¾ cup *(180 ml)* mayonnaise

¼ cup *(60 ml)* stone-ground mustard

3 tablespoons Crown Maple syrup (Golden Color, Delicate Taste), plus more to taste

1   Shred the cabbage in a food processor with the grater attachment or with a very sharp knife. Transfer to a large bowl and lightly season with salt; set aside for 30 minutes, then squeeze the excess liquid out of the cabbage to get it as dry as possible. (You will have about 2 cups/200g cabbage.)

2   Cut the stems and fronds from the fennel. Discard the stems and set aside the fronds; cut the remaining bulb into thick slices. Shred the fennel slices in the food processor through the grater attachment (or with a very sharp knife), then add it to the bowl with the cabbage.

3   Shred the apple slices, then transfer to the bowl with the fennel and cabbage. Set aside.

4   Grind the fennel seeds to a fine powder with a mortar and pestle, then put in a small bowl. Add the mayonnaise, mustard, and maple syrup and whisk together until smooth. Pour the dressing over the cabbage mixture and toss to coat.

5   Chop about 2 tablespoons of the reserved fennel fronds, then scatter them over the top of the slaw. Refrigerate for about 30 minutes to let the flavors mingle, then season with salt and maple syrup to taste.

CHILLED

SWEET POTATO SOUP

WITH MAPLE-SMOKED CHILE SAUCE

PREP TIME: **15 MINUTES** | COOK TIME: **30 MINUTES**

This cool winter soup might be just as good warmed up, especially with a drizzle of smoky maple chile sauce on top. (To be fair, I love anything spicy, so this is one of my all-time favorite dishes.) The flavors are straight out of a global explorer's cookbook—you have sweet potatoes that can be traced back to both Africa and prehistoric Polynesia, dried peppers brought up to the colonies by the Spanish conquerors of Mesoamerica, and, of course, maple syrup from North America. How can so many different flavors peacefully coexist in one dish?

The three dried chiles used in this sauce are the most commonly used chiles for preparing classic Mexican mole dishes. Many grocery stores now carry these chiles at the end of the spice aisle, but if you can't find them, go to the best Latin American grocery store you can find and ask for them by name.

1 Put the dried chiles, vinegar, 1½ teaspoons salt, and the maple syrup in a food processor. Process the chiles, drizzling in ½ cup (120 ml) of the oil slowly as you go, until you have a smooth mixture that resembles a homemade barbecue sauce. (Add up to ½ cup / 120 ml water if needed.) Set the sauce aside. (You will have about 1 ½ cups / 360 ml chile sauce; in a sealable container, it will last up to 1 month in the refrigerator.)

2 Preheat the oven to 350°F (175°C); line a baking sheet with foil.

3 Combine the sweet potatoes with the remaining ¼ cup (60 ml) vegetable oil, the maple sugar, the black pepper, and the remaining 1 teaspoon salt in a large bowl and toss to coat the sweet potatoes thoroughly. Spread the sweet potatoes on the baking sheet and bake for 25 to 30 minutes, or until soft and slightly browned on the edges. Let cool.

4 Place the roasted potatoes in a food processor. Add the yogurt and puree the mixture, adding up to 5 cups (1.2 L) broth as necessary, until you have a smooth soup consistency. Season with additional salt, pepper, and maple sugar to taste, then transfer to a sealable container and chill until ready to serve.

5 Serve the soup in bowls and top generously with the chile sauce.

SERVES 4

1 dried ancho chile

2 dried pasilla chiles

4 dried árbol chiles

2 tablespoons distilled white vinegar

2½ teaspoons kosher salt, plus more to taste

¼ cup *(60 ml)* Crown Maple syrup (Dark Color, Robust Taste)

¾ cup *(120 ml)* vegetable oil

4 pounds *(1.8 kg)* sweet potatoes (about 4 large), peeled and cut into large chunks

1 teaspoon Crown Maple sugar, plus more to taste

1 teaspoon freshly ground black pepper, plus more to taste

½ cup *(120 ml)* plain full-fat Greek yogurt

Up to 5 cups *(1.2 L)* chicken or vegetable broth

MAPLE-ROASTED BRUSSELS, SHALLOTS, AND

FARRO SALAD

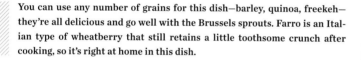

PREP TIME: **5 MINUTES** | COOK TIME: **30 TO 45 MINUTES**

Thank goodness the days of the maligned Brussels sprout are gone—no more steaming or boiling until it turns to mush. Now Brussels sprouts are one of the girls' favorite vegetables, especially in this slightly sweet salad. Brussels sprouts love fat, sugar, and roasting, and this delicious dish of sprouts, shallots, and chewy grains is a great vehicle for maple syrup. Don't worry if the sprouts come apart in the oven while roasting—a few extra-crispy leaves means more to nibble on while you assemble the dish.

You can use any number of grains for this dish—barley, quinoa, freekeh—they're all delicious and go well with the Brussels sprouts. Farro is an Italian type of wheatberry that still retains a little toothsome crunch after cooking, so it's right at home in this dish.

1 Preheat the oven to 375°F (190°C); line a baking sheet with aluminum foil.

2 Put the farro in a small saucepan and cover with 3 cups (720 ml) water and a pinch of salt. Bring to a boil, then reduce to a simmer and cover. Cook the farro for 25 minutes, or until the grains are tender but still have a little chew to them. Drain in a colander. Transfer to a large bowl and toss with the 1 tablespoon oil.

3 While the farro cooks, roast the vegetables: Spread the Brussels sprouts and shallots on the prepared baking sheet. Drizzle the maple syrup, the remaining ¼ cup (60 ml) oil, and the vinegar over the top, and season with salt and pepper. Use your hands to toss the vegetables right on the sheet.

4 Roast the vegetables for 25 to 30 minutes, turning halfway through, until the shallots have softened and the Brussels sprouts are crisped around the edges.

5 Add the vegetables to the bowl with the farro, and add the parsley. Toss to combine, and add more maple syrup, vinegar, and salt and pepper to taste. Serve warm.

SERVES 4

1 cup *(200 g)* dried farro

Kosher salt to taste

1 tablespoon plus ¼ cup *(75 ml)* olive oil

2 pounds *(910 g)* Brussels sprouts, trimmed and halved

4 to 5 medium shallots, sliced

2 tablespoons Crown Maple syrup (Amber Color, Rich Taste), or more to taste

1 tablespoon red wine vinegar, or more to taste

Freshly ground black pepper to taste

¼ cup *(13 g)* chopped fresh flat-leaf parsley

ROASTED

SQUASH SOUFFLÉ

WITH MAPLE STREUSEL

PREP TIME: **10 MINUTES** | COOK TIME: **1 TO 1¾ HOURS**

This dish is a Turner family favorite, one that we make almost every year at Thanksgiving. The girls can barely contain themselves when they see Lydia bring this out to the table; what is it about kids and sweet dishes at Thanksgiving? This is our equivalent of sweet potato pie with marshmallows—a little extra sweet at an extra-sweet holiday. We've given you cook times both for a big soufflé for the table and for personal-size soufflés for each dinner guest.

SERVES 6
6 MINI SOUFFLÉS OR 1 LARGE

1 MAKE THE SOUFFLÉ: Bring a large pot of water to a boil. Add the squash pieces and cook until tender, 15 to 20 minutes. Remove the squash to a cutting board and let cool completely. Peel and cut the squash down into bite-size pieces. Transfer to a large bowl.

2 Preheat the oven to 350°F (175°C). Butter a large glass or ceramic baking dish, or four small ovenproof ramekins, and lightly dust the inside with flour.

3 Mash the boiled squash until smooth, then stir in the flour, sugar, baking soda, and salt. Mix in the eggs, melted butter, and vanilla, then stir in the milk. (You will have a thick but rather liquid mixture.)

4 Transfer the squash mixture to the casserole dish. If using small ramekins, bake the soufflés for 35 minutes; if using a large casserole, bake for 45 minutes, until the soufflé has puffed up and browned slightly.

5 MAKE THE STREUSEL: Combine all the ingredients together with a fork or your hands in a small bowl. Remove the soufflés from the oven and sprinkle the streusel on top, then return to the oven and bake for an additional 30 minutes (for small soufflés) or 50 minutes (for a large soufflé), until the topping is a rich golden brown. Serve warm.

FOR THE SOUFFLÉ:

3 pounds *(1.4 kg)* butternut squash (about 2 large squash), cut into large pieces

¼ cup *(55g)* unsalted butter, melted, plus more softened butter for greasing

1 cup *(125 g)* all-purpose flour, plus more for dusting

1 cup *(200 g)* sugar

1 teaspoon baking soda

¼ teaspoon kosher salt

2 large eggs

1 teaspoon vanilla extract

1¾ cups *(420 ml)* whole milk

FOR THE STREUSEL:

¼ cup *(30 g)* all-purpose flour

2 tablespoons Crown Maple sugar

4 tablespoons *(55 g)* cold unsalted butter, cut into small pieces

¼ cup *(30 g)* finely chopped pecans

⅛ teaspoon freshly grated nutmeg

CLASSIC MAPLE

CORN PUDDING

PREP TIME: **10 MINUTES** | COOK TIME: **1 HOUR**

We first had corn pudding on a trip to Boston to spend time with my sister Martha and her husband, Dick, and the recipe has stuck with us for many years. If we had attended the first Thanksgiving, it would not have been surprising to see this classic pudding on the table—and probably sweetened with the last of the year's maple sugar. But this is an easy enough dish to make throughout the year, especially in the summertime when corn is at its sweetest and most abundant. (To make this dish gluten-free, you can easily swap in cornmeal for the flour. The texture will be slightly coarser, but the corn flavor will be more pronounced.)

1   Heat the oven to 350°F (175°C); grease a 1½-quart (1.4-L) baking dish. Set a kettle full of water on the stovetop and bring to a boil.

2   Put the corn, maple syrup, and salt in a food processor.

3   Mix the eggs and milk together in a separate bowl.

4   Process the corn mixture to break down the kernels, pour in the egg-milk mixture and the melted butter, then process until smooth. Add the flour and baking powder and pulse together until combined.

5   Spoon the mixture into the prepared dish and sprinkle with the nutmeg. Place the filled dish in a larger baking dish or roasting pan; pour boiling water from the kettle into the larger dish, until it comes about halfway up the sides of the smaller baking dish. (This will keep the pudding moist and evenly heated as it cooks.)

6   Transfer the pans to the oven and bake for 45 minutes, or until a knife inserted into the center of the pudding comes out clean. The pudding will be set but still jiggle. Remove the smaller baking dish from the water bath, and bake the pudding for an additional 15 minutes, until it has completely set. Serve hot.

SERVES 4 TO 6

3 tablespoons unsalted butter, melted, plus more for greasing

2 cups *(290 g)* fresh or frozen corn kernels (from 2 to 3 ears)

⅓ cup *(75 ml)* Crown Maple syrup (Dark Color, Robust Taste)

1 teaspoon kosher salt

2 large eggs

1 cup *(240 ml)* whole milk

½ cup *(65 g)* all-purpose flour

2 teaspoons baking powder

½ teaspoon freshly grated nutmeg

CLASSIC MAPLE

BAKED BEANS

PREP TIME: 50 MINUTES, PLUS 6 HOURS SOAKING TIME | COOK TIME: 4½ HOURS

I cooked this just the other night—or rather, enjoyed it the other night. I'd put it in the oven in the morning and I came home to the delicious smell of finished baked beans in the oven. Baked beans are often prepared with molasses, so because we're using very fine syrup, it might not look as lacquered or super dark as what you're used to. This isn't a fast recipe, but the work is worth it.

1   Cover the beans with water in a large bowl. Set aside for 6 hours to soak.

2   Drain the beans and put them in a large Dutch oven with a lid. Add the salt and enough cool water to cover by a few inches. Bring to a boil, then lower the heat and simmer gently, stirring occasionally, until the beans are just tender, 30 to 40 minutes. Drain and set aside in a separate bowl.

3   Preheat the oven to 300° (150°C); bring a kettle full of water to a boil.

4   Put the Dutch oven over medium-high heat. Cook the bacon until it browns and renders most of its fat, 7 to 10 minutes. Add the onion and garlic and cook for another 2 to 3 minutes, stirring, until softened. Stir in the beans and remove from the heat.

5   Mix together the maple syrup, vinegar, mustard powder, and pepper in a small bowl. Stir into the pot; pour in enough boiling water to cover the beans.

6   Cover the pot and move it to the oven. Bake until the beans are very tender but still retain their shape, 2 to 3 hours, checking every hour and adding more water to cover as necessary.

7   Remove from the oven, uncover, stir, and season with salt to taste. Raise the oven temperature to 400° (205°C).

8   Return the uncovered pot to the oven and continue cooking for 1½ hours, stirring every 45 minutes until the sauce has thickened and the top is brown. Garnish with the parsley.

SERVES 6

2¼ cups *(1 pound/455 g)* dried navy beans

1 teaspoon kosher salt, plus more to taste

8 ounces *(225 g)* slab bacon, coarsely chopped

1 large onion, finely chopped

2 garlic cloves, minced

¾ cup *(180 ml)* Crown Maple syrup (Very Dark Color, Strong Taste)

1 tablespoon apple cider vinegar

1 tablespoon dry mustard powder or mustard seeds

1 teaspoon freshly ground black pepper

Chopped fresh flat-leaf parsley for garnish

If you wish to use canned beans instead, skip the first two steps of soaking and precooking, and pick up from the beginning of step 3. You will need 4 15-ounce cans of navy beans, rinsed and drained.

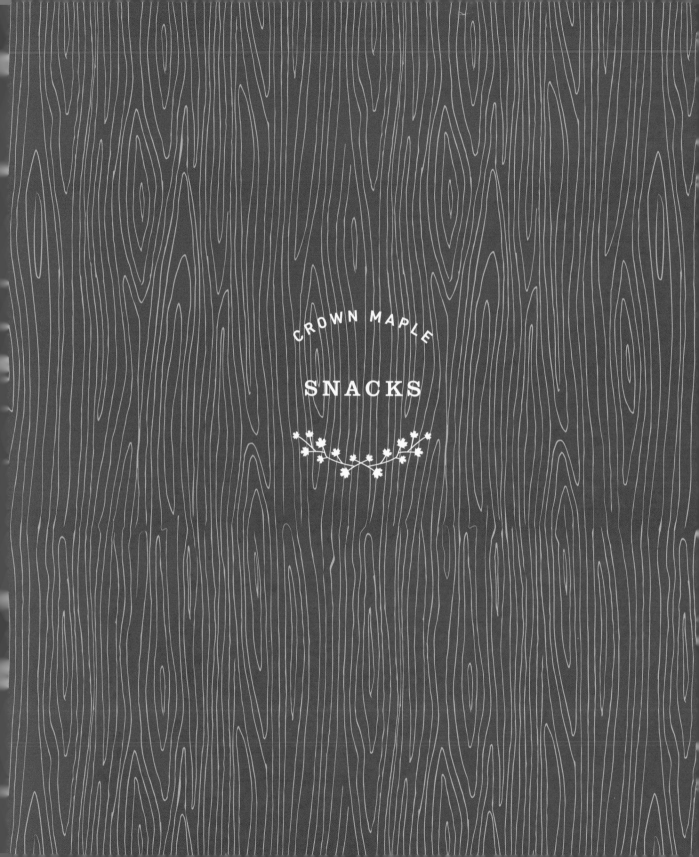

CROWN MAPLE

SNACKS

MAPLE
COCONUT CHIPS

PREP TIME: **5 MINUTES** | COOK TIME: **15 MINUTES**

These coconut chips are ridiculously easy to make, and impossible to put down. Though they're probably some of the healthiest things I could enjoy as a snack, I find myself inhaling them like they're potato chips. This is also an extremely adaptable recipe where you can mix in whatever flavors you like—you could do a spicy variation by stirring some cayenne pepper into the syrup, or one with Indian flavors by mixing in some garam masala and turmeric. The possibilities are endless, and given that it won't take you much time to eat through one batch, I recommend you make a few batches just to try them out. (You can find raw coconut chips in most grocery stores with a large health food aisle, or you can order them in bulk online.)

1 Preheat the oven to 325°F (165°C). Line a baking sheet with parchment paper and spray lightly with nonstick spray.

2 Toss together the coconut chips, maple syrup, and salt in a large bowl. Spread out on the prepared baking sheet.

3 Bake the chips, stirring every few minutes, until evenly toasted, about 15 minutes. Let the chips cool completely, then break them up into small clusters and store in an airtight container for up to 1 week (or plan to eat them well before then).

MAKES 2 CUPS
(ABOUT 210 G)

2 cups *(200 g)* raw coconut chips

¼ cup *(60 ml)* Crown Maple syrup (Very Dark Color, Strong Taste)

Pinch of kosher salt

MAPLE BUTTERED

POPCORN

PREP TIME: **5 MINUTES** | COOK TIME: **10 MINUTES**

The first time I ever tried this maple popcorn, it nearly knocked me over with surprise. I had expected a caramel corn–like confection, something I'd get stuck in my teeth. But this freshly popped, lightly sugared and salted, buttery treat is absolutely perfect; like kettle corn, it's impossible to resist. Sure, you could easily dress a bowl of fresh popcorn with maple syrup, if you want that sticky sweetness, but this may be even better. We always prepare this as a late-night favorite whenever we have movie night at home.

SERVES 4

2 tablespoons vegetable oil

½ cup *(80 g)* raw popcorn kernels

¼ cup *(½ stick / 55 g)* unsalted butter

⅓ cup *(50 g)* Crown Maple sugar

½ teaspoon kosher salt

1   Put the oil in a large, deep saucepan. Turn the heat to medium, add a few kernels of corn, and cover the pan. When you hear the kernels pop, remove the lid and add the rest of the popcorn.

2   Cover the pan and shake, holding the lid on, until the popcorn stops popping, 5 to 7 minutes. Transfer the popped kernels to a large bowl.

3   Melt the butter in a small saucepan, and pour half of it over the popcorn. Add half the maple sugar and ¼ teaspoon of the salt and toss to coat. Add the remaining butter, maple sugar, and salt and toss again. Serve warm.

MAPLE
COCONUT CHIPS

CANDIED
MIXED NUTS

MAPLE BUTTERED
POPCORN

CANDIED

MIXED NUTS

PREP TIME: **5 MINUTES** | COOK TIME: **1 HOUR**

Created by our brilliant chef, Sherri, these nuts have a great brittle-like crunch. Leave me alone with these at a cocktail party, and I would inhale them by the handful. (They're also fantastic as the topping on an ice cream sundae.) This is a great, very adaptable recipe, and can easily be made more savory with some added spices or cayenne pepper. They're also great to give away during the holidays; put them in a Mason jar and add a decorative ribbon for a lovely, simple, delectable gift.

1 Preheat the oven to 250°F (120°C). Line a rimmed baking sheet with a silicone mat, or line with parchment paper and spray lightly with nonstick cooking spray.

2 Combine the nuts in a medium bowl. Whisk together the egg whites, maple syrup, vanilla, and salt in a separate bowl until frothy, and pour over the nuts. Toss the nuts in the syrup mixture, then stir in the maple sugar and stir once more to coat.

3 Spread the nuts on the prepared baking sheet. Bake, stirring every 15 minutes, for 1 hour, until the nuts have completely candied in the syrup.

4 Let the nuts cool, then crumble into bite-size chunks and store in an airtight container for up to 2 weeks.

MAKES 3 CUPS
(336 G)

1 cup *(140 g)* whole almonds

1 cup *(95 g)* walnut halves

1 cup *(100 g)* pecan halves

2 large egg whites

2 tablespoons Crown Maple syrup (Very Dark Color, Strong Taste)

1 teaspoon vanilla extract

½ teaspoon kosher salt

1 cup *(145 g)* Crown Maple sugar

POWERFULLY MAPLE

FRUIT & NUT BARS

PREP TIME: **10 MINUTES** | COOK TIME: **20 MINUTES**

These chewy, crunchy, nutty bars are way better than any processed energy bar you could buy. Not only are the flavors more pronounced, with a nutty maple taste, but the texture is more natural as well, softer and chewier than a store-bought nut bar. Plus, they're naturally loaded with real power-food ingredients like flax seeds and rolled oats, and they travel exceptionally well. Lydia actually made a huge batch of these for my nephew at West Point (about an hour from Madava), and he shared them with his fellow cadets. They're an ideal grab-and-go food for me as well—just add an apple or two in a bag, and you're ready for the day.

1 Preheat the oven to 325°F (165°C). Line a large baking sheet with parchment paper.

2 In a food processor, pulse the oats, pecans, cashews, maple syrup, peanut butter, figs, flax seeds, and coconut oil until the mixture is coarsely chopped and comes together in a ball. Add the currants and coconut and pulse until just incorporated.

3 Shape the bars: Take a heaping tablespoonful of dough and roll it between your hands until it's about the length and thickness of a breakfast sausage. Press the log of dough onto the prepared baking sheet, flattening with your fingers, until you have a bar that is about ¾ to 1 inch (2 to 2.5 cm) thick. (If you form the bars thicker, they will have a chewier, less granola bar–like consistency.) Make the remaining bars and place them ½ inch (12 mm) apart on the baking sheet.

4 Bake the bars for 20 minutes, until they are browned around the edges. Let them cool completely on the baking sheet, then store in an airtight container for up to 5 days.

MAKES 1 DOZEN

---

1 cup *(90 g)* rolled oats

1 cup *(100 g)* pecan halves

½ cup *(60 g)* roasted cashews

½ cup *(120 ml)* Crown Maple syrup (Amber Color, Rich Taste)

¼ cup *(60 ml)* smooth peanut butter

5 dried figs, quartered

1 tablespoon flax seeds

1 tablespoon melted coconut oil

1 cup *(145 g)* dried currants, cranberries, or blueberries

½ cup *(45 g)* unsweetened coconut flakes

These are exceptionally easy to make gluten-free—just swap out the rolled oats for gluten-free oats, or even your favorite gluten-free grain like quinoa or barley.

MAPLE-APPLE-WALNUT

SNACK CAKE

PREP TIME: **5 MINUTES** | COOK TIME: **20 TO 25 MINUTES**

This recipe was Lydia's grandmother's—she used to prepare it for herself and her grandfather. He had a sweet tooth, so she would always have something on hand for him to snack on with a glass of milk (Lydia and her sisters also benefitted from this tradition)! This cake brings back many memories of spending the summer with her grandparents. Made with freshly picked apples, there is really nothing better than this simple snack cake. We all crave a little treat when we get home at the end of a long day, and this is the perfect thing to reach for instead of cookies or potato chips.

1 Preheat the oven to 375°F (190°C); grease a 9-inch (23-cm) square baking pan with oil.

2 Combine the maple sugar, eggs, oil, and maple syrup together in a medium bowl and mix well.

3 In a separate bowl, sift together the flour, salt, cinnamon, and baking soda.

4 Fold the wet ingredients into the dry ingredients to just barely combine. Stir in the apples and walnuts until everything is completely combined.

5 Spread the batter in the prepared pan and bake until it is a deep golden brown and a knife inserted near the center comes out clean, 20 to 25 minutes.

6 Let cool completely and cut into squares; dust liberally with confectioners' sugar and serve. Leftover cake should be covered with foil and either refrigerated or moved to a cool, dry place for up to 1 week.

SERVES 12
(3-INCH/7.5-CM)
SQUARES OF CAKE

¾ cup *(110 g)* plus 2 tablespoons Crown Maple sugar

3 large eggs

½ cup *(120 ml)* vegetable oil, plus more for greasing

2 tablespoons Crown Maple syrup (Dark Color, Robust Taste)

1 cup *(125 g)* all-purpose flour

½ teaspoon kosher salt

½ teaspoon ground cinnamon

½ teaspoon baking soda

1 cup *(180 g)* finely diced apples (Fujis or Gala apples are best here; leave the peel on)

½ cup *(60 g)* chopped walnuts

Confectioners' sugar for serving

CARAMELIZED ONION AND MAPLE-MUSHROOM

FLATBREAD

PREP TIME: **15 MINUTES** | COOK TIME: **45 MINUTES**

This could easily be a family dinner (especially if you're in a household that loves pizza), but we prefer to serve this flatbread sliced up in little pieces and spread around to guests, or as a side dish with our maple salmon (page 137) or a pasta dish. The mushrooms and maple are a surprisingly great combination, especially with a bit of sweet onion to pull them together. Just be sure to cook or drain off all but a very little of the mushroom juices before assembling the pizza, or you run the risk of a soggy crust (not so fun when you're eating leftovers the next day, as we usually do).

This recipe recommends the use of a pizza stone, but if you don't have one, you can improvise with a standard baking sheet: Flip a baking sheet so it is bottom-side up, and preheat it in the oven as it comes to full temperature. Lightly flour the hot baking sheet before sliding the raw pizza dough onto it, and bake as otherwise directed.

1   Preheat the oven (and a pizza stone or overturned baking sheet) to 500°F (260°C). Sprinkle some flour or cornmeal on the back of a baking sheet (or pizza peel, if you have one). Working with your hands or a well-floured rolling pin, flatten the dough into a large disk on top of the baking sheet, then use your hands to flatten it until it is even and less than ¼ inch in thickness, lifting and turning as you work to keep the dough from sticking to the sheet. Use the baking sheet or pizza peel to transfer the crust to the pizza stone and parbake, rotating every 15 seconds or so, for 60 seconds. Return the crust to the back of the baking sheet and set aside until ready to assemble the flatbread.

recipe continues

> **MAKES 1**
> (9-INCH/23-CM) PIZZA
> OR FLATBREAD; SERVES
> 10 TO 12 IN SMALL
> APPETIZER PORTIONS

1 batch *(22 oz.)* raw pizza or flatbread dough

¼ cup *(60 ml)* olive oil

2 large onions, thinly sliced

3 tablespoons Crown Maple syrup (Dark Color, Robust Taste), plus more for serving

1 teaspoon apple cider vinegar

1 to 2 garlic cloves, minced

½ teaspoon dried thyme or rosemary

Kosher salt and freshly ground black pepper to taste

2 *(8-ounce/225-g)* packages sliced portobello mushroom caps, diced

4 ounces *(115 g)* fresh mozzarella, torn into small pieces

½ teaspoon crushed red pepper flakes

1 cup *(20 g)* arugula, torn into small pieces

½ cup *(50 g)* grated Parmesan or Pecorino cheese

2   Heat the oil in a very large skillet set over high heat. Add the onions and stir to coat. Drizzle in 2 tablespoons maple syrup, the vinegar, garlic, and thyme, and season with salt and pepper. Stir to coat. Cook for 15 minutes, or until the onions have turned translucent. Remove to a bowl and set aside.

3   Add the mushrooms to the now-empty pan and season with salt and pepper. (Try to space the mushrooms somewhat apart, so they have space to brown.) Cook, stirring occasionally, until the mushrooms start to brown, about 10 minutes. Reduce the heat to low, then add the remaining 1 tablespoon maple syrup, cover the pan, and cook until the mushrooms have released their juices, about 15 minutes. Once finished, use a slotted spoon to transfer the mushrooms to the bowl with the onions, draining off as much of their residual cooking liquid as possible.

4   Brush the parbaked crust with oil, then scatter the torn mozzarella over the top. Top evenly with the onions and mushrooms. Season with more salt and pepper, then sprinkle with the crushed red pepper flakes.

5   Bake the flatbread for 5 minutes, until the cheese has melted and the edges have crisped. Remove from the oven and scatter the arugula and Parmesan over the flatbread. Return to the oven and bake for 1 minute more. Drizzle a final bit of maple syrup over the top just before slicing and serving. Leftover flatbread should be wrapped in tinfoil and will keep in the refrigerator for 3 to 4 days.

PARSNIP, MAPLE, AND

TAHINI DIP

PREP TIME: **10 MINUTES** | COOK TIME: **20 TO 25 MINUTES**

The general rule of thumb is that sweetness likes sweetness—when maple syrup meets carrots, sweet potatoes, squash, anything orange and rich in beta-carotene, it amplifies and mutes the sweetness all at once, bringing the very best of the vegetable forward. But something truly crazy happened when we tried out maple syrup on parsnips. The parsnip, a butter-yellow cousin of the carrot, is one of the few vegetables that can be left in the ground once grown to maturity rather than harvested right away—because, like maple, they get even sweeter after winter frosts. But when we roasted these parsnips in maple syrup, then pureed them with tahini and garlic, they went from vegetal to totally mind-blowing, tasting more like roasted bananas spread on a peanut-butter sandwich. My daughter Maddie often makes a batch of this dip to enjoy with raw veggies as an afternoon snack. It usually only lasts a day in our house; it's also great for lunches as a dip with pita wedges.

MAKES 2 TO 3 CUPS
(500 TO 750 G)

2 cups *(270 g)* chopped parsnips

2 large garlic cloves, halved

¼ cup *(60 ml)* Crown Maple syrup (Amber Color, Rich Taste), or more to taste

Up to 4 tablespoons *(60 ml)* olive oil

½ teaspoon kosher salt, or more to taste

½ cup *(120 ml)* tahini

3 tablespoons fresh lemon juice (from 1½ lemons), or more to taste

Freshly ground black pepper to taste

Raw broccoli florets and snap peas for serving

1 Preheat the oven to 400° (205°C); line a baking sheet with foil or a silicone mat.

2 Spread the parsnips and garlic on the baking sheet. Drizzle the maple syrup and 2 tablespoons of the oil over the vegetables, sprinkle with the salt, and toss with your hands to coat. Roast the vegetables until soft, 20 to 25 minutes.

3 Let the vegetables cool slightly, then puree in a food processor fitted with the metal blade with the tahini and lemon juice until you have a smooth puree the texture of hummus. (You may need to add an additional 2 tablespoons oil to make it smooth.)

4 Season to taste with additional salt, pepper, lemon juice, and maple syrup before serving. Serve warm with the broccoli and snap peas, or chill to let the flavors intensify before serving. (This can be kept in the refrigerator in a sealed container for up to 1 week.)

BAKED BRIE

WITH MAPLE AND PEAR CONFIT

PREP TIME: **10 MINUTES** | COOK TIME: **10 TO 15 MINUTES**

A serving size is somewhat useless in a recipe like this—whoever has access to it will eat as much of it as they can. This is a great appetizer for last-minute guests at our house, especially because it has such a pretty presentation. The warm brie topped with a slightly savory maple and pear spread is good on crackers or bread, or eaten directly with a spoon before anyone can complain.

1   Preheat the oven to 350°F (175°C).

2   Slice the top rind off the round of brie. Place the brie cut-side up in a small baking dish. (You want the walls of the dish to be as close to the cheese as possible. This prevents the cheese from burning as it spreads.) Fan the slices of pear over the brie to completely cover the exposed surface of the cheese.

3   Stir together the maple sugar, pepper, and orange zest in a small bowl. Sprinkle the sugar mixture evenly over the sliced pears.

4   Transfer the brie to the oven and bake for 7 to 10 minutes, until the cheese just slightly oozes when poked with a fork. Serve warm with dried fruit and lots of crackers and toasted bread on the side.

SERVES 4 TO 6

---

1 *(8-inch/20-cm)* round of brie cheese

1 large ripe red pear, very thinly sliced

2 teaspoons Crown Maple sugar

1 teaspoon freshly ground black pepper

Grated zest of 1 orange

Dried fruit, crackers, and toast for serving

BEVERAGES

MACA-OAT-MAPLE

SMOOTHIE

PREP TIME: **5 MINUTES**

My brother-in-law, Jebb, is a big maca fan, and so is my daughter Maddie, and whenever we're on vacation together in the Hamptons, we love to make these smoothies. This recipe actually makes an ideal nonvacation food for me to take into the sugarhouse when I'm too busy for a sit-down meal. It's also a great vehicle for delivering a ton of nutritional impact with not a lot of food prep. This smoothie has not only chia seeds (which are great for digestion and rich with omega-3s and protein), but maca, a root plant often called "Peruvian gin-seng" that, when powdered, provides a great stamina boost. Exactly what you need when you're in for a long week in the sugarhouse, trying to keep up with the thaw.

1 Blend all the ingredients together in a blender until smooth. Add more maple syrup for additional sweetness if you'd like, then pour into two tall glasses and serve.

SERVES 2

2 cups *(480 ml)* unsweetened almond milk

2 ripe bananas, peeled, sliced, and frozen

2 tablespoons Crown Maple syrup (Very Dark Color, Strong Taste), or more to taste

2 tablespoons rolled oats

1 tablespoon maca powder

1 tablespoon chia seeds

¼ teaspoon ground cinnamon

CHERRY-ALMOND

SMOOTHIE

PREP TIME: **5 MINUTES**

We always keep the ingredients for this smoothie on hand, and it's incredibly adaptable for pretty much any kind of frozen fruit–and–nut combination you have on hand. Blueberries and pecans? Bananas and walnuts? Apricots and pistachios? Try them all! None will be overwhelmed by the additional maple, and you can increase or decrease the sweetness to your liking.

 If using fresh cherries, add up to ½ cup of ice when preparing this smoothie.

1 Blend all the ingredients together in a blender until smooth. Taste and add more maple syrup for additional sweetness if you'd like, or more almond milk for a milkier consistency. Pour into a glass and serve.

SERVES 1

½ cup *(6 ounces/180 ml)* vanilla or plain Greek yogurt

½ cup *(50 g)* frozen cherries

1 tablespoon Crown Maple syrup (Very Dark Color, Strong Taste)

1 tablespoon ground almonds or ground flax seeds

2 tablespoons almond milk

½ teaspoon almond extract

½ teaspoon vanilla extract

MAPLE-VANILLA
ORANGE SODA

PREP TIME: **5 MINUTES** | COOK TIME: **5 MINUTES, PLUS COOLING TIME**

This tastes exactly like an old-fashioned cream soda—though of course much fresher and more naturally sweet. If you really want to take it over the top, add a scoop of maple or vanilla ice cream, or to make it adult, stir in a little bourbon. But right now this is as kid-friendly—and adult-nostalgia-inducing—as you can get. (The orange rind in the syrup keeps it from being too sweet, so if you prefer your sodas on the sweet side, just remove the rind when preparing the syrup.)

SERVES 4

3 navel oranges, halved, plus a few extra slices for garnish

1 whole vanilla bean, split

¾ cup *(180 ml)* Crown Maple syrup (Amber Color, Rich Taste)

½ teaspoon Crown Maple sugar (optional)

Sparkling water or club soda

1 Juice the oranges and strain out any residual seeds or pulp. You will have about 2 cups (480 ml) juice. Slice about 2 inches (5 cm) of rind from one of the juiced halves, and set aside.

2 Scrape the seeds from the vanilla bean into a small saucepan. Add the maple syrup, reserved orange rind, and ½ cup (120 ml) water. Bring to a boil, then reduce the heat to medium and simmer for 5 minutes to thicken, stirring all the while. (Use a wet pastry brush to wipe down any sugar crystals from the walls of the pot.) Remove from the heat, cover, and let sit until cool.

3 Remove the vanilla bean and orange rind, and pour the syrup into a small container. (You will have about 1 cup/240 ml syrup, which will last in a sealable container in the refrigerator for up to 2 weeks.)

4 If using maple sugar, spread it on a small plate. Wet the edges of four tall glasses, then tip the wet edges into the maple sugar to make a sugar rim.

5 Pour 2 to 3 tablespoons of the syrup into each of the glasses. Top the syrup with ½ cup (120 ml) orange juice. Add a few ice cubes, top with sparkling water or club soda, and stir with a long spoon to combine. Float a small slice of orange in each glass, and serve.

GINGER-MAPLE

LEMONADE

PREP TIME: **5 MINUTES**

This is a very lightly sweetened lemonade that will cut through any summer heat. The ginger gives it a nice spicy bite, one that isn't completely hidden by the sweet maple. The sweetness of artificial lemonade can often be overpowering, but if you're more of a sweet lemonade fan, feel free to increase the amount of syrup. This recipe reminds the girls of picking lemons off their Aunt Elise's lemon tree in California—they were always eager to make lemonade knowing that they were responsible for the picking. For us, it's lemonade made for a sophisticated grown-up palate, just as good cut with vodka as it is with seltzer. (If you prefer your lemonade pink, replace the ginger with ¼ cup [60 ml] pink grapefruit juice, and add more maple to sweeten accordingly.)

Keep your ginger in the freezer; not only will it last longer, but when you need to grate some into this lemonade, you don't even need to peel it. Just put your grater right to the ginger and go to work.

MAKES 1½ QUARTS
(1.4 L)

4 large lemons, plus extra slices of lemon for garnish

1 tablespoon grated fresh ginger

½ cup *(120 ml)* Crown Maple syrup (Amber Color, Rich Taste)

Crushed ice

1   Squeeze the lemons on a citrus juicer and remove any residual pulp or seeds. You should have about 1 cup (240 ml) juice.

2   Combine the lemon juice, ginger, and maple syrup in a pitcher, and top with 4 cups (960 ml) cool water. Stir with a long spoon. Refrigerate until ice cold.

3   Fill glasses halfway with crushed ice. Taste the lemonade and add maple syrup to your preferred level of sweetness, then stir and pour over the ice in each glass. Serve with an extra round of sliced lemon.

MAPLE
BRANDY ALEXANDER

PREP TIME: **5 MINUTES**

Originally, the Alexander cocktail was made with gin instead of brandy—unsurprisingly, because it was developed during the Prohibition era, when cocktails were made to be a decadent close to the evening. You'll want to mix and taste as you prepare this drink, to get the right balance of crème de cacao to brandy to syrup. This is, I'll concede, a very sweet cocktail, but also very deep in flavor. It's also Lydia's preferred drink—perfect to sip slowly after dinner.

 The rim of the glass should be wet with vodka—water will simply liquefy the sugar, whereas the vodka will evaporate and the sugar will stay behind.

1 Spread the maple sugar on a small plate. Wet the rim of two martini glasses with vodka, then dip each glass's rim in the sugar to coat.

2 Combine the maple syrup, brandy, crème de cacao, and cream in a cocktail shaker. Fill the shaker with ice, and shake vigorously for 1 minute.

3 Strain the cocktail through the shaker into the prepared glasses and serve.

SERVES 2

2 to 3 tablespoons Crown Maple sugar

Vodka, for wetting the rim of the glasses

½ cup *(120 ml)* brandy

½ cup *(120 ml)* crème de cacao

2 tablespoons Crown Maple syrup (Very Dark Color, Strong Taste)

2 tablespoons heavy cream

ROBB'S CROWN MAPLE

OLD-FASHIONED

PREP TIME: **5 MINUTES**

Maple and bourbon is a classic pairing—the smoky flavor of bourbon so perfectly matches the sweetness of the maple, you have to wonder why anyone ever bothered making this drink with white sugar. (Given that the Old-Fashioned dates back to 1806, it's nearly as old as the first industrial maple producers.) This is the beverage we hand to guests when they come in the door. It's my personal favorite, and a Turner family favorite as well (it was the signature drink at my nephew's wedding). Just be sure you find a bourbon that's not too sweet for this cocktail—I prefer Woodford Reserve or Maker's Mark, but you might want to use your favorite brand instead.

1 Pour the maple syrup into a cocktail shaker or large glass. Pour the bitters over the syrup to saturate, then squeeze in the juice from 1 orange section and 1 lemon section.

2 Add the unsqueezed fruit sections, then press with a pestle to muddle the fruit with the syrup. Add the bourbon and stir well. Add 1 or 2 ice cubes and top with 1 to 2 inches (2.5 to 5 cm) sparkling water. Stir again. Pour over ice in two glasses, and garnish each glass with a cherry.

SERVES 2

2 tablespoons Crown Maple Syrup (Dark Color, Robust Taste)

3 to 4 dashes Angostura bitters

2 sections orange

2 sections lemon

¼ cup *(60 ml)* good-quality bourbon

Ice cubes

Sparkling water

2 stemmed Maraschino cherries

MULLED MAPLE

CRANBERRY CIDER

PREP TIME: **10 MINUTES** | COOK TIME: **15 TO 20 MINUTES**

Sometimes I think the more all-American the flavors are, the more maple syrup belongs in the dish. There's nothing more fall-like, or more reminiscent of the New England landscape, than cranberries, and whether you're enjoying it hot or cold, this cider brings the flavors of the holiday season together in sippable form. We've gone apple picking as a family almost every year since the girls were little, driving halfway between New Jersey and Pennsylvania to meet Lydia's sisters and parents (and to find some of the best apples in the country). We always buy fresh-pressed cider after we finish the day's picking, and the smell of the cider on the stovetop reminds me of those trips, and of the next apple-picking season to look forward to.

1 Combine all the ingredients in a large saucepan over medium heat and bring to a boil. Reduce the heat and simmer for 15 to 20 minutes to concentrate the flavors.

2 Strain out the solid ingredients and pour the punch into a tall pitcher. Serve warm or chilled.

SERVES 4

2 cups *(480 ml)* apple cider

2 cups *(480 ml)* cranberry juice

1 cup *(95 g)* fresh or frozen cranberries

½ cup *(120 ml)* Crown Maple syrup (Very Dark Color, Strong Taste)

2 cinnamon sticks

2 whole cloves

1 vanilla bean, split

Peel of 1 orange in whole strips

MAPLE

EGGNOG

PREP TIME: **10 MINUTES** | COOK TIME: **30 MINUTES, PLUS CHILLING TIME**

We've served this eggnog at Christmas parties, usually in small shot glasses with platters of homemade Christmas cookies nearby. There's almost nothing better than a good eggnog during the holidays, and this beats the pants off the premade stuff available in the grocery store. (Plus, why wait until December to make a good batch of eggnog?)

 You can use beaten egg whites in lieu of the whipped cream.

1 In a saucepan over medium heat, whisk together the milk, maple sugar, and salt.

2 If using the vanilla bean, split it down the middle with a paring knife, scrape the seeds with the back of the knife, and whisk the seeds and the bean into the milk mixture.

3 Whisk the egg yolks together in a large bowl.

4 When the milk begins to steam and the sugar has dissolved, slowly pour the hot mixture into the yolks, whisking constantly.

5 Return the mixture to the pan; reduce the heat to medium-low and stir constantly until the mixture coats the back of a spoon or reaches 180°F (82°C) (this will ensure the mixture has been pasteurized and is safe to consume).

6 Remove from the heat and strain the mixture into a large metal container; chill in an ice bath until completely cold, 30 to 45 minutes. (If adding liquor, carefully whisk it into the eggnog midway through chilling.)

7 Whisk the cream in a medium bowl until very soft peaks form. Fold ⅔ cup (40 g) of the whipped cream into the eggnog. Serve very cold in frosted mugs or glasses. Garnish with additional whipped cream and nutmeg.

SERVES 4 TO 6

2⅔ cups *(645 ml)* whole milk

¾ cup *(110 g)* Crown Maple sugar

⅛ teaspoon kosher salt

1 vanilla bean (optional; you can also use 1 teaspoon vanilla extract)

4 large egg yolks

1 cup *(240 ml)* heavy cream

⅓ cup *(75 ml)* dark rum (optional)

Freshly grated nutmeg

PEACH-MAPLE

PUNCH

PREP TIME: **5 MINUTES**

Maple sugaring season is always a celebratory occasion, and this punch is perfect for such a celebration. While peaches are best enjoyed in summertime (and we often go peach picking during the warmer months in the Hudson Valley), good-quality peach nectar can now be found year-round, and really carries the contrasting sweetness of maple syrup well. We've prepared this punch with sparkling water, but a sharp ginger beer also works (don't use ginger ale, or you'll find it much too sweet.) Or, if you're feeling really festive, sparkling Prosecco or champagne might also do the trick!

1   Pour the peach nectar into a large pitcher. Stir in the maple syrup (start with 1 tablespoon), then add the peaches, lime, and lemon. Top with the sparkling water, then taste and adjust the maple content to your liking. (If the mixture seems too thick or fruity, add more sparkling water or ginger beer to lighten it up.) Muddle the entire mixture with a tall spoon to crush the fruit slightly, and chill until ready to serve.

2   Just before serving, add the mint to the pitcher and stir with a wooden spoon to gently bruise the leaves. Add ice cubes to four tall glasses, fill each glass three-quarters full with the punch, and top with more sparkling water if desired. Serve cold.

SERVES 4

3 cups *(720 ml)* peach nectar or peach juice, chilled

Up to 4 tablespoons *(60 ml)* Crown Maple syrup (Dark Color, Robust Taste)

2 ripe peaches, cut into thick wedges

1 lime, thinly sliced

1 lemon, thinly sliced

1 cup *(240 ml)* sparkling water or ginger beer, plus more for topping off to taste

¼ cup *(13 g)* torn mint or basil leaves (optional)

Ice cubes

CROWN MAPLE

DESSERTS

FUDGY DARK

BROWNIES

PREP TIME: **20 MINUTES** | BAKE TIME: **40 TO 45 MINUTES**

You'd think that the maple flavor would disappear in the face of something so rich and chocolaty. But the maple sugar in this recipe makes its presence known in these super decadent brownies—something about the maple sugar combined with the texture of the maple pearls keeps the interior of the brownies fudgy, even with a super cakey exterior.

1 Preheat the oven to 350°F (175°C). Spray a 9 by 13-inch (23 by 33-cm) metal or glass baking pan with nonstick cooking spray.

2 In the bowl of a stand mixer fitted with the paddle attachment, cream the maple sugar, butter, and maple syrup together until well combined. Continue to beat at medium speed for 5 more minutes.

3 Meanwhile, carefully melt the chocolate either in the microwave or over a double boiler, being careful not to scorch the chocolate or let any water come into contact with it, until completely smooth; set aside.

4 Add the eggs, one at a time, to the creamed butter mixture, beating well after each addition; add the melted chocolate and mix well, then add the cake flour and salt. Scrape down the bowl and beat on medium speed for 5 more minutes, then fold in the maple pearls.

5 Spread the batter in the prepared pan, smooth the top, and garnish with the remaining 2 tablespoons maple pearls. Bake until a toothpick inserted into the center of the pan comes out clean with just a few crumbs, 40-45 minutes.

6 Let cool on a wire rack for 5 minutes, then cut into 18 pieces by cutting into 3 rows and 6 columns.

MAKES 18 BROWNIES

2½ cups *(350 g)* Crown Maple sugar

1 cup *(2 sticks/230 g)* unsalted butter, room temperature

1 tablespoon Crown Maple syrup (Dark Color, Robust Taste)

10 ounces *(280 g)* semisweet chocolate, chopped

4 large eggs, room temperature

1½ cups *(195 g)* cake flour

½ teaspoon kosher salt

½ cup *(100 g)* plus 2 tablespoons Crown Maple pearls

Cake flour is crucial to a recipe like this—finely milled, super-soft flour makes for a much better brownie than coarser bread flour or even all-purpose. For a quick substitute, measure out 1 cup (128 g) all-purpose flour, then remove 1 tablespoon and replace it with 1 tablespoon cornstarch. Sift together, and you'll have a smoother, fluffier flour that's brownie-ready.

CHEWY MAPLE

SUGAR COOKIES

PREP TIME: 10 MINUTES, PLUS 2 HOURS FOR CHILLING | BAKE TIME: 8 TO 12 MINUTES

Sometimes the very best thing about a cookie is the simplest thing—and these chewy, sweet, buttery cookies are maybe the simplest, and best, expression of how good maple syrup can be used as a sugar substitute. You could always spice these up with your favorite blend of cinnamon, ginger, and allspice, but then you're entering more of a snickerdoodle territory—and why mess with perfection?

 These are also great rolled in crunchy maple sugar pearls rather than regular maple sugar.

MAKES 2 DOZEN COOKIES

½ cup *(1 stick/115 g)* unsalted butter, at room temperature

½ cup *(120 ml)* vegetable oil

1 cup *(145 g)* Crown Maple sugar, plus more for rolling the cookies

1 tablespoon Crown Maple syrup (Very Dark Color, Strong Taste)

1 large egg

2¼ cups *(290 g)* all-purpose flour

½ teaspoon baking soda

½ teaspoon cream of tartar

½ teaspoon kosher salt

1   In the bowl of a stand mixer fitted with the paddle attachment, cream together the butter, oil, and maple sugar. Add the maple syrup and egg and mix well.

2   In a separate bowl, sift together the flour, baking soda, cream of tartar, and salt. Add the dry mixture to the wet mixture and stir until combined into a smooth dough.

3   Transfer the dough to a sheet of plastic wrap and shape into a ball. Let the dough chill in the refrigerator for at least 2 hours.

4   Preheat the oven to 350°F (175°C); line two baking sheets with parchment paper or silicone mats.

5   Spread some maple sugar in a shallow bowl. Drop rounded tablespoons of the dough into the maple sugar and roll around to coat. Place on the prepared baking sheets, leaving about 1 inch (2.5 cm) between them.

6   Bake the cookies, turning and rotating the pans halfway through, until the edges are just golden and cookies are set, 8 to 12 minutes.

7   Cool the cookies for 2 to 3 minutes on the pan, then transfer to wire racks to cool completely. Store extra cookies in an airtight container for up to 1 week.

MAPLE CRÈME

SANDWICH COOKIES

PREP TIME: **20 MINUTES, PLUS 1 HOUR FOR CHILLING** | BAKE TIME: **8 TO 10 MINUTES**

Every time I have one of these cookies, I'm reminded of just how maple syrup can improve pretty much any dish on the planet. One bite of these takes me way beyond the gross-out maple crème cookies on grocery store shelves. Why bother with extra chemical preservatives or hydrogenated fats? A batch of homemade cookies is a huge step up for your afternoon milk-and-cookie break.

1 MAKE THE COOKIES: In the bowl of a stand mixer fitted with the paddle attachment, cream the butter, maple sugar, and salt together. Add the maple syrup and eggs, one at a time, scraping well after each addition. Add the flour and mix until a smooth dough forms. Transfer the dough to the refrigerator and let chill completely, about 1 hour.

2 Preheat the oven to 325°F (165°C); line two baking sheets with parchment paper. Lightly dust a clean surface with flour.

3 Transfer the dough to the floured surface and pat into a large rectangle of ⅛ inch (3 mm) thick; cut out shapes using a maple leaf cookie cutter. (For Oreo-size sandwich cookies, use a 1½-inch/4-cm cutter.) Cut out cookies and reroll dough as necessary.

4 Transfer the cookies to the prepared baking sheets and bake, turning and rotating the pans halfway through baking, for 8 to 10 minutes, until just set and barely brown. Transfer the cookies to a wire rack and let cool completely.

5 WHILE THE COOKIES COOL, MAKE THE ICING: In the bowl of a stand mixer fitted with the paddle attachment, cream together the confectioners' sugar, butter, and salt; gradually drizzle in the maple syrup and beat until light and fluffy, about 10 minutes. Transfer the frosting to a sealable plastic bag with a spatula, then close and twist the bag to force the frosting down into one of the corners of the bag. Chill the frosting until ready to assemble the cookies, then snip off the tip of one corner to pipe the frosting.

6 Pipe about a nickel-size dollop of frosting onto half of the cooled cookies and top each with another cookie. Store in an airtight container for up to 4 days.

MAKES 15
MAPLE LEAF SANDWICH
COOKIES, OR 45 OREO-SIZE
SANDWICH COOKIES

FOR THE COOKIES:

1 cup *(2 sticks/225 g)* unsalted butter, at room temperature

1½ cups *(220 g)* plus 2 tablespoons Crown Maple Sugar

½ teaspoon kosher salt

2 tablespoons Crown Maple syrup (Dark Color, Robust Taste)

2 large eggs

2¼ cups *(290 g)* all-purpose flour

FOR THE ICING:

3 cups *(370 g)* confectioners' sugar

1 cup *(2 sticks/225 g)* unsalted butter, at room temperature

½ teaspoon kosher salt

¼ cup plus 2 tablespoons *(90 ml)* Crown Maple syrup (Dark Color, Robust Taste)

CHOCOLATE
SPICE COOKIES

PREP TIME: 20 MINUTES, PLUS 1 HOUR FOR CHILLING | BAKE TIME: 12 TO 15 MINUTES

This recipe is our own spin on a cookie recipe from Yotam Ottolenghi's Jerusalem, *one of our favorite cookbooks—but we've given it a spice spin that comes straight from the Mexican tradition of* mole, *a family of savory sauces that combine chocolate, chile peppers, and an array of spices that often includes cinnamon, cloves, and star anise. These cookies taste much like Mexican wedding cookies, which is just as a holiday cookie should taste—a balance of spice, citrus, and sweetness. I especially love these cookies when they're still a little warm and soft, perfect for dunking in a cup of maple-sweetened coffee.*

1 MAKE THE COOKIES: Line a baking sheet with parchment paper or a silicone mat.

2 Grind the spices together in a spice grinder or with a mortar and pestle until you have a fine powder. Set aside.

3 In a medium bowl, combine the chocolate, ground spices, flour, cocoa powder, baking powder, baking soda, and salt, and mix together. Set aside.

4 In a stand mixer fitted with the paddle attachment, combine the butter, maple sugar, vanilla, and orange zest. Cream the ingredients together for about 1 minute. Add the dry ingredients, in ½-cup (70-g) increments, until well incorporated. Mix until everything comes together into a smooth dough (adding an extra tablespoon or two of water as necessary).

5 Divide the dough into tablespoon-size chunks and roll each into a round ball. Place the balls on the prepared baking sheets, staggering them about 2 inches (5 cm) apart so they have room to spread. Chill in the refrigerator for about 1 hour.

6 Preheat the oven to 350°F (175°C). Bake the cookies for 12 to 15 minutes, until they have spread and puffed up but are still slightly soft. Remove and

MAKES 16 COOKIES

FOR THE COOKIES:

½ teaspoon ground cinnamon

¼ teaspoon ground cloves

¼ teaspoon cayenne pepper

1 star anise pod

5 ounces *(140 g)* dark chocolate, finely chopped

2 cups *(250 g)* all-purpose flour

1½ teaspoons unsweetened cocoa powder

½ teaspoon baking powder

¼ teaspoon baking soda

¼ teaspoon kosher salt

½ cup *(1 stick/115 g)* unsalted butter, at room temperature

⅔ cup *(100 g)* Crown Maple sugar

1 teaspoon vanilla extract

½ teaspoon grated orange zest

let them cool on the pan for 5 minutes. Transfer the slightly cooled cookies to a wire rack set over a sheet of parchment paper.

7 MAKE THE GLAZE: Whisk together the confectioners' sugar and maple syrup with ¼ cup water in a small bowl until you have a thin, smooth icing.

8 Dip a spoon in the glaze and drizzle a little over each of the warm cookies to coat the surface. Let the glaze set on the cookies before serving; any leftovers can be kept in an airtight container for up to 3 days.

Infusing maple syrup is a great way to add extra flavors to your sweetener. Commercial syrups with artificial thickeners won't take another flavor well, but our syrup is so pure it's easy to add a little extra flavor, like you can to natural honey or agave or to homemade simple syrup. For a good pie-spiced syrup, add a strip of orange peel, a stick of cinnamon, and a spoonful or two of whole cloves, cardamom pods, or other spices of choice to ½ cup (120 ml) maple syrup in a saucepan, and heat to an active simmer. Cover, remove from the heat, and let steep for 30 minutes, then strain out the spices and pour the seasoned syrup into a clean sealable container. This will keep for up to 2 weeks in the refrigerator, and it is perfect for the next time you bake a pie or want a little extra flavor in your baked goods.

FOR THE GLAZE:

1⅓ cups *(165 g)* confectioners' sugar

3 tablespoons Crown Maple syrup (Amber Color, Rich Taste)

MAPLE-BACON-BOURBON-PEANUT

CHOCOLATE CHIP

COOKIES

PREP TIME: **15 MINUTES, PLUS 30 MINUTES FOR CHILLING** | BAKE TIME: **22 MINUTES**

Crunchy peanuts, salty bacon, sweet chocolate, and maple syrup—have we gone too far? You might think so, and certainly there's no need to improve upon a perfect chocolate chip cookie. But this is one of those times where texture is all. Salty and sweet, this is a cookie for grown-ups—or for the most sophisticated kid in the room. (Just don't bring it to the school bake sale.)

 Don't be shy about cooking the bacon all the way to its very crispiest; otherwise you'll find the cookies unnecessarily chewy.

1   Fry the bacon in a skillet over medium heat until very crispy, about 10 minutes; transfer the finished bacon to a paper towel–lined plate. Chop the cooled bacon into small pieces. You should have about ½ cup (115 g) chopped bacon.

2   In a stand mixer fitted with the paddle attachment, cream the butter, maple syrup, bourbon, vanilla, sugars, and salt together. Stir in the eggs one at a time until incorporated, then add the flour and baking soda and stir to combine. Stir in the bacon, chocolate chips, and peanuts until incorporated throughout. Put the bowl in the refrigerator for 30 minutes, to let the dough firm up slightly.

3   Preheat the oven to 350°F (175°C). Line a baking sheet with a silicone mat or parchment paper.

4   Drop heaping teaspoon–size balls of the dough onto the prepared baking sheet, spacing them about 2 inches (5 cm) apart so they have room to spread. Bake for 12 minutes, until they are fragrant and puffed up and have turned almond brown. Transfer to a wire rack to cool slightly, then serve warm. Leftover cookies can be stored in an airtight container for up to 5 days.

MAKES 24 COOKIES

8 slices thick-cut bacon

½ cup *(1 stick / 115 g)* unsalted butter, at room temperature

1 tablespoon Crown Maple syrup (Amber Color, Medium Taste, or Dark Color, Robust Taste)

3 tablespoons good-quality bourbon

1 tablespoon vanilla extract

1 cup *(200 g)* granulated sugar

½ cup *(75 g)* Crown Maple sugar

1 teaspoon fine sea salt

2 large eggs

2¼ cups *(290 g)* all-purpose flour

1 teaspoon baking soda

½ cup *(85 g)* chocolate chips

½ cup *(70 g)* chopped roasted peanuts

MAPLE

LEMON BARS

PREP TIME: **20 MINUTES** | BAKE TIME: **45 TO 50 MINUTES**

These bars are exactly the kind of lick-your-fingers treat that you hope to find at a bake sale. Some lemon bars may remind you of slightly crystallized cakes you'd see at a high tea, but these are much more the gooey, pucker-sweet bars I remember from my childhood. The longer you refrigerate the bars, the more the curd on top will firm up . . . but you might just want to eat them with a knife and fork, if you're worried about getting your fingers sticky.

1 Preheat the oven to 350°F (175°C). Line a 9-inch (23-cm) square baking pan with parchment paper, so a little paper hangs over the sides of the pan. Lightly spray the paper with nonstick cooking spray.

2 MAKE THE CRUST: In a stand mixer fitted with the paddle attachment, cream the butter, confectioners' sugar, and salt together. When thoroughly mixed, add the flour and mix well. Press evenly into the bottom of the prepared pan and bake for 25 minutes, until the crust is light golden brown. Remove and let cool completely. Turn the oven temperature down to 300°F (150°C).

3 MAKE THE FILLING: In the bowl of a stand mixer fitted with the whisk attachment, whip the eggs, sugars, flour, baking powder, salt, and lemon zest and juice together until you have a smooth yellow mixture.

4 Pour the lemon filling over the prepared crust and bake until set and golden brown, 20 to 25 minutes. (The bars are done when the center still jiggles but doesn't run when the pan is tilted.) Remove from the oven and let the bars cool to room temperature. Transfer the bars to the refrigerator and chill, to set completely.

5 Cut the bars carefully into 3-inch (7.5-cm) squares, making sure to press the knife all the way through the bars to the crust, and dipping the knife in hot water and wiping dry after each cut. Dust liberally with confectioners' sugar and serve. Refrigerate any remaining bars in an airtight container for up to 4 days.

MAKES 9 BARS

FOR THE CRUST:

¾ cup *(1½ sticks / 170 g)* unsalted butter, at room temperature

½ cup *(65 g)* confectioners' sugar, plus more for dusting

¼ teaspoon fine sea salt

1¼ cups *(160 g)* all-purpose flour

FOR THE FILLING:

4 large eggs

½ cup *(75 g)* plus 2 tablespoons Crown Maple sugar

½ cup *(100 g)* plus 2 tablespoons granulated sugar

¼ cup *(30 g)* all-purpose flour

¾ teaspoon baking powder

¼ teaspoon fine sea salt

Grated zest of 1 lemon

½ cup *(120 ml)* fresh lemon juice (from about 3 lemons)

MAPLE

ICE CREAM

PREP TIME: **5 MINUTES, PLUS CHILLING TIME** | COOK TIME: **20 MINUTES**

While not much about maple's origin story is known, there are several accounts from early settlers that a version of maple ice cream was enjoyed even by that era's Native Americans. During each winter's "sugar moon" celebrations, children would collect the first sap as it dripped out of the trees and pour it from their baskets out on banks of fresh snow. Enjoying bowls of snow and hardened syrup might be called Maple Ice Cream 1.0—but we like our version even better, especially when you load it up with fresh sundae toppings. (Our girls love a mix of unusual textures in their maple sundaes: granola, toasted coconut, dark cocoa nibs, fresh berries, and chopped walnuts all go perfectly.) The soft, buttery flavor of the maple ice cream is perfect during any season—why wait until the snow to enjoy your maple cold?

MAKES ABOUT I QUART
(960 ML)

2 cups *(480 ml)* heavy cream

1 cup *(240 ml)* whole milk

1 cup *(240 ml)* Crown Maple syrup (Dark Color, Robust Taste)

6 large egg yolks

1 Warm the cream, milk, and maple syrup in a large saucepan, but do not let the mixture boil. Set aside a medium bowl with a fine-mesh sieve, and set that bowl over an ice-water bath.

2 In a separate bowl, whisk together the egg yolks. Slowly pour an equal volume of the warm milk mixture into the egg yolks, whisking constantly, then scrape the warmed yolks back into the saucepan.

3 Return the saucepan to medium heat and cook, stirring constantly with a heat-safe spatula, for 15 to 20 minutes, until the custard thickens and coats the spatula so much that you can draw a line through it with your finger. (You can also test the temperature of the custard with a candy thermometer to see if it's done—it should be between 170 and 176°F/ about 77°C.) Pour the custard through the sieve into the bowl set over the ice bath, and stir until cool.

4 Chill the maple custard completely, then freeze it in your ice cream maker according to the manufacturer's directions. Enjoy with your favorite ice cream toppings.

CARROT CAKE

CUPCAKES

WITH MAPLE–CREAM CHEESE FROSTING

PREP TIME: **5 MINUTES, PLUS 30 MINUTES FOR CHILLING** | BAKE TIME: **25 MINUTES**

Adapted from Nicole Spiridakis' wonderful gluten-free cookbook Flourless, *these may be the most festive—and healthiest—cupcakes you'll ever have. I don't like a too-sweet carrot cake, and this one rides that perfect line between muffin and cupcake (though the maple–cream cheese frosting really takes it over the top). Make sure to let the cakes fully chill in the refrigerator before frosting.*

MAKES 12

1 Preheat the oven to 350°F (175°C). Line a 12-cup cupcake tin with cupcake liners.

2 Put the butter, eggs, coconut, about 2½ cups (280 g) of the carrots, the maple sugar, cornstarch, vanilla, baking powder, and salt in the bowl of a food processor fitted with the steel blade and process until a smooth batter forms, at least 1 minute. Stir in the remaining carrots, the raisins, and the walnuts.

3 Divide the batter among the prepared cups, filling each about three-quarters full. Bake the cupcakes until the tops are lightly browned and firm to the touch, and until a toothpick inserted into the center of one comes out clean, about 25 minutes. Remove the cupcakes from the oven and let cool in the tin for 5 minutes before turning out onto a wire rack. Move the cupcakes to the refrigerator for at least 30 minutes, until they have cooled completely.

4 In a large bowl, using an electric mixer, combine the cream cheese, butter, and maple syrup and beat on medium speed until well combined and smooth. When ready to frost, spread each cupcake with an equal amount of frosting and refrigerate for at least 30 minutes before serving. Store at room temperature in an airtight container, or in the fridge, for up to 5 days.

7 tablespoons *(100 g)* unsalted butter, at room temperature

3 large eggs

1 cup *(85 g)* unsweetened coconut flakes

3 large carrots, grated *(about 3 cups / 335 g)*

⅔ cup *(100 g)* Crown Maple sugar

½ cup *(65 g)* cornstarch

1 teaspoon vanilla extract

1½ teaspoons baking powder

½ teaspoon fine sea salt

½ cup *(75 g)* raisins

½ cup *(60 g)* chopped walnuts

8 ounces *(225 g)* cream cheese, at room temperature

2 tablespoons unsalted butter, at room temperature

3 tablespoons Crown Maple syrup (Amber Color, Medium Taste)

MAPLE-MASCARPONE

POUND CAKE

WITH SUGARED BERRIES

PREP TIME: **5 TO 10 MINUTES** | BAKE TIME: **1 HOUR 20 MINUTES**

This is a wonderfully rich and simple pound cake, where the sweetness of the maple sugar and syrup is detectable, but far from overwhelming—the definition of what pound cake should be, a vehicle for whatever you serve with it. Mascarpone is a soft, slightly tart Italian cream cheese, best known for its place in the classic dessert tiramisù. You can make this with cream cheese if you absolutely can't find mascarpone, but this is a great time to try it if it's brand new to you. (It especially holds up against the slightly citrusy berries that end up soaking right through the cake.)

1   Preheat the oven to 325°F (165°C). Generously grease a 9 by 5-inch (23 by 12-cm) loaf pan.

2   In the bowl of a stand mixer fitted with the paddle attachment, cream together the butter, ¼ cup (35 g) of the maple sugar, and the salt until the mixture is completely smooth, 2 to 3 minutes, stopping to occasionally scrape down the sides of the bowl.

3   In a medium bowl, whisk together the maple syrup, eggs, and ¼ cup (35 g) maple sugar. With the mixer running on low speed, gradually add the egg mixture and mascarpone to the butter mixture, alternating between the ingredients in small amounts, waiting until each addition is incorporated before adding more.

4   Sift the flour and baking powder together in a separate bowl. Add the flour mixture to the mascarpone batter, 1 cup (125 g) at a time, mixing at low speed, until each cup of flour is well incorporated and the batter is completely smooth.

5   Pour the batter into the prepared pan and smooth the top with a clean knife. Bake for 35 minutes, until it is puffed and slightly browned on the edges, but still jiggles and is somewhat liquid in the center. Reduce the oven temperature to 300°F (150°C), tent the loaf with foil, and bake for another 45 minutes. The cake is finished when a toothpick inserted into the center comes out clean and the top of the cake is cracked but still moist. Remove and let cool on a rack.

6   Combine the blackberries, raspberries, and triple sec in a small bowl. Sprinkle the remaining 1 tablespoon maple sugar over the top and toss to coat.

7   Cut the warm pound cake into thick slices and serve each with a spoonful of sugared berries on top.

MAKES I
(9-INCH/23-CM) LOAF

½ cup *(1 stick/115g)* unsalted butter, at room temperature, plus more for greasing

½ cup *(75 g)* plus 1 tablespoon Crown Maple sugar

1 teaspoon kosher salt

¼ cup *(60 ml)* Crown Maple syrup (Dark Color, Robust Flavor)

4 large eggs

¾ cup *(175 g)* mascarpone cheese, at room temperature

2 cups *(255 g)* all-purpose flour

1½ teaspoons baking powder

1½ cups *(215g)* ripe blackberries

1½ cups *(215g)* ripe raspberries

1 tablespoon triple sec

VELVETY MAPLE

CHEESECAKE

PREP TIME: **15 MINUTES, PLUS OVERNIGHT CHILLING AFTER BAKING** | BAKE TIME: **1 HOUR**

This cheesecake is sublime, and I think it is especially so because of the dark, not-too-sweet syrup lacing both the crust and the filling. The crumbly graham crackers are perfect for creating a chewy base to the cheesecake, almost like a gingersnap or snickerdoodle. Just don't slice into the cake too early: The reward for waiting until it chills completely is a rich yet light, sweet, and creamy cake. This recipe has been a go-to dessert for Lydia and her family for ages, and it's one we always look forward to, especially around Easter time. (It also freezes beautifully, in case you don't eat it all at once.)

MAKES 1
(10-INCH/25-CM)
CHEESECAKE

3 full sleeves graham crackers (about 30 cracker sheets)

½ cup *(1 stick/115 g)* unsalted butter, melted

1½ cups *(360 ml)* Crown Maple syrup (Dark Color, Robust Taste), plus more for drizzling

4 *(8-ounce/232-g)* packages cream cheese, at room temperature

4 large eggs

1 tablespoon vanilla extract

½ cup *(120 ml)* heavy cream

1   Preheat the oven to 350°F (175°C). Lightly mist a 10-inch (25-cm) springform pan with cooking spray.

2   In a food processor, process the graham crackers into fine crumbs. You should have about 3½ cups (210g) of crumbs. Transfer the crumbs to a large bowl and stir together with the melted butter and ½ cup (120 ml) of the maple syrup, until you have a mixture that resembles crumbly wet sand that easily clumps together when you squeeze it between your fingers.

3   Press the crust in the bottom and up about 1 inch (2.5 cm) of the sides of the pan, packing it with your fingers so you have an even layer of crust. Wrap the underside of the pan with a sheet of foil and place the pan on a baking sheet.

4   In a stand mixer fitted with the paddle attachment, or in the food processor (thoroughly clean it to make sure there is no graham cracker residue), beat the cream cheese on low speed (or pulse) until smooth, scraping down the sides to incorporate. Add the remaining 1 cup (240 ml) maple syrup and beat to combine. Add the eggs, one at a time, beating after each is added. Add the vanilla and cream, beating until the mixture is well combined and smooth.

5   Pour the filling into the crust; it will rise very high on the sides but will not overflow the crust. Transfer the pan (on the baking sheet) to the oven and bake for 1 hour. The edges will be lightly golden but the cake will not be fully set. Remove and let cool completely, then gently cover with plastic wrap. Transfer the cake to the refrigerator and let chill overnight, or at least 8 hours. (Any less time than that, and the center of the cake will be runny, even if the sides are set.)

6   After it is chilled, release the cake from the springform pan. Add a thin drizzle of syrup over the top of the cake, slice, and serve immediately. Leftover cheesecake can be covered with plastic wrap and refrigerated for up to 1 week.

MAPLE-BOURBON

PECAN PIE

PREP TIME: **20 MINUTES, PLUS 1 HOUR FOR CHILLING** | BAKE TIME: **30 TO 45 MINUTES**

Pecans, like maple syrup, are an indigenous American ingredient that has inspired fanaticism across the country, especially in the southern United States. While you could make this with molasses or even Karo syrup (yikes), why not make a marriage between these two original ingredients? Even the most traditional of Southern tasters would agree that maple syrup has earned its place in this iconic dish—it takes a classic recipe and adds a much richer flavor profile to it without turning it into something too sweet or sugary.

1 MAKE THE CRUST: In the bowl of a food processor, combine the butter, flour, and salt, and pulse a few times until the mixture looks like crumbled feta cheese. Add half of the ice water and pulse again. The mixture should start to come together to form a rough ball; if it still seems dry, add the remaining water and pulse until it comes together.

2 Remove the dough from the food processor to a clean work surface and form it into a ball. Wrap in plastic wrap and refrigerate for at least 1 hour. (This can be done a few days in advance; when you are ready to use the dough, remove it from the refrigerator 20 to 30 minutes beforehand.)

3 Preheat the oven to 300°F (150°C). Lightly grease a deep-dish 9-inch (23-cm) pie plate.

4 Dust the dough and a work surface with flour. Using a rolling pin, roll the dough out evenly in all directions, forming a circle about 10 inches (25 cm) wide and ⅛ inch (3 mm) thick. (Turn the dough in between rolls, dusting with more flour if necessary, to prevent it from sticking to the work surface and help it to roll out more evenly.)

recipe continues

MAKES I
(9-INCH/23-CM)
DEEP-DISH PIE

FOR THE CRUST:

¾ cup *(1½ sticks/170 g)* cold unsalted butter, cut into pea-size pieces, plus more for greasing

1 cup *(125 g)* all-purpose flour, plus more for rolling

Pinch of kosher salt

3 to 4 tablespoons *(45 to 60 ml)* ice water

5 Drape the dough into the prepared pie plate, leaving ½ inch (12 mm) of dough hanging over the edge. Trim off the excess and crimp the crust around the edge of pie plate with a fork. Place the pie plate on a baking sheet and spread the pecans in the crust; set aside.

6 MAKE THE PIE FILLING: Combine the maple syrup, maple sugar, butter, bourbon, and salt in a saucepan over medium heat; whisk constantly until the sugar is dissolved and the butter is melted, about 3 minutes. Remove from the heat and whisk in the flour until smooth. Let cool until warm but no longer hot.

7 In a small bowl, whisk the eggs together; add ½ to ¾ cup (120 to 180 ml) warm syrup mixture to the eggs and whisk together. Whisk the egg-syrup mixture back into the saucepan of remaining syrup to combine. Pour over the pecans in the crust.

8 Carefully place the pie (on the baking sheet) in the center of the oven and bake until the pecans are golden and the pie is puffy and jiggles slightly when moved, but does not ooze, about 45 minutes. Cool completely before slicing and refrigerate any leftovers. Leftover pecan pie can be kept in the refrigerator for up to 1 week.

FOR THE FILLING:

2 cups *(200 g)* pecan halves

2 cups *(480 ml)* Crown Maple syrup (Very Dark Color, Strong Taste)

½ cup *(75 g)* Crown Maple sugar

½ cup *(1 stick/115 g)* unsalted butter

¼ cup *(60 ml)* good-quality bourbon

½ teaspoon kosher salt

2 heaping tablespoons all-purpose flour

6 large eggs

COPR. DETROIT PUBLISHING CO.

ACKNOWLEDGMENTS

TO THE CROWN MAPLE TEAM: Danielle Simmons, Tyge Rugenstein, and our woods crew and café team: Thank you for your hard work and dedication to this project.

TO THE ABRAMS TEAM: To Camaren Subhiyah, Sarah Massey, Danielle Deschenes, Michael Sand, John Gall, Erin Hotchkiss, Emily Albarillo, Erin Slonaker, Mary Hern, and Denise LaCongo; It's an honor to be published by you, and it was a pleasure working with you.

TO OUR BOOK COLLABORATORS AND SUPPORTERS: Michael Farrell and Stephen Childs at Cornell's Sugar Maple Research & Extension Field Station in Lake Placid, New York, whose advice has proved invaluable to us since the beginning. Thank you to the folks outside the maple world—Betsy Amster and Paula Johnson for their guidance; Paulina Do, Yvonne Kemper, Michael Kozar, Laura March, Leona Scanlan, Corinne Segal, and Stuart Shapiro for their taste-testing assistance . . . and to Nicholas Carbone for being the best guinea pig and culinary scientist imaginable.

LASTLY, TO MY FAMILY: To my wife, Lydia, the one and only Mother Maple, for your recipes and inspiration. Part Three couldn't be without you. To my girls, Madeline and Ava, for making my life as sweet as the syrup we have the privilege to create.

ABOUT THE AUTHOR

ROBB TURNER grew up in a small town in northern Illinois. During his younger years, he had a great love of the outdoors and spent a great deal of time working and playing on his family's farm. Robb earned a Bachelor of Science in Engineering from the U.S. Military Academy at West Point and a Master of Business Administration from Harvard Business School. He is a co-founder of Crown Maple and co-founder of ArcLight Capital Partners. In 2009, he began looking for the perfect location for a family retreat and subsequently purchased 400 acres of untouched forest in Dover Plains, New York. They named the property Madava Farms after daughters Madeline and Ava. Robb soon acquired an additional 600 acres of nearby hardwood forest to protect it from development—and thus began a journey that led to the launch of Crown Maple, now a leading U.S. maple syrup producer with a following that connects the worlds of Cornell University, forestry experts, and trendsetting New York chefs. Robb and his family reside in Montclair, New Jersey.

JESSICA CARBONE is a native New Englander and culinary writer, editor, and historian based in Washington, DC.

WORKS CONSULTED

ABBOTT, ELIZABETH. *Sugar: A Bittersweet History*. New York: The Overlook Press, 2011.

AGRICULTURE AND AGRI-FOOD CANADA. "Taste of Maple Syrup." Chart © 2004, AAFC/Centre ACER Inc. Available at: http://www.finemapleproducts.com/en/information/133/taste-of-maple-syrup

ALBERS, JAN. *Hands on the Land: A History of the Vermont Landscape*. Cambridge, MA: The MIT Press, 2000.

ALLEN, R. L. *The American Farm Book*. New York: Saxton, 1849.

AMERICAN FOOD ROOTS. "World War I Sugar Substitutes No Sacrifice Today," published January 6, 2015, accessed July 5, 2015. Available at: http://www.americanfoodroots.com/wwi/world-war-i-sugar-substitutes-no-sacrifice-today.

AUSTEN, IAN. "Canadian Maple Syrup 'Rebels' Clash with Law." *New York Times*, August 20, 2015, BU1. Available at: http://www.nytimes.com/2015/08/23/business/international/canadian-maple-syrup-producers-clash-with-law.html?_r=0.

BALL, DAVID W. "The Chemical Composition of Maple Syrup." *Journal of Chemical Education*, 2007, 84 (10). DOI: 10.1021/ed084p1647.

BEAHRS, ANDREW. *Twain's Feast: Searching for America's Lost Foods in the Footsteps of Samuel Clemens*. New York: Penguin, 2011.

BENTLEY, E. V. "Adulterations and Imitations." *Ohio Farmer (1856–1906)*, March 17, 1898; 93, 11; 229.

BERNHARDT, JASE, VICTORIA KELLY, ALLISON CHATRCHYAN, AND ARTY DEGAETANO. "Climate and Air Quality of Dutchess County." Written October 2008, revised October 2010, accessed August 9, 2015; 1–40. Available at: http://www.co.dutchess.ny.us/CountyGov/Departments/Planning/nrichaptwo.pdf.

BERRY, THOMAS SENIOR. *Western Prices before 1861: A Study of the Cincinnati Market*. Cambridge, MA: Harvard University Press, 1943.

BLAKE, JOHN L. *The Farmer's Every-Day Book*. Auburn, NY: Derby Miller, 1850.

BROWER, W. C. Sap-Collecting System. U.S. Patent 1186741 A, filed December 17, 1914, and issued June 13, 1916.

BROWN, JOSHUA E. "Remaking Maple: New Method May Revolutionize Maple Syrup Industry." University of Vermont press office, released November 6, 2013, accessed July 29, 2015. Available at: http://www.uvm.edu/~uvmpr/?Page=news&storyID=17209.

"Bulk Price per Pound." Conversation thread via MapleTrader.com, April 2014, accessed July 20, 2015. Available at: http://mapletrader.com/community/showthread.php?23288-Bulk-Price-per-Pound.

BUTTERFIELD, ROY L. "The Great Days of Maple Sugar." *New York History*, vol. 39, no. 2 (April 1958), 151–64.

CBS News/AP. "Vt.: Log Cabin Syrup Not the Real Thing." Published September 9, 2010, accessed July 10, 2015. Available at: http://www.cbsnews.com/news/vt-log-cabin-syrup-not-the-real-deal/.

CHEN, JOANNE. *The Taste of Sweet: Our Complicated Love Affairs with Our Favorite Treats*. New York: Crown, 2008.

CHILDS, STEPHEN. "Chemistry of Maple Syrup." *Cornell Maple Bulletin*, issue 202, 2007.

CHIN, AVA. "On Tap on Staten Island: Maple Syrup." *New York Times*, March 13, 2011.

COCHRANE, WILLARD W. *The Development of American Agriculture: A Historical Analysis* (2nd ed.). Minneapolis: University of Minnesota Press, 1993.

COHEN, YORAM, AND JULIUS GLATER. "A Tribute to Sidney Loeb, the Pioneer of Reverse Osmosis Desalination Research." Published March 15, 2010. DOI: 10.5004/dwt.2010.1762.

COOK, D. M. Improvements in Pans for Evaporating Cane-Juice. U.S. Patent 20631 A, issued June 22, 1858.

COOPER, DAN. "The History of Wood Flooring." *Old-House Journal*, December/January 2013. Accessed July 13, 2015. Available at: http://www.oldhouseonline.com/the-history-of-wood-flooring/.

COWPER, WILLIAM. "The Negro's Complaint." Written February 1788. Published in *The Gentleman's Magazine*, Dec., 1793; afterwards in 1800. Accessed July 27, 2015. Available at: http://www.luminarium.org/eightlit/cowper/negroscomplaint.htm.

CULPEPER, NICHOLAS. *Culpeper's Complete Herbal*. London: Joseph Smith, 1832.

CURTIS, PAUL D., AND KRISTI L. SULLIVAN. "Wildlife Damage Management Fact Sheet Series: White-Tailed Deer." Published 2001 by the Cornell Cooperative Extension, Wildlife Damage Management Program. Available at: http://wildlifecontrol.info/pubs/Documents/Deer/Deer_factsheet.pdf.

DAWSON, TODD E. "Hydraulic Lift and Water Use by Plants: Implications for Water Balance, Performance, and Plant-Plant Interactions." *Oecologia*, vol. 95, no. 4 (1993), 565–74.

DE CHARLEVOIX, PIERRE-FRANÇOIS-XAVIER. *Journal d'un Voyage dans l'Amerique Septentrionnale*, vol. 1. Paris: Giffart, 1744.

DENNY, ELLEN, AND THOMAS SICCAMA. "Sugar Maple (*Acer Saccharum*) in the Hubbard Brook Forest." Last updated August 2001, accessed July 25, 2015. Available at: http://www.hubbardbrook.org/w6_tour/tree-stop/sugar-maple/maple-tree.htm.

DENYS, NICOLAS. *Histoire Naturelle*. Paris: Barbin/Nobel Press, 1672.

DINAPOLI, THOMAS P., AND KENNETH B. BLEIWAS."The Role of Agriculture in the New York State Economy." Albany, NY: Office of the State Comptroller, 2010. Accessed August 7, 2015. Available at: http://www.osc.state.ny.us/reports/other/agriculture21-2010.pdf.

DMITRIEVA, KATIA, AND ILAN KOLET. "Syrup Shortage? Prices Are Soaring." *Chicago Tribune*, December 21, 2012. Available at: http://articles.chicagotribune.com/2012-12-21/news/ct-talk-syrup-prices-1221-20121221_1_maple-syrup-maple-leaf-syrup-consumption.

DOUGLAS, SHARON M. "Anthracnose Diseases of Trees." Last updated June 2011, via the Connecticut Agricultural Experiment Station, accessed August 10, 2015. Available at: http://www.ct.gov/caes/lib/caes/documents/publications/fact_sheets/plant_pathology_and_ecology/anthracnose_diseases_of_trees_06-03-11r.pdf.

DUCHESNE, LOUIS, DANIEL HOULE, MARC-ANDRÉ CÔTÉ, AND TRAVIS LOGAN. "Modelling the Effect of Climate on Maple Syrup Production in Québec, Canada." *Forest Ecology and Management*. Published September 19, 2009, accessed June 30, 2015. DOI: 10/1016/j.foreco.2009.09.035.

EIGHMEY, RAE KATHERINE. *Food Will Win the War: Minnesota Crops, Cooks, and Conversation During World War I*. St. Paul: Minnesota Historical Society Press, 2010.

EVANS, FRANCIS A. *The Emigrant's Directory and Guide to Obtain Lands and Effect a Settlement in the Canadas*. Dublin: William Curry, Jr. and Company, 1833.

FALK, LAURA WINTER. *Culinary History of the Finger Lakes: From the Three Sisters to the Riesling*. Mount Pleasant, SC: History Press, 2014.

FOOD AND NUTRITION BOARD OF THE INSTITUTE OF MEDICINE. "Manganese." In *Dietary Reference Intakes for Vitamin A, Vitamin K, Arsenic, Boron, Chromium, Copper, Iodine, Iron, Manganese, Molybdenum, Nickel, Silicon, Vanadium, and Zinc*, 394–419. Washington, D.C.: National Academy of Sciences, 2005.

FROST, ROBERT. "Maple." In *The Poetry of Robert Frost: The Collected Poems, Complete and Unabridged*, ed. Edward Connery Lathem. New York: Henry Holt, 1969.

GLYNWOOD CENTER INC. "The State of Agriculture in the Hudson River Valley." Report commissioned 2010, accessed June 28, 2015. Available at: http://www.glynwood.org/wp-content/uploads/2015/02/State-of-Agriculture-2010.pdf.

GRIGGS, N.S. Sap Collection System. U.S. Patent US2877601 A, filed February 28, 1956, and issued March 17, 1959.

HERD, TIM. *Maple Sugar: From Sap to Syrup: The History, Lore, and How-to Behind This Sweet Treat*. North Adams, MA: Storey Publishing, 2011, Kindle edition.

HILLS, J. L. *Vermont Agricultural Report, 1893*. Vermont Agricultural Experiment Station.

HOFFARD, WILLIAM H., AND PHILIP T. MARSHALL. "How to Identify and Control the Sugar Maple Borer." Prepared by Forest Service, Northeastern Area State and Private Forestry, 1978. Available at: http://www.na.fs.fed.us/spfo/pubs/howtos/ht_mapleborer/mapleborer.htm.

HOLMES, MATTHEW. "'Pure' Maple Syrup?" *Gastronomica: The Journal of Critical Food Studies*, vol. 6, no. 1 (Winter 2006), 67–71.

HORSLEY, STEPHEN B., ROBERT P. LONG, SCOTT W. BAILEY, RICHARD A HALLETT, AND THOMAS J. HALL. "Factors Associated with the Decline in Disease of Sugar Maple on the Allegheny Plateau." *NRC Canada*, vol. 30 (March 7, 2000), 1365–78.

HUMBERT, ROGER P. *The Growing of Sugar Cane*. Kindle edition: Elsevier Books, 2013.

HUSBAND, JULIE AND JIM O'LOUGHLIN. *Daily Life in the Industrial United States, 1870-1900*. Santa Barbara, CA: ABC-Clio/Greenwood, 2004.

"Indian Method to Make as Good Sugar as the Islands Afford." *New-York Gazette*, January 9, 1764.

KAUFMAN, CATHY K. "Salvation in Sweetness? Sugar Beets in Antebellum America." In *Vegetables: Proceedings of the Oxford Symposium on Food and Cookery*, ed. Susan R. Friedland, 94–104. London: Prospect Books, 2008.

"Komline-Sanderson—Dissolved Air Flotation." Last modified January 2015, accessed July 20, 2015. Available at: http://www.komline.com/docs/dissolved_air_flotation.html.

KURLANSKY, MARK. *The Food of a Younger Land: A Portrait of American Food—Before the National Highway System, Before Chain Restaurants, and Before Frozen Food, when the Nation's Food was Seasonal, Regional, and Traditional—from the Lost WPA Files*. New York: Riverhead Books, 2010. Kindle edition.

LAFITAU, JOSEPH FRANÇOIS. *Moeurs des Sauvages Ameriquains*, vol. 2. Paris: Saugrains, 1724.

LES PRODUITS D'ÉRABLE DE QUÉBEC. "Maple Syrup's Beginnings." Accessed June 1, 2015. Available at: http://www.siropderable.ca/Afficher.aspx?page=46&langue=en.

"Letter From Thomas Jefferson to C. P. de Lasteyrie, 15 July 1808," Founders Online, National Archives. Available at: http://founders.archives.gov/documents/Jefferson/99-01-02-8329.

LI, LIYA, AND NAVINDRA P. SEERAM. "Quebecol, a Novel Phenolic Compound Isolated from Canadian Maple Syrup." Journal of Functional Foods (Impact Factor: 4.48), vol. 3, no. 2 (April 2011), 125-1–28. DOI: 10.1016/j.jff.2011.02.004.

"Liquid Sugar UV Disinfection Systems," via American Air and Water®, last updated 2012. Available at: http://www.americanairandwater.com/liquid-sugar-uv/liquid-sugar-uv.htm.

LONG, LUCY. *Regional American Food Culture*. Part of the Food Cultures in America series, ed. Ken Albala. Santa Barbara, CA: Greenwood Press, 2009.

"Maple Sugar: Some Facts About the Trade and How the Article Is Adulterated." *New York Times*, March 18, 1888.

"Maple Syrup First Choice: Favored Sweet Used in Cooking Recipes." *Los Angeles Times*, October 23, 1935, 33.

MEIER, ERIC. "Differences Between Hard Maple and Soft Maple." Accessed August 2, 2015. Available at: http://www.wood-database.com/wood-articles/differences-between-hard-maple-and-soft-maple/.

MINTZ, SIDNEY W. *Sweetness and Power: The Place of Sugar in Modern History*. New York: Viking Penguin, 1985.

MOSHER, ELI. Improvements in Sap-Conductors. U.S. Patent 26858 A, issued January 1, 1860.

NEARING, HELEN, AND SCOTT NEARING. *The Maple Sugar Book*. New York: Chelsea Green, 1950.

NEWPORT ARBORETUM. "Sugar Maple." Last modified May 2015, retrieved May 25, 2015. Available at: http://newportarboretum.org/home/portfolio/sugar-maple/.

OWEN, JUNE. "Maple Syrup Has Cut Crop and Raised Prices—Yellow Pike Shipments Heavy." *New York Times*, May 5, 1956.

OSNAS, JEANNE L.D. "Maple Syrup Mechanics: Xylem, Sap Flow, and Sugar Content." Botanist in the Kitchen, posted March 18, 2013. Available at: https://botanistinthekitchen. wordpress.com/2013/03/18/maple-syrup-mechanics/.

PARKER, ARTHUR C. *The Code of Handsome Lake, the Seneca Prophet.* Originally published 1913. Charleston, SC: Nabu Press, 2011.

PERKINS, TIMOTHY, AND MARK ISSELHARDT. "The 'Jones Rule of 86,' Revisited." University of Vermont Proctor Maple Research Center. *Maple Syrup Digest*, vol. 25A, no. 3 (October 2013), 26–28. Available at: http://www.uvm. edu/~pmrc/jones.pdf.

PFLÜG, MELISSA A. *Ritual and Myth in Odawa Revitalization: Reclaiming a Sovereign Place.* Norman: University of Oklahoma Press, 1998.

PICARD, MARTIN. *Sugar Shack au Pied de Cochon.* Montreal: Au Pied de Cochon, 2012.

PINNACLE FOODS INC. PRESS RELEASE BY ELENA MAGG. "Log Cabin the First National Brand to Debut All Natural Pancake Syrup." 2010. Available at: http://pinnaclefoods. com/media/detail/log-cabin-the-first-national-brand-to-debut-all-natural-pancake-syrup.

PITCOFF, WINTON. "Boiling It Down: The Untapped Potential of America's Sugar Bushes." *Farming Magazine*, January 1, 2014, accessed July 11, 2015. Available at: http:// www.farmingmagazine.com/maple/boiling-it-down-the-untapped-potential-of-americas-sugar-bushes/.

PRESS OFFICE OF GOVERNOR ANDREW CUOMO. "Governor Cuomo Launches New Farmers Grant Fund to Support Agribusiness in New York." Accessed July 22, 2015. Available at: http://www.governor.ny.gov/news/governor-cuomo-launches-new-farmers-grant-fund-support-agribusiness-new-york.

RAPP, JOSHUA M., AND ELIZABETH E. CRONE. "Maple Syrup Production Declines Following Masting." *Forest Ecology and Management*, September 27, 2014, accessed June 15, 2015. DOI: http://dx.doi.org/10.1016/j.foreco.2014.09.041.

RASPUZZI, DAWSON. "Maple Syrup Prices Jump." *Rutland Herald*, January 11, 2009, accessed July 15, 2015. Available at: http://www.rutlandherald.com/article/20090111/ NEWS04/901120299/1050.

RED HAWK, BOB. "The Story of the Maple Tree," ed. Louise St. Amour. Last modified 2005, retrieved May 19, 2015. Available at: http://lenapenation.org/The%20Story%20 of%20the%20Maple%20Tree.pdf.

RUSH, BENJAMIN. *An Account of the Sugar Maple-Tree of the United States.* Philadelphia: Aitken, 1792.

SAVOIE, LAUREN. "Tapping into Maple Syrup's Secrets." *Cook's Illustrated*, September/October 2015, 26–27.

SCHWANER-ALBRIGHT, OLIVER. "Maple Syrup, an Untapped Luxury." *New York Times*, March 11, 2009.

SOULE, G. H. Maple-Sap Evaporator. U.S. Patent 1049935 A, filed November 16, 1911, and issued January 7, 1913.

STOUT, MILTON W. "The Maple Sugar Industry: Some of Its Problems." *Ohio Farmer*, February 10, 1906; 109, 6; 126.

STOWE, HARRIET BEECHER. *Uncle Tom's Cabin*. Boston: John P. Jewett, 1852.

STROUD, ELLEN. *Nature Next Door: Cities and Trees in the American Northeast*. Seattle: University of Washington Press, 2012.

SUGAR ACT OF 1764. Full text accessed July 5, 2015. Available at: http://ahp.gatech.edu/sugar_act_bp_1764.html.

THEOBALD, MARY MILEY. "Thomas Jefferson and the Maple Sugar Scheme." Last modified 2012, retrieved May 20, 2015. Available at: www.history.org/foundation/journal/Autumn12_newformat/maplesugar.cfm.

THÉVET, ANDRÉ DE. *Les Singularitez de la France Antarctique Autrement Nommée Amérique*. Originally published in Paris 1558. In André Thévet's *North America: A Sixteenth Century View*. Montreal, Quebec: McGill-Queen's Press, 1986.

THOMAS JEFFERSON'S ESTATE AT MONTICELLO. "The Trees of Monticello." Accessed July 1, 2015. Available at: http://www.monticello.org/site/house-and-gardens/trees-monticello.

THOMAS JEFFERSON'S ESTATE AT MONTICELLO. "Sugar Maple." Accessed July 1, 2015. Available at: http://www.monticello.org/site/house-and-gardens/trees-monticello.

TRAGER, JAMES. *The Food Chronology: A Food Lover's Compendium of Events and Anecdotes, from Prehistory to the Present*. New York: Henry Holt, 1995.

UNIVERSITY OF RHODE ISLAND. "URI Scientist Discovers 54 Beneficial Compounds in Pure Maple Syrup." Press release, March 30, 2011, accessed August 3, 2015. Available at: http://news.uri.edu/releases/?id=5758.

University of Vermont Libraries and the Agriculture Network Information Center. "Plants, Pests, and Diseases: Sugar Maple Tree Distribution." Accessed 8-1-2015, available at: http://library.uvm.edu/maple/plants/.

USDA. "Climate Change May Impact Maple Syrup Production." Press release, October 8, 2010, accessed June 4, 2015. Available at: http://www.fs.fed.us/news/releases/climate-change-may-impact-maple-syrup-production.

USDA. "United States Standards for Grades of Maple Syrup." Washington, D.C., March 2015. Available at: http://www.regulations.gov/#!documentDetail;D=AMS-FV-15-0006-0001.

USDA NATURAL AGRICULTURAL STATISTICS SERVICE. "Crop Production (June 2015)." Released June 11, 2015; accessed July 18, 2015. Available at: https://www.nass.usda.gov/Statistics_by_State/New_England_includes/Publications/Crop_Production/Maple%20Syrup%202015.pdf.

USDA NATURAL AGRICULTURAL STATISTICS SERVICE. "Maple Syrup Production, 2013," June 2013. Available at: www.nass.usda.gov.

WARNER, DEBORAH JEAN. *Sweet Stuff: An American History of Sweeteners from Sugar to Sucralose*. Washington, D.C.: Smithsonian Institution Scholarly Press, 2011.

WARREN, JAMES R. "Crescent Manufacturing Company." Last updated September 13, 2004, accessed June 26, 2015. Available at: http://www.historylink.org/index.cfm?DisplayPage=output.cfm&File_Id=2006.

WATERWORTH, KRISTI. "Tree Borer Management: Signs of Tree Borer Insects." Last updated March 25, 2015, accessed July 17, 2015. Available at: http://www.gardeningknowhow.com/ornamental/trees/tgen/tree-borer-insects.htm.

WESTOVER, ROBERT H., U.S. FOREST SERVICE. "Changing Climate May Substantially Alter Maple Syrup Production." Last modified September 11, 2012. Available at: www.blogs. usda.gov/2012/09/11/changing-climate-may-substantially-alter-maple-syrup-production.

WHEELER, GEORGE E. Process of Evaporating Maple-Sap or Other Fluids. U.S. Patent 438787 A, filed August 29, 1988, and issued October 21, 1890.

WHITNEY, GORDON G., AND MARIAN M. UPMEYER. "Sweet Trees, Sour Circumstances: The Long Search for Sustainability in the North American Maple Products Industry." *Forest Ecology and Management*, vol. 200, nos. 1–3 (October 25, 2004), 313–33.

WHYNOTT, DOUGLAS. *The Sugar Season: A Year in the Life of Maple Syrup, and One Family's Quest for the Sweetest Harvest*. New York: Da Capo Press, 2014. Kindle edition.

WOLOSON, WENDY A. *Refined Tastes: Sugar, Confectionery, and Consumers in Nineteenth-Century America*. Baltimore, MD: Johns Hopkins University Press, 2002.

"World War I Sugar Substitutes No Sacrifice Today." *American Food Roots*, January 6, 2015.

YACOUBOU, JEANNE, M.S. "Is Your Sugar Vegan? The Vegetarian Resource Group Journal, Issue 4, 2007. https://www.vrg.org/journal/vj2007issue4/2007_issue4_sugar.php.

INDEX

pecan
    Glazed Maple-Pecan Scones, 107–8
    Maple-Bourbon Pecan Pie, 204, *205*, 206
    Maple-Pecan Sticky Buns, 110, *111*, 112
Pennsylvania State College, 40
phloem, 16
photosynthesis, 59
pie, 204, *205*, 206
plastic sap-gathering pipeline system
    patent, 40, *41*
poison squad, 36
pomegranate, 133
popcorn, 159, *160*, *161*
pork
    Maple and Pomegranate-Glazed Ham,
        133
    Maple-Braised Pork Chops and
        Peaches, 132
    Maple Pulled Pork, 130, *131*
potato hash, 113, *114*, 115
poultry
    Fennel and Coriander-Spiced Maple
        Duck Breasts, *134*, 135
    Maple Teriyaki Chicken, 136
pound cake, *200*, 201
Powerfully Maple Fruit & Nut Bars, 163
pricing, 87–88
production, 44
pudding, 154
pulled pork, 130, *131*
Pumpkin Pancakes, 116, *117*
pumps, 67
punch, 185
Pure Food and Drug Act (1906), 36–37

Quaker Reformation, 29
Quakers, 28–29
Quebec, 44

red maple, 53, 54
refrigerated railway cars, 32
regional cuisine, 39–40, 44
research centers, 10, 40, 43
restorative powers, of maple, 21
reverse-osmosis filtration, 41, 69, 70, 74–76,
    76–77
Revolutionary War, 30
Richmond, Roaldus, 39
Roasted Squash Soufflé with Maple
    Streusel, *152*, 153
Robb's Crown Maple Old-Fashioned, *180*,
    181
Roosevelt, Franklin D., 8

rules and regulations, 38–39
Rush, Benjamin, *28*, 30

salad. *See also* slaw
    Maple-Roasted Brussels, Shallots, and
        Farro Salad, 150, *151*
    Spiced Maple Cauliflower Salad, *144*,
        145
    Strawberry and Spinach Salad with
        Miso-Maple Dressing, 146
salmon, 137
sap
    flow, 59–61
    lines, 66–69, *68*
    season, 61
    spout, 25, *32*
    sweetness, 18, 58–59
Sarony, Napoleon, 23
sauce, *148*, 149
sausage, 113, *114*, 115
scones, 107–8
seafood. *See* fish
Seneca tribe prayer, 22
"Seven Ways to Save Sugar," 38
shallots, 150, *151*
Simmons Family Chili, *126*, 127–28
Sinclair, Upton, 36
"Sketchbook of Landscapes in the State of
    Virginia" (Miller), 29, *29*
slaw, 147
smoothies
    Cherry-Almond Smoothie, 175
    Maca-Oat-Maple Smoothie, 174
snacks
    Baked Brie with Maple and Pear Confit,
        170, 171
    Candied Mixed Nuts, *160*, *161*, 162
    Caramelized Onion and Maple-
        Mushroom Flatbread, 165, *166*, 167
    Maple-Apple-Walnut Snack Cake, 164
    Maple Buttered Popcorn, 159, *160*, *161*
    Maple Coconut Chips, 158, *160*
    Parsnip, Maple, and Tahini Dip, 168, *169*
    Powerfully Maple Fruit & Nut Bars, 163
soda, 176, *177*
soft maple, 53
soil, 56–58
soufflé, *152*, 153
Soule, George H., 34
soup, *148*, 149
Spanish-American War of 1898, 37
spice cookies, 192–93
Spiced Maple Cauliflower Salad, *144*, 145

Spicy Hot Maple Syrup, 99
spinach, 146
spouts, 25, *32*
squash, *152*, 153
Stamp Act of 1765, 26
steam-away, 78, 80
sticky buns, 110, *111*, 112
storing, 84–85
Stowe, Harriet Beecher, 29
Strawberry and Spinach Salad with Mi-
    so-Maple Dressing, 146
streusel, *152*, 153
sucrose, 58, 59
sucrose molecule, *71*
sugar. *See also* cane sugar
    consumption, 36
    cookies, 189
    dance, 17
    moon, 18
    substitute, 92–95
    Sugared Berries, *200*, 201
Sugar Act of 1764, 26, 27
sugar beet industry, 37
sugarbushes, 14, 43, 52–55
sugarhouses, 69–70
sugar maple (*Acer saccharum*), 14, 53, 54
sugar maple borer, 52, *52*
Sugar Maple Research and Extension Field
    Station, 10
Sully, Thomas, *28*
sustainability, 43–46, 53, 61, 95
sweeteners, 45, 92–95, *94*
sweetness, 18, 59–59
sweet potato soup, *148*, 149
syrup, 44–45
syrup grade, 84, 85, 96, 97

tahini, 168, *169*
tapping, 22, 24–25, 44, 64–65
taps, 62–69, *67*
tasting, 84–85
tea, 100
technological advances, 32–34, *34*, 40–46
teriyaki, 136
Thévet, André, 18, 22
Thomas, Robert B., 30
Towle, P. J., 34
trading, 26
transparency, 36
transpiration, 59, *60*
trees, 14–17, *15*, 54, *55*
trout, 138–39

PHOTO CREDITS:

All photographs © 2016 Tina Rupp with the exception of the following:

Agriculture and Agri-Food Canada: p. 93; Michael Bohne, U.S. Forest Service: p. 52; "Well, I hardly know which to take first!" Wood engraving in *The Boston Globe,* May 28 1898. Courtesy of the Library of Congress Prints and Photographs Division: p. 36; D.M. Cook, 1858: p. 33; Detroit Publishing Co., circa 1906, via the Library of Congress Prints and Photographs Division: pp. 3, 207; Ellenbogen Creative Group: pp. 6, 9, 10, 47, 51, 62, 63, 101, 208; Christine Engelbrecht. Used with permission from Iowa State University Extension and Outreach: p. 53 (bottom); Larry Frank/Flickr Creative Commons: p. 53 (top); "Scene in a Sugar Bush, Otsego County, New York," Photographed by A.S. Avery, Morris, New York, reproduced as woodcut engraving in *Harpers' Weekly,* page 256, May 1867: p. 25 (bottom); Nelson Steven Griggs, 1959: p. 41; Paul Kane, via Wikimedia Commons: p. 18; Canyon Maple (*Acer grandidentatum*), from Southeast Arizona. Photograph by Mike Kuhns: p. 15 (middle); Mrs. Dick Gahbowh boiling sap for maple sugar and syrup, Mille Lacs, 1925. Courtesy of the Minnesota Historical Society: p. 25 (top); Joseph Francois Lafitau, 1724, via the Library of Congress: p. 21; Advertisement by the Log Cabin Products Company of 250 Park Avenue, New York, NY. Published in March 1929 issue of *Good Housekeeping*: p. 35; File photographs Madava Farms: pp. 46, 67, 81, 82, 87; Mural

© Sean Mellyn 2012: p. 50; Sketch from Lewis Miller's "Sketchbook of Landscapes in the State of Virginia," circa 1853. Courtesy of the Colonial Williamsburg Foundation. Gift of Dr. and Mrs. Richard M. Kain in memory of George Hay Kain: p. 29; Eli Mosher, 1860: p. 32; Dan Mullen/Flickr Creative Commons: p. 15 (far right, above); Pedrick/Flickr Creative Commons: p. 15 (far right, bottom); Illustration courtesy of Pierre Pomet, 1748. Courtesy of University of Virginia Library, Special Collections Department: p. 27; Bigleaf Maples in the Purisima Creek Open Space Preserve, San Mateo County, California. Photograph by Tom Radulovich, via Wikimedia Commons: p. 15 (top left); Roland Reed, via the Library of Congress: 20; Florida Maple (*Acer floridanum*) at Three Rivers State Recreation Area, Jackson Co., Florida. Photograph by Tim Ross, via Wikimedia Commons: p. 15 (top right); Tyge Rugenstein: pp. 56, 58, 68, 70, 83, 84; Eli Sagor/Flickr Creative Commons: p. 55; Lithograph by Napoleon Sarony, c. 1850, based on the cartoon by Andrew Morris: p. 23; Michael Stahl: p. 211; Thomas Sully, *Benjamin Rush,* c. 1813, oil on canvas, The Trout Gallery at Dickinson College, Carlisle, PA: p. 28; Fay Turner: p. 7; Chart compiled via USDA Nutrient Database and Canadian Nutrient File: p. 94; *The Vermont Watchman,* Jan. 21st, 1891, Page 3, Image 3. Courtesy of the Library of Congress: p. 34; Ron Wolf, via Collection of the Colorado School of Mines Geology Museum. Golden, Colo: p. 14